CW00794045

Andy
852437

Colloquial **Chinese**

The Colloquial 2 Series
Series adviser: Gary King

The following languages are available in the Colloquial 2 series:

Chinese
Dutch
French
Italian
Russian
Spanish
Spanish of Latin America

Accompanying cassettes and CDs are available for the above titles. They can be ordered through your bookseller, or send payment with order to Taylor & Francis Ltd/ Routledge Ltd, ITPS, Cheriton House, North Way, Andover, Hants SP10 5BE, UK, or to Routledge Inc, 270 Madison Avenue, New York, NY 10016, USA.

Colloquial **Chinese**

The next step in language learning

Kan Qian

Routledge
Taylor & Francis Group

LONDON AND NEW YORK

First published 2007
by Routledge
2 Park Square, Milton Park, Abingdon, Oxon, OX14 4RN

Simultaneously published in the USA and Canada
by Routledge
270 Madison Ave, New York, NY 10016

Routledge is an imprint of the Taylor & Francis Group, an informa business

© 2007 Kan Qian

Typeset in 10/12pt Sabon
by Graphicraft Limited, Hong Kong
Printed and bound in Great Britain by
TJ International Ltd, Padstow, Cornwall

British Library Cataloguing in Publication Data
A catalogue record for this book is available from the British Library

Library of Congress Cataloging-in-Publication Data
Kan, Qian, 1960–
  Colloquial Chinese 2 / Qian Kan.
    p.   cm. – (Colloquial 2 series)
  Chinese and English.
  Includes indexes.
    1. Chinese language–Conversation and phrase books–English.   2. Chinese
  language–Grammar.   I. Title.   II. Series.
  PL1125.E6K37 2006
  495.1'83421–dc22

                                                              2006007103

ISBN13: 978-0-415-32818-0 (book)
ISBN13: 978-0-415-32816-6 (audio cassettes)
ISBN13: 978-0-415-32817-3 (audio CDs)
ISBN13: 978-0-415-32815-9 (pack)

Contents

Introduction

Intended readership

This book is designed for English speakers who have done a beginner's course in Chinese, and who would like to continue with their learning at an intermediate level. The book can be used as a self-study course or as supplementary material for a taught course.

The text has taken into consideration the fact that whereas some learners may have learnt *pinyin* only, others may have learnt both *pinyin* and characters. Throughout the book, both *pinyin* and simplified characters are used so that learners can choose to learn either or both. For a minority of learners who have learnt the traditional form of Chinese characters, there is an appendix of the texts and dialogues in traditional form at the end of the book (Appendix A).

Objectives

By the end of the book, learners should be able to:

▶ conduct a meaningful conversation in Chinese on a variety of topics
▶ have a better command of Chinese, and as a result use more sophisticated sentence structures such as the passive voice, the **ba**-sentence, topic structure, etc.
▶ read simple authentic texts such as articles from Chinese newspapers or popular magazines with the help of a dictionary
▶ write letters and diaries in Chinese.

Structure of the book and how to use it

This book contains about 1,500 words (not individual characters), amongst which about 1,100 are new words. It is divided into 12 units covering a wide range of issues that are relevant to modern China today, ranging from marriage and work to computers and the internet. It is important to follow the sequence of the units as they appear in the book because they get progressively more difficult.

As *pinyin* is used throughout the book with the characters, the following conventions are adopted:

▶ syllables are linked together to correspond to their English equivalents rather than to represent each Chinese character (e.g. **bàozhǐ** instead of **bào zhǐ** for 报纸 'newspaper')

▶ tone marks do not reflect the tone change, except for 不 (i.e. 不 in isolation is the fourth tone **bù** but becomes the second tone if it is followed by another fourth tone, for example 'bú dàn' for 'not only'). For tone change rules, see *Colloquial Chinese* (Kan Qian, Routledge, 1995: Introduction)

▶ neutral tones are not marked

▶ four-character fixed expressions are linked with hyphens (e.g. 名胜古迹 **míng-shèng-gǔ-jī** for 'places of historical interest')

▶ proper nouns such as place names, personal names and titles of books have their first letter capitalized (e.g. 天津 **Tiānjīn** (a city))

Two dialogues appear in each of the first four units. From Unit 5 onwards, however, each unit has a combination of text(s) and dialogue(s). New words in both *pinyin* and characters that occur in each text/dialogue are listed under the heading 'Vocabulary' with their English translations. It is a good idea to become familiar with those words before learning the dialogue/text. In order to facilitate the identification of new words in the first four units, all the words that appear under 'Vocabulary' are underlined in the *pinyin* text. Additional terms and expressions that are relevant to a particular topic are provided under the heading 'Additional useful words'. Grammatical points and key phrases are explained under the heading 'Language points' and are cross-referenced throughout the book. In order to explain clearly some difficult grammatical structures, literal translations are given in italics wherever necessary. An index to grammar and language points is included at the end of the book. In order to reinforce the words and structures introduced in each unit, between seven and ten exercises appear in each unit. At the same time, words and grammar points introduced in the previous units are recycled and practised repeatedly in these exercises. They are carefully designed to improve the basic language skills: speaking, listening, reading and writing. In the first seven units, unfamiliar words in

Exercises are provided before the exercises. From Unit 8 onwards, however, learners are encouraged to check unfamiliar words in the Chinese–English glossary on page 265. At the end of each unit, there is either a passage for reading comprehension or a listening comprehension exercise. The key to all exercises, including reading/listening comprehension exercises, is on page 212.

In order to help learners gain an appreciation of what it is like to read authentic materials, a short extract from a Chinese newspaper or popular magazine is included at the end of Units 10, 11 and 12 under the heading 'Authentic text'. These texts are in characters only, but new words are provided in both pinyin and characters along with their English translation. As these are original texts, there will inevitably be grammar points or sentence structures that are not covered in this book. To help those learners who wish to take on the challenge·and try to read some or all of these texts, a full English translation of all three authentic texts is provided on page 262.

Finally, as language is closely linked with its culture, throughout the book, relevant cultural points are explained under the heading 'Culture notes' in each unit, and again an index to culture notes can be found on page 296.

Acknowledgements

My gratitude goes to Kan Jia for countless hours of word processing, pinyin annotation and proof reading the Chinese texts. I am extremely grateful to Gerry Lydon who gave hours of his time polishing the English texts. I would like to thank the following people: Andrew Brown and Paul Guest for putting themselves in the position of a learner and providing some very useful comments and suggestions; Boping Yuan for his valuable suggestions on some difficult grammatical points; the Routledge team for their support throughout the writing of this book; Victoria Coleman, René Frank, Jin Miao, Kan Yigang, Paul Stilley, Wang Shiyue, Wu Han, Zhang Lan and Zhang Ping for allowing me to use their photographs in the book. I would also like to thank www.istock.com for permission to use some of their images.

Finally, this project received a grant from the Faculty of Oriental Studies at the University of Cambridge, for which I am extremely grateful.

1 中文以及中国

Zhōngwén yǐjí Zhōngguó

The Chinese language and China

In this unit, you will learn about:

- ▶ using 得 (**de**) to link a verb and an adverb
- ▶ pattern 连... 也... (**lián ... yě ...**)
- ▶ using 不是 (**bú shì**) in yes-no questions
- ▶ 的 (**de**) as the past particle and to introduce a noun clause
- ▶ making comparisons using 比... 得多 (**bǐ... deduō**)

and you will revise:

- ▶ the difference between 多少 (**duō shǎo**) and 几 (**jǐ**)
- ▶ the difference between 一个月 (**yī ge yuè**) and 一月 (**yī yuè**)

Dialogue 1 (CD 1; 1)

学中文 Xué Zhōngwén
Learn Chinese

Tom is travelling in China. He is on a train sitting next to a Chinese woman named Lili.

LILI	你会说中文吗？
TOM	会，不过说得不好。
LILI	你的口音很不错。
TOM	过奖，过奖。我的四声总是有问题。
LILI	你太谦虚了。学了几年中文了？
TOM	整整三年了。
LILI	认识多少个汉字？
TOM	差不多一千个，可是只会写五百个左右。
LILI	那也很不简单。我连一句外语也不会说。

Peking University
Photographer: Paul Stilley

Dialogue 1 in pinyin ♦

LILI Nǐ huì shuō Zhōngwén ma?

TOM Huì, <u>búguò</u> shuō de bù hǎo.

LILI Nǐde <u>kǒuyīn</u> hěn <u>bú cuò</u>.

TOM <u>Guò jiǎng</u>, guò jiǎng. Wǒde <u>sì shēng</u> zǒngshì <u>yǒu wèntí</u>.

LILI Nǐ tài <u>qiānxū</u> le. Xué le jǐ nián Zhōngwén le?

TOM <u>Zhěngzhěng</u> sān nián le.

LILI <u>Rènshi</u> duō shǎo ge <u>hànzì</u>?

TOM <u>Chàbuduō</u> yī qiān gè, <u>kěshì</u> zhǐ huì <u>xiě</u> wǔ bǎi gè zuǒyòu.

LILI Nà yě hěn <u>bù jiǎndān</u>. Wǒ <u>lián</u> yī <u>jù</u> <u>wàiyǔ</u> <u>yě</u> bú huì shuō.

Vocabulary ♦

不过	**búguò**	however
口音	**kǒuyīn**	accent
不错	**bú cuò**	quite good (*lit.* not bad)
过奖	**guò jiǎng**	I am flattered (*lit.* over praise)
四声	**sì shēng**	four tones
有问题	**yǒu wèntí**	to have problems
谦虚	**qiānxū**	be modest
整整	**zhěngzhěng**	exactly
认识	**rènshi**	to recognize
汉字	**hànzì**	Chinese character
差不多	**chàbuduō**	nearly
可是	**kěshì**	but
写	**xiě**	to write
不简单	**bù jiǎndān**	extraordinary (*lit.* very not simple)
连...也...	**lián ... yě ...**	even
句	**jù**	sentence
外语	**wàiyǔ**	foreign language

Language points ♦

1.1 Use of 得 (de) to link a verb and an adverb

This 得 (de) is used to link a verb and an adverb. It is known as a complement of manner in grammatical terms. Most Chinese adjectives and adverbs share the same form. The simplest pattern is: verb + 得 (**de**) + adverb. The adverb is usually modified by another degree adverb. To negate, put 不 (**bù**) after 得 (**de**). For example:

> 我 妹妹 写 得 非常 好。
> **Wǒ mèimei** <u>xiě</u> *de* <u>fēicháng</u> <u>hǎo</u>
>   verb   degree adverb adverb
> My sister writes very well.

> 她 跑 得 不 快。
> **Tā** <u>pǎo</u> *de* <u>bú</u> <u>kuài</u>.
>   verb   negator adverb
> *lit.* *she run   not   fast*
> She doesn't run fast.

Please note that if the verb is a 'verb + object' form such as 做饭 (**zuòfàn**, to cook), 开车 (**kāichē**, to drive), the first element of the verb is repeated before adding the complement. So the pattern is:

verb + repeat the first element of the verb + 得 (**de**) + adverb

For example:

> 我妈妈做饭做得特别好。
> **Wǒ māma zuòfàn zuò de tèbié hǎo.**
> My mum cooks very well/My mum is a very good cook.

> 他开车开得不太好。
> **Tā kāichē kāi de bú tài hǎo.**
> He drives poorly/He is a poor driver.

In the dialogue above, the sentence 不过说得不好 (**búguò shuō de bù hǎo**, *lit. but I speak not very well*) is a reply to the question 你会说中文吗？(**Nǐ huì shuō Zhōngwén ma?**, Can you speak Chinese?). So 说中文 (**shuō Zhōngwén**, speak Chinese) is omitted in the reply. If it is not omitted, it should be 我说中文说得不好 (**Wǒ shuō Zhōngwén shuō de bù hǎo**, *lit. I speak Chinese speak not very well*).

1.2   Use of 不错 (**bú cuò**)

Literally, 不错 (**bú cuò**) means 'not bad'. But really it is used when you wish to say 'quite good'. If you wish to say 'really good', put 很 (**hěn**, very) or 真 (**zhēng**, really) in front of 不错 (**bú cuò**). For example:

他的英文很不错。
Tāde Yīngwén hěn bú cuò.
His English is really good.

1.3   Omission of personal pronouns when acting as subject

In Chinese, it is very common to omit the personal pronoun such as
我, 你, 她 (**wǒ, nǐ, tā,**/I, you, she) when it occurs in the subject
position, if the context makes it clear who is being talked about.
In the dialogue above, the pronoun 你 (**nǐ**) is omitted in the question 认识多少个汉字? (**Rènshí duō shǎo gè hànzì?** How many
characters do you recognize?). In other words, a Chinese sentence or
question can start with a verb. See the second question in the following exchange:

A   你什么时候去中国？
    Nǐ shénme shíhòu qù Zhōngguó?
    When are you going to China?

B   下个星期。
    Xià gè xīngqī.
    Next week.

A   去多久？
    Qù duō jiǔ?
    How long are you going for? (*lit. go for how long?*)

B   一个月左右。
    Yī gè yuè zuǒyòu.
    About a month.

1.4   Use of 认识 (rènshi)

When this verb is followed by a person, it means 'to know'; and
when it is followed by an object, it means 'to recognise'. For example:

你认识王先生吗？
Nǐ rènshi Wáng xiānsheng ma?
Do you know Mr Wang?

我不认识这种水果。
Wǒ bú rènshi zhè zhǒng shuǐguǒ.
I don't recognise this kind of fruit.

1.5 Pattern 连 … 也 … (lián … yě …, 'even')

This is a very useful pattern which means 'even'. 连 (lián) is always placed before whatever you wish to emphasise and 也 (yě) is placed before the verb. For example:

他连上海话也会说。
Tā lián Shànghǎi huà yě huì shuō.
He can even speak the Shanghai dialect.

Please note that 都 (dōu) can be used instead of 也 (yě). If the verb is negated, the negation word 不 or 没 (bù or méi) is placed after 也 (yě) or 都 (dōu). For example:

你怎么连这个字都不认识？
Nǐ zěnme lián zhè gè zì dōu bú rènshi?
How come you don't even recognise this character?

1.6 Difference between 多少 (duō shǎo) and 几 (jǐ)

Although both of these question words mean 'how many' in English, they have different implications. When 多少 (duō shǎo) is used, the speaker anticipates a large number (normally above ten) in the reply, and when 几 (jǐ) is used, the assumed number is usually less than ten. For example:

A 你有多少本中文书？
　　Nǐ yǒu duō shǎo běn Zhōngwén shū?
　　How many Chinese books have you got?

B 大概二十本。
　　Dàgài èrshí běn.
　　Approximately 20.

A 你有几个兄弟姐妹？
　　Nǐ yǒu jǐ ge xiōngdì jiěmèi?
　　How many brothers and sisters have you got?

B 一个姐姐，两个弟弟。
　　Yī gè jiějie, liǎng gè dìdi.
　　One elder sister and two younger brothers.

Please note that when followed by countable nouns, an appropriate measure word must be used after 几 (jǐ), but it is optional after

多少 (**duō shǎo**). For example, in the examples above, 本 (**běn**) can be omitted from 你有多少本中文书？ (**Nǐ yǒu duō shǎo běn Zhōngwén shū?**), but 个 (**gè**) cannot be omitted from 你有几个兄弟姐妹？ (**Nǐ yǒu jǐ gè xiōngdì jiěmèi?**).

Please also note that 多少 (**duō shǎo**) can also mean 'how much' when followed by uncountable nouns. For example:

你带了多少钱？
Nǐ dài le duō shǎo qián?
How much money have you got?

Culture note

Modesty

Modesty is regarded as a virtue in Chinese culture, and it is reflected in every aspect of everyday life. For example, when someone pays you a compliment, you are not supposed to accept it. Instead, depending on what the compliment is, you always try to deny it. For instance, if someone praises your cooking by saying '你做的饭真好吃' (**Nǐ zuò de fàn zhēn hǎochī**, Your food is really tasty), the most common reply would be '不好, 不好' (**Bù hǎo, bù hǎo**) or '哪里, 哪里' (**Nǎlǐ, nǎlǐ**), meaning 'not at all'. However, due to Western influence, young people these days are starting to accept the compliment by saying '谢谢' (**xièxie**, thank you).

Exercises

Useful words for the following exercises

电影	**diànyǐng**	film, picture
简单	**jiǎndān**	simple
听力	**tīnglì**	listening ability
总是	**zǒngshì**	always
质量	**zhìliàng**	quality

Exercise 1

Fill in the gaps using appropriate words from the vocabulary list for Dialogue 1 above:

a 他的女朋友会说三种_____。
Tāde nǚ péngyou huì shuō sān zhǒng_____.

b 我看过那个电影，_____不太喜欢。
Wǒ kàn guò nà ge diànyǐng, _____bú tài xǐhuān.

c 这么简单的字，你怎么不_____?
Zhème jiǎndān de zì, nǐ zěnme bù_____?

d 在听力方面，我总是_____。
Zài tīnglì fāngmiàn, wǒ zǒngshì_____.

e 我在中国住了_____八年。
Wǒ zài Zhōngguó zhù le_____bā nián.

f 这两件衣服_____一样贵，但是黑的质量不好。
Zhè liǎng jiàn yīfú_____yīyàng guì, dànshì hēide zhìliàng bù hǎo.

Exercise 2

Translate into Chinese:

a Your four tones are quite good.
b When he speaks *putonghua*, he has a Shanghai accent.
c I lived in Britain for a year, but I can't even speak one sentence of English.
d She is extraordinary. She can even speak Cantonese.

Exercise 3

Ask questions using 多少 (**duō shǎo**) or 几 (**jǐ**) based on the following answers:

a 我家有五个人。
Wǒ jiā yǒu wǔ ge rén.

b 我们班有十六个人。
Wǒmen bān yǒu shíliù ge rén.

c 他会说三种外语。
　Tā huì shuō sān zhǒng wàiyǔ.

Exercise 4 (CD 1; 2)

What do you say in the following situations?

a You want to find out if the person you speak to can speak English. You ask . . .
b You wish to find out how long the person you speak to has been learning Chinese. You ask . . .
c When someone pays you a compliment, saying that you speak very good Chinese. You reply . . .

Dialogue 2 (CD 1; 3)

我对中国的印象　Wǒ duì Zhōngguó de yìnxiàng
My impressions of China

Jane has been to China recently and her Chinese friend Zhang Xin is chatting to her about her trip . . .

ZHANG XIN	你不是去中国了吗？什么时候回来的？
JANE	是啊！去了整整一个月。昨天回来的。
ZHANG XIN	你对中国的印象怎么样？有空聊聊吗？
JANE	当然有空。总的来说，印象很好。
ZHANG XIN	你能不能具体点？
JANE	北京、上海这些大城市比我想像的现代化得多。给我印象最深的是那些名胜古迹，比如北京的故宫、西安的碑林等。再就是中国饭菜品种多样、味道鲜美！
ZHANG XIN	你还去了其他什么地方？
JANE	差不多七、八个城市。比如青岛、成都等。我还游了三峡。真是美极了！
ZHANG XIN	你说的都是好的方面，有什么是你不喜欢的？
JANE	交通太拥挤，特别是北京；还有就是噪音，到处都吵吵闹闹。
ZHANG XIN	我完全同意。

The Three Gorges
Photographer: René Frank

Dialogue 2 in pinyin ♦

ZHANG XIN	Nǐ bú shì qù Zhōngguó le ma? Shénme shíhòu huí lái de?
JANE	Shì a! Qù le zhěngzhěng yī gè yuè. Zuótiān huílái de.
ZHANG XIN	Nǐ duì Zhōngguó de <u>yìnxiàng</u> zěnme yàng? Yǒu kòng <u>liáoliáo</u> ma?
JANE	Dāngrán yǒu kòng. <u>Zǒngde láishuō</u>, yìnxiàng hěn hǎo.
ZHANG XIN	Nǐ néng bù néng <u>jùtǐ diǎn</u>?
JANE	Běijīng, Shànghǎi, zhèxiē dà chéngshì bǐ wǒ <u>xiǎngxiàng</u> de <u>xiàndàihuà</u> de duō. <u>Gěi</u> wǒ yìnxiàng zuì shēn de shì nàxiē <u>míng-shèng-gǔ-jī</u>, bǐrú Běijīng de <u>Gùgōng</u>, Xī'ān de <u>Bēi Lín</u> děng. <u>Zài jiù shì</u> Zhōngguó fàncài – <u>pǐnzhǒng</u> <u>duō</u> <u>yàng</u>, <u>wèidào</u> <u>xiānměi</u>!
ZHANG XIN	Nǐ hái qù le qítā shénme dìfāng?
JANE	Chābuduō qī, bā gè chéngshì. Bǐrú <u>Qīngdǎo</u>, <u>Chéngdū</u> děng. Wǒ hái <u>yóu</u> le <u>Sānxiá</u>. Zhēn shì měi jí le!
ZHANG XIN	Nǐ shuō de dōu shì hǎo de <u>fāngmiàn</u>, yǒu shénme shì nǐ bù xǐhuān de?
JANE	<u>Jiāotōng</u> tài <u>yǒngjǐ</u>, <u>tèbié</u> shì Běijīng; <u>hái yǒu jiù shì</u> <u>zàoyīn</u>, <u>dàochù</u> dōu <u>chǎo-chǎo-nào-nào</u>.
ZHANG XIN	Wǒ <u>wánquán</u> <u>tóngyì</u>.

Vocabulary ♦

印象	yìnxiàng	impression
聊聊	liáoliao	to chat
总的来说	zǒngde láishuō	generally speaking
具体点	jùtǐ diǎn(r)	a bit detailed
想像	xiǎngxiàng	to imagine
现代化	xiàndàihuà	modernised
名胜古迹	míng-shèng-gǔ-jī	places of historical interest
故宫	Gù Gōng	Forbidden City (Palace Museum)
碑林	Bēi Lín	Forest of Tablets
再就是	zài jiù shì	another thing is
品种	pǐnzhǒng	goods; items
多样	duō yàng	various kinds
味道	wèidào	flavour
鲜美	xiānměi	tasty, delicious

青岛	**Qīngdǎo**	(city name)
成都	**Chéngdū**	(city name)
游	**yóu**	to tour around
三峡	**Sān Xiá**	The Three Gorges
方面	**fāngmiàn**	aspect
交通	**jiāotōng**	transport
拥挤	**yǒngjǐ**	crowded, be crowded
特别	**tèbié**	especially
还有就是	**hái yǒu jiù shì**	another thing is . . .
噪音	**zàoyīn**	noise, undesired sound
到处	**dàochù**	everywhere
吵吵闹闹	**chǎo-chǎo-nào-nào**	noisy; be noisy
完全	**wánquán**	completely
同意	**tóngyì**	to agree

Language points ♦

1.7 Expressions of summary

There are many expressions used to summarise. The common ones are:

总的来说 (**zǒng de lái shuō**), generally speaking
总而言之 (**zǒng ér yán zhī**), in summary/in short
总之 (**zǒng zhī**), in summary/in short
简而言之 (**jiǎn ér yán zhī**), in short

1.8 Use of 不是 (**bú shì**) in yes-no questions

Let us start by comparing the following two sentences:

a 你去中国了吗？
   Nǐ qù Zhōngguó le ma?
   Did you go to China?

b 你不是去中国了吗？
   Nǐ bú shì qù Zhōngguó le ma?
   Isn't it the case that you went to China?

The speaker of sentence a has no idea if the listener went to China or not. It is just a general yes-no question. Whereas the speaker of sentence b thinks that the listener has gone to China. The implied meaning is 'I thought you went to China. How come you are here?' So there is an element of surprise. Let us look at some other examples:

你不是喜欢吃西餐吗？
Nǐ bú shì xǐhuān chī xīcān ma?
Don't you like Western food?
(possible implication: I thought you liked Western-style food. Why haven't you eaten much today?)

1.9 Use of 的 (de) to indicate the past

When an event took place in the past, 是 (**shì**) may be used in conjunction with 的 (**de**) to emphasise the adverbials or other modifying elements. 是 (**shì**) is always placed before the element being emphasised and 的 (**de**) comes at the end of the sentence. For example:

A 你是什么时候大学毕业的？
   Nǐ shì shénme shíhòu dàxué bìyè de?
   When did you graduate from the university?

B 是一九八八年毕业的。
   Shì yījiǔbābā nián bìyè de.
   (I) graduated in 1988.

However, in spoken language, 是 (**shì**) is often omitted. For example:

我在中国大饭店见到他的。
Wǒ zài Zhōngguó Dà Fàndiàn jiàndào tā de.
lit. *I at China Hotel meet him* [particle]
    I saw him at the China Hotel.

1.10 Comparison

You may be familiar with patterns such as 'A + 比 (**bǐ**) + B + adjective' or 'A + 比 (**bǐ**) + B + adjective + specific'. For example:

王林比李勇高。
Wáng Lín bǐ Lǐ Yǒng gāo.
Wang Lin is taller than Li Yong.

王林比李勇高三公分。
Wáng Lín bǐ Lǐ Yǒng gāo sān gōngfēn.
Wang Lin is three centimetres taller than Li Yong.

However, if you simply do not know exactly how much taller Wang Lin is compared to Li Yong, but you know that he is much taller, then use the pattern 'A 比 B + adjective + 得多 (**deduō**)'. For example:

王林比李勇高得多。
Wáng Lín bǐ Lǐ Yǒng gāo deduō.
Wang Lin is much taller than Li Yong.

In Dialogue 2, the sentence 北京、上海这些大城市比我想象的现代化 得多 (**Běijīng, Shànghǎi zhèxiē dà chéngshì bǐ wǒ xiǎngxiàng de xiàndàihuà deduō**) can be translated as 'Big cities such as Beijing and Shanghai are much more modernised than I had imagined.'

1.11   Use of 的 (de) to introduce a noun clause

In English, noun clauses are introduced by 'what' (e.g. What you've imagined . . . /what you liked . . .). In Chinese, when 的 (de) follows a verb or verbal phrase, it signals a noun clause. It can function as subject. For example:

你说的都是好的方面, . . .
<u>Nǐ shuō</u> de dōu shì hǎo de fāngmiàn
[verb]
lit.   you've just said [de] all were good aspects, . . .
What you've just said were all positive aspects of things, . . .

给我　印象　　最深　　的　是她如此自信。
<u>Gěi wǒ yìnxiàng　zuì shēn</u>　de　shì tā rúcǐ zìxìn.
[verbal phrase]
lit.   give me impression most deep [de] is she so be confident.
What impressed me most was that she was so confident.

1.12   Difference between 一个月 (yī ge yuè) and 一月 (yī yuè)

You will by now know that the measure word **ge** is used in between a number and a noun. So 一个月 (**yī ge yuè**) means 'one month', and 三个月 (**sān ge yuè**) means 'three months'. Whereas 一月 (**yīyuè**)、 二月 (**èyuè**)、三月 (**sānyuè**), etc., are names for the months, i.e. January, February, March, etc.

1.13   Use of emphatic 都 (dōu)

You may have noticed that 都 (**dōu**) is often used in conjunction with expressions such as 所有的 (**suǒyǒude**, all), 每 (**měi**, every),

到处 (**dàochù**, everywhere). And it is always placed before the verb or the modal verb. For example:

所有的人都喜欢她。
Suǒyǒude rén dōu xǐhuān tā.
All the people like her.

到处都能看到骑自行车的人。
Dàochù dōu néng kàndao qí zìxíngchē de rén.
You can see cyclists everywhere.

Exercises

Useful words for doing the following exercises

饭馆	**fànguǎn**	restaurant
绿绿的	**lǜlǜde**	green
草地	**cǎodì**	grass field
北方的	**běifāngde**	northern
农村	**nóngcūn**	countryside
毕业	**bìyè**	to graduate

Exercise 5

Fill in the gaps using appropriate words from the vocabulary list for Dialogue 2:

a 我特别想在奶奶家多住几天，可是我爸爸不_____。
   Wǒ tèbié xiǎng zài nǎinai jiā duō zhù jǐ tiān, kěshì wǒ bàba bù_____.

b 这个小饭馆做的饭不但_____鲜美，价钱也不贵。
   Zhè gè xiǎo fànguǎn zuò de fàn búdàn_____xiānměi, jiàqián yě bù guì.

c 现在，商店里的商品_____多样，要什么有什么。
   Xiànzài, shāngdiàn lǐ de shāngpǐn_____duōyàng, yào shénme yǒu shénme.

d 这条街上有一个自由市场，所以_____吵。
   Zhè tiáo jiē shàng yǒu yī gè zìyóu shìcháng, suǒyǐ_____chǎo.

e 在学习汉语_____，玛丽有很多好主意。
Zài xuéxí Hànyǔ_____, Mǎlì yǒu hěnduō hǎo zhǔyì.

f 在英国，_____都可以看到绿绿的草地。
Zài Yīngguó, _____dōu kěyǐ kàndào lǜlǜde cǎodì.

Exercise 6

Decide if the measure word 个 (gè) is needed in the following sentences, and then translate them into English:

a 我去了五、六_____城市，还去了北方的农村。
Wǒ qù le wǔ、liù_____chéngshì, hái qù le běifāngde nóngcūn.

b 她打算今年九_____月去中国。
Tā dǎsuàn jīn nián jiǔ_____yuè qù Zhōngguó.

c 我下_____月就要毕业了。
Wǒ xià_____yuè jiù yào bìyè le.

d 去年，我在北京住了六_____月。
Qù nián wǒ zài Běijīng zhù le liù_____yuè.

Exercise 7

Translate into Chinese:

a Generally speaking, my impression of China is very good.
b This city is a lot more crowded than I had imagined.
c I really like this small town. It's beautiful and quiet. Another thing is that the local people are very friendly.
d Can you be a bit more specific?
e When did you come to Beijing?

Listening comprehension (CD 1; 5)

为什么学中文 Wèishénme xué Zhōngwén?
Why learn Chinese?

You will hear a dialogue between two Chinese people – Linfang and Xiaoyan. Try not to read the script. Bear the following questions

in mind whilst listening to the dialogue and try to answer them afterwards:

1	谁开始学中文了？	Shéi kāishǐ xué Zhōngwén le?
2	这个人学了多久中文了？	Zhè ge rén xué le duō jiǔ Zhōngwén le?
3	这个人为什么学习中文？	Zhè ge rén wèishénme xuéxí Zhōngwén?

Key words ♦

You may find the following words useful in understanding the dialogue:

开始	**kāishǐ**	to start
觉得	**juéde**	to feel, to think of
才	**cái**	only just
因为	**yīnwéi**	because
夏天	**xiàtiān**	summer
父母	**fùmǔ**	parents
难怪	**nánguài**	no wonder
只	**zhǐ**	only
原因	**yuányīn**	reason
之一	**zhī yī**	one of
交流	**jiāoliú**	to communicate

Script in characters ♦

LINFANG	小燕，听说你的男朋友开始学中文了。是真的吗？
XIAOYAN	是啊！已经快三个月了。
LINFANG	怎么样？他觉得难不难？
XIAOYAN	总的来说，他觉得很难，不过他很喜欢。
LINFANG	你们认识了这么久，他为什么现在才学中文？
XIAOYAN	因为我们今年夏天要去北京见我的父母！
LINFANG	难怪！他想给你父母一个好印象。
XIAOYAN	这只是原因之一。他真的想同中国人交流。

Script in pinyin ♦

LINFANG	Xiǎoyàn, tīngshuō nǐde nán péngyou kāishǐ xué Zhōngwén le. Shì zhēnde ma?
XIAOYAN	Shì a! Yǐjīng kuài sān gè yuè le.
LINFANG	Zěnme yàng? Tā juéde nán bù nán?
XIAOYAN	Zǒngde láishuō, tā juéde hěn nán, búguò tā hěn xǐhuān.
LINFANG	Nǐmen rènshí le zhème jiǔ, tā wèishénme xiànzài cái xué Zhōngwén?
XIAOYAN	Yīnwéi wǒmen jīnnián xiàtiān yào qù Běijīng jiàn wǒde fùmǔ!
LINFANG	Nánguài! Tā xiǎng gěi nǐ fùmǔ yī gè hǎo yìnxiàng
XIAOYAN	Zhè zhǐ shì yuányīn zhī yī. Tā zhēnde xiǎng tóng Zhōngguórén jiāoliú.

2 在中国旅行
Zài Zhōngguó lǚxíng
Travelling in China

In this unit you will learn about:

▶ asking for advice
▶ giving reasons for doing or not doing something
▶ expressions regarding means of transport
▶ apologising and returning a compliment
▶ describing a location
▶ giving directions
▶ end of sentence 了 (le)

Dialogue 1 (CD 1; 6)

准备旅行　Zhǔnbèi lǚxíng
Planning the trip

Mary is learning Chinese at a university in Beijing. Li Liang is her Chinese friend and has done a lot of travelling within China, so Mary is asking for his advice ...

MARY　　你什么时候有空？我想请你帮我出出主意。
LI LIANG　什么方面的主意？
MARY　　在中国旅游方面的。听说你玩了不少地方。
LI LIANG　没问题。现在就可以。咱们找个地方坐下来慢慢说。
MARY　　太好了！刚好快到吃中饭的时间了。我请你吃中饭，咱们一边吃一边聊。
LI LIANG　你的这个建议棒极了。走吧！

(After they have sat down with their lunch ...)

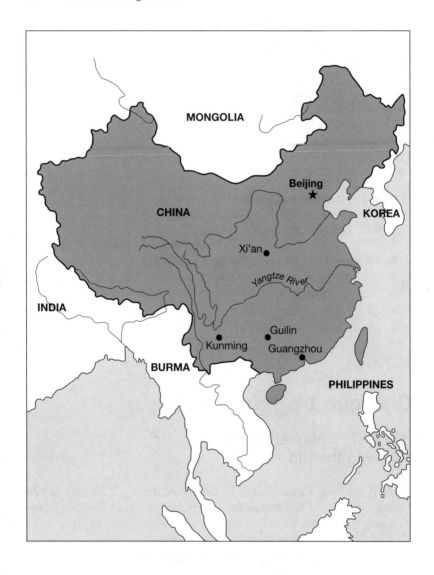

LI LIANG　　你先说说，你想去哪几个城市？准备去多久？

MARY　　　我有两个星期的时间，想去西安，三峡，广州等。

LI LIANG　　我觉得，你最好去完三峡后去云南，不去广州。

MARY　　　为什么？

LI LIANG　　一是因为云南有许多自然风景，二是因为三峡和云南都在
　　　　　　中国的西南部。广州你可以下次去桂林的时候再去。

MARY　　　有道理。去云南坐火车好还是飞机好？

LI LIANG　　坐火车好，因为这样你可以看到沿途美丽的景色。

Dialogue 1 in pinyin ◆

MARY   Nǐ shénme shíhòu yǒu kòng? Wǒ xiǎng qǐng nǐ <u>bāng</u> wǒ <u>chūchu</u> <u>zhǔyi</u>.

LI LIANG   Shénme fāngmiàn de zhǔyi?

MARY   Zài Zhōngguó lǚyóu fāngmiàn de. Tīngshuō nǐ <u>wán</u> le bù shǎo dìfang.

LI LIANG   Méi wèntí. Xiànzài jiù kěyǐ. Zánmen zhǎo gè dìfang zuò xiàlai mànmàn shuō. ⎜⎱ ⎩⎧⎝ ⎡⎼⎬

MARY   Tài hǎo le! Gānghǎo kuài dào chī zhōngfàn de shíjiān le. Wǒ qǐng nǐ chī zhōngfàn, Zánmen <u>yībiān</u> chī <u>yībiān</u> liáo.

LI LIANG   Nǐde zhè ge <u>jiànyì</u> <u>bàngjíle</u>. Zǒu ba!

(After they have sat down with their lunch . . .)

LI LIANG   Nǐ xiān shuōshuo, nǐ xiǎng qù nǎ jǐ ge chéngshì, <u>zhǔnbèi</u> qù duō jiǔ?

MARY   Wǒ yǒu liǎng ge xīngqī de shíjiān, xiǎng qù Xī'ān, Sān Xiá, Guǎngzhōu <u>děng</u>.

LI LIANG   Wǒ juéde nǐ zuìhǎo qù wán Sān Xiá hòu qù <u>Yúnnán</u>, bú qù Guǎngzhōu.

MARY   Wèishénme?

LI LIANG   Yī shì yīnwéi Yúnnán yǒu xǔduō <u>zìrán</u> fēngjǐng, èr shì yīnwéi Sān Xiá hé Yúnnán dōu zài Zhōngguó de <u>xīnán bù</u>. Guǎngzhōu nǐ kěyǐ xià cì qù Guìlín de shíhòu zài qù.

MARY   <u>Yǒu dàolǐ</u>. Qù Yúnnán zuò huǒchē hǎo háishì fēijī hǎo?

LI LIANG   Zuò huǒchē hǎo, yīnwéi zhè yàng nǐ kěyǐ kàndào <u>yán tú měilì</u> de <u>jǐngsè</u>.

Vocabulary ◆

帮	bāng	to help
出出	chūchū	to give; to come up with
主意	zhǔyi	advice; idea
玩	wán	to tour
一边 . . . 一边 . . .	yībiān . . . yībiān . . .	(to be doing something) while (doing something else)
建议	jiànyì	suggestion
棒极了	bàngjíle	super

准备	**zhǔnbèi**	to be planning
等	**děng**	etc.
云南	**Yúnnán**	(a province in China)
自然	**zìrán**	natural
西南部	**xīnán bù**	southwest part
有道理	**yǒu dàolǐ**	you have a point there; it makes sense
沿途	**yán tú**	on its way; throughout the journey
美丽	**měilì**	beautiful
景色	**jǐngsè**	scenery

Language points ♦

2.1 Use of 玩 (wán)

The basic meaning of 玩 (**wán**) is 'to play' and 'to enjoy oneself'. This verb is used very often in colloquial expressions. For example,

> 有空到我们家来玩。
> **Yǒu kòng dào wǒmen jiā lái wán(r).**
> *lit.* *have time come to our home play*
> Please come to our house when you have time.

> 好好玩。
> **Hǎohāo wán(r).**
> Have a good time.

The sentence in the above dialogue 听说你玩了不少地方 (**tīngshuō nǐ wán le bù shǎo dìfang**) can be translated as 'I hear that you've travelled a lot' or 'I hear that you've been to many places.'

Please note that 玩 (**wán**) is often pronounced with the retroflex 'r' in northern China.

2.2 Pattern 快到 . . . 的时间了 (kuài dào . . . de shíjiān le)

This phrase means 'it is nearly (the) time for . . .' or 'it is nearly . . . time'. There are two points to be noted here. First, a verbal phrase is put before 的 (**de**) to modify 时间 (**shíjiān**, time). For example:

> 快到上课/睡觉/吃饭/出发的时间了。
> **Kuài dào shàng kě/shuìjiào/chīfàn/chū fā de shíjiān le.**
> *lit.* *soon reach going to class/going to bed/eating/setting off time*
> It is nearly time for class/bed/meal/setting off.

Second, putting 了 (le) at the end of the sentence (known as 'end-of sentence *le*') indicates an updating or changing of the situation and influences the meaning of a sentence as a whole. One of the functions of the sentence particle 了 (le) is to suggest that circumstances have reached a particular point, as in the above sentence. See Language points 6.7 in Unit 6 and 10.2 in Unit 10 for more discussions of it.

2.3 Use of 一边...一边... (yībiān ... yībiān ..., 'while')

Use this structure to describe two actions that are taking place at the same time. Put the verb straight after 一边 (yībiān). For example:

我喜欢一边看电视一边吃饭。
Wǒ xǐhuān yībiān kàn diànshì yībiān chīfàn.
I like watching TV whilst eating.

2.4 Giving reasons

To answer the question introduced by 为什么 (wèishénme, why), 因为 (yīnwéi, because) is often used to start the answer. If two or more points need to be given, you can list them as in Dialogue 1 above:

一是因为云南有许多自然风景，二是因为...
yī shì yīnwéi Yúnnán yǒu xǔduō zìrán fēngjǐng, èr shì yīnwéi ...
First, it's because Yunnan has a lot of natural scenery, and second it's because ...

2.5 Use of 再 (zài, 'then')

In 再见 (zàijiàn, good-bye), or 请再说一遍 (qǐng zài shuō yī biàn, please say it again), 再 (zài) means 'again'. In the above dialogue, it means 'then', and it is used to indicate that one action takes place after another. For example:

广州你可以下次去桂林时再去。
Guǎngzhōu nǐ kěyǐ xià cì qù Guìlín shí zài qù.
As for Guangzhou, next time when you go to Guilin, you can go there then.

Please note that 广州 (**Guǎngzhōu**) is the object of the second 去 (**qù**). By bringing it to the beginning of the sentence, it puts emphasis on it. It becomes the topic of the sentence. We shall look at the topical structure in detail in Unit 7.

2.6 Means of transport

Here are the words often used:

火车	**huǒchē**	train
飞机	**fēijī**	aeroplane
船	**chuán**	ship; boat
车	**chē**	car
长途车	**chángtúchē**	coach (*lit.* long-distance bus)
公共汽车	**gōnggòng qìchē**	bus (*lit.* public bus)
出租汽车	**chūzū qìchē**	taxi

When travelling by train, aeroplane, sea, or any of the above means of transport, always use 坐 (**zuò**, *lit. to sit*) or 乘 (**chéng**, to take) + means of transport. 乘 (**chéng**) is more formal than 坐 (**zuò**).

2.7 Use of 请 (**qǐng**)

请 (**qǐng**) can mean 'please' when placed before the verb, or 'to invite, to treat' when it is placed before a personal pronoun. For example:

请坐。
Qǐng zuò.
Please sit down.

我请你吃中饭。
Wǒ qǐng nǐ chī zhōngfàn.
I'll buy you/treat you to lunch.

However, the following sentence can take on both meanings:

请你帮我出出主意。
Qǐng nǐ bāng wǒ chūchu zhǔyi.
i Please help me come up with some ideas.
ii (I) invite you to help me come up with some ideas.

2.8 Use of 完 (**wán**)

Place 完 (**wán**) after the verb to indicate the finishing of an action. For example:

你	最好	去	完	三峡	后	去 云南...
Nǐ	**zuìhǎo**	**qù**	**wán**	**Sān Xiá**	**hòu**	**qù Yúnnán.**

lit. *you better off go [finish] San Xia after go Yunnan*
You're better off going to Yunnan after touring the Three Gorges.

2.9 Use of 好 (hǎo) at the end of a sentence

When 好 (hǎo) is placed at the end of a sentence (in both statement and question), it means 'better'. For example:

我认为这件衣服好。
Wǒ rènwéi zhè jiàn yīfú hǎo.
I think this piece of clothing is better.

你觉得上海好还是北京好？
Nǐ juéde Shànghǎi hǎo háishì Běijīng hǎo?
Which do you think is better – Shanghai or Beijing?

Exercises

Useful words for doing the following exercises

酒吧	**jiǔbā**	bar
聊天	**liáotiān**	to have a chat; to chat
修一修	**xiū yi xiū**	to fix (it)
乡村	**xiāngcūn**	countryside
站	**zhàn**	stop
恰恰相反	**qiàqià xiāngfǎn**	be just the opposite

Exercise 1

Fill in the gaps using appropriate words from the vocabulary list for Dialogue 1:

a 我准备明年夏天去中国旅游，你能不能帮我_____主意？
   Wǒ zhǔnbèi míng nián xiàtiān qù Zhōngguó lǚyóu, nǐ néng bù néng bāng wǒ_____zhǔyi?

b 他们在酒吧里_____喝酒_____聊天。
   Tāmen zài jiǔbā lǐ_____hē jiǔ_____liáotiān.

c 我的自行车坏了，你能不能_____我修一修？
   Wǒde zìxíngchē huài le, Nǐ néng bù néng_____wǒ xiū yi xiū?

d 英国的乡村很美，有许多_____景色。
   Yīngguó de xiāngcūn hěn měi, yǒu xǔduō_____jǐngsè.

e 这是一列慢车，_____要停很多站。
   Zhè shì yī liè màn chē, _____yào tíng hěnduō zhàn.

Exercise 2

Complete the following sentences using the word/phrase provided in brackets and then translate the completed sentences into English:

a _____，小王怎么还没来？(快到...的时间了)
_____, Xiǎo Wáng zěnme hái méi lái? (kuài dào
... de shíjiān le)

b 我不太喜欢这个电影，_____。(一是因为..., 二是
因为....)
Wǒ bù tài xǐhuān zhè ge diànyǐng, _____. (yī shì
yīnwéi..., èr shì yīnwé...)

c 上海人喜欢饭后喝汤，而广东人却恰恰相反，他们_____
_____。(再)
Shànghǎirén xǐhuān fàn hòu hē tāng, ér Guǎngdōngrén què qiàqià
xiāngfǎn, tāmen_____. (zài)

Exercise 3

Translate the following sentences into Chinese:

a Lao Wang, I'd like to invite you to dinner this Sunday.
b The scenery on the journey to Yunnan was superb. I'm so pleased
that I went there by train.
c What he said just now makes sense.
d Enjoy your holiday.
e It's nearly time for supper. We must hurry up.

Dialogue 2   (CD 1; 8)

上城墙 Shàng chéng qiáng
Visiting the city wall

*Mark is in Xi'an, travelling on his own. He is planning to visit the
city wall, but is not sure where the entrance is. He asks a young
Chinese man, Wang Meng, for help...*

Terracotta warriors
www.istock.com

MARK	对不起，我想参观城墙。知道从哪儿上去吗？
WANG MENG	真不好意思，我也不太清楚。我也是外地人，刚好也想到城墙上走走。这样吧，我去打听一下，然后咱们可以一起去。
MARK	太好了，多谢。

(a few minutes later . . .)

WANG MENG	打听清楚了，离这儿不远的南门有个入口处。我们顺着这条街一直走到底，就可以看见大门了。
MARK	要走多久？
WANG MENG	大约十分钟。

(after having visited the wall . . .)

MARK	多亏了你，我今天玩得高兴极了。
WANG MENG	我也是。你的汉语这么好，而且对中国的文化也有很深的了解，真让我佩服。
MARK	多谢夸奖。我明天准备去兵马俑。你去过兵马俑吗？
WANG MENG	还没去过呢。
MARK	咱们一起去，好吗？
WANG MENG	那太棒了！

Dialogue 2 in pinyin

MARK   Duìbùqǐ, wǒ xiǎng <u>cānguān</u> <u>chéng qiáng</u>. Nǐ zhīdào cóng nǎr <u>shàngqu</u> ma?

WANG MENG   Zhēn <u>bù hǎoyìsi</u>, wǒ yě <u>bù tài qīngchu</u>. Wǒ yě shì <u>wàidìrén</u>, gānghǎo yě xiǎng dào chéng qiáng shàng zǒuzou. <u>Zhè yàng ba</u>, wǒ qù <u>dǎtīng</u> yīxià, <u>ránhòu</u> zánmen kěyǐ yīqǐ qù.

MARK   Tài hǎo le, duō xiè.

(a few minutes later . . .)

WANG MENG   Dǎtīng qīngchǔ le, <u>lí</u> zhèr <u>bù yuǎn</u> de nán mén yǒu gè <u>rùkǒuchù</u>. Wǒmen <u>shùnzhe</u> zhè <u>tiáo jiē</u> yīzhí <u>zǒu dào dǐ</u>, jiù kěyǐ kànjiàn dàmén le.

MARK   Yào zǒu duō jiǔ?

WANG MENG   Dàyuē shí fēnzhōng.

(after having visited the wall . . .)

MARK   <u>Duōkuī le</u> nǐ, wǒ jīntiān wán de gāoxìng jí le.

WANG MENG   Wǒ yě shì. Nǐde Hànyǔ zhème hǎo, <u>érqiě</u> duì Zhōngguó de wénhuà yě yǒu hěn shēn de <u>liǎojiě</u>, zhēn ràng wǒ <u>pèifú</u>.

MARK   Duō xiè <u>kuājiǎng</u>. Wǒ míngtiān zhǔnbèi qù <u>Bīngmǎyǒng</u>. Nǐ qù guò Bīngmǎyǒng ma?

WANG MENG   Hái méi qù guò ne.

MARK   Zánmen yīqǐ qù, hǎo ma?

WANG MENG   Nà tài bàng le!

Vocabulary ♦

参观	**cānguān**	to visit
城墙	**chéng qiáng**	city wall
上去	**shàngqu**	to go up
不好意思	**bú hǎoyìsi**	I am sorry; I'm a bit embarrassed
不太清楚	**bú tài qīngchu**	I'm not sure
外地人	**wàidìrén**	stranger, outsider
这样吧	**zhè yàng ba**	I'll tell you what
打听	**dǎtīng**	to find out

然后	ránhòu	then
离... 不远	lí . . . bù yuǎn	to be not far from . . .
入口处	rùkǒuchù	entrance
顺着	shùnzhe	along
条	tiáo	(measure word for winding and slender objects such as street, river)
街	jiē	avenue
走到底	zǒu dào dǐ	to walk to the very end
多亏了	duō kuī le	thanks to . . . ; because of . . .
而且	érqiě	furthermore
了解	liǎojiě	understanding
佩服	pèifu	to admire, admiration
夸奖	kuājiǎng	praise, compliment
兵马俑	Bīngmǎyǒng	Terracotta warriors and horses

Language points ♦

2.10 To apologise or to return a compliment

不好意思 (bù hǎoyìsī) is a colloquial expression and is often used in situations where you wish to apologise, or to return a compliment. For example (to apologise):

A 小王，我能借一下你的自行车吗？
   Xiǎo Wáng, wǒ néng jiè yīxià nǐde zìxíngchē ma?
   Xiao Wang, could I borrow your bike please?

B 真不好意思，我的自行车坏了。
   Zhēn bù hǎoyìsī, wǒde zìxíngchē huài le.
   Really sorry, my bike has broken down.

(to return a compliment):

A 大卫，你的中文说得真棒。
   Dàwèi, nǐde Zhōngwén shuō de zhēn bàng.
   David, you speak such good Chinese.

B 不好意思。谢谢夸奖。
   Bù hǎoyìsī. Xièxie kuājiǎng.
   Not at all. Thank you for your compliment.

2.11 Describing a location

To describe the distance of one place in relation to another, the following structure is often used: 'somewhere + 离 (lí) + somewhere + adjective'. For example:

图书馆　　　离　　中文系　　　　　　很近。
Túshūguǎn lí　　Zhōngwén xì　　　hěn jìn.
lit. *library　　from Chinese Department very close*
The library is quite close to the Chinese Department.

Please note that adverbs such as 很 (**hěn**, very), 比较 (**bǐjiào**, rather) must be used before the adjective.

2.12 Giving directions

This pattern is often used in giving directions: '顺着 (**shùnzhe**, along/down) + somewhere + verbal phrase'. The prepositional phrase 顺着 . . . (**shùnzhe**, along) must be placed before the verbal phrase. For example:

顺着　　这条路　　一直 走，　　第一个 红绿灯
Shùnzhe zhè tiáo lù yīzhí zǒu,　　dì yī gè hónglǜdēng
lit. *along　　this road　　straight walk, the first traffic light*
往　　左　拐。
wǎng　zuǒ guǎi.
lit. *toward left turn*
Walk straight down this road, turn left at the first traffic light.

2.13 Pattern: 'somebody + 对 (duì) + something + 有 (yǒu) + noun phrase'

This pattern is used when somebody has an understanding/interest about something. For example:

我 对　　中国　　有　　一些 了解。
Wǒ duì　　Zhōngguó yǒu　　yīxiē liǎojiě.
lit. *I　about China　　have some understanding*
I have some understanding about China.

他 对　　古典音乐　　没有　　兴趣。
Tā duì　　gǔdiǎn yīnyuè méi yǒu　　xìngqù.
lit. *he about classical music not have interest*
He is not interested in classical music.

2.14   Use of '真让 (zhēn ràng) + somebody + adjective'

It is a very useful pattern, which means 'It really makes one . . .'. For example:

真让我头疼。
Zhēn ràng wǒ tóuténg.
It really gives me a headache.

The indefinite pronoun 人 (rén, someone) can be used here as well. For example:

真让人羡慕。
Zhēn ràng rén xiànmù.
It's really admirable.

Please note that 让 (**ràng**) can be replaced by 令 (**lìng**) but the latter is more formal in style.

Culture note

Terracotta warriors and horses

China's first emperor Qin Shihuang (259–210 BC) was buried 35 km from Xi'an. Buried with him were thousands of life-sized clay figures of warriors and horses. They were discovered accidentally in 1974 by some peasants sinking a well. After years of excavation by archaeologists, the vast Museum of Emperor Qin Shihu Huang's Terracotta Warriors and Horses (**秦始皇兵马俑**, **Qín Shǐhuáng Bīngmǎyǒng**), which nonetheless covers only a third of the site, was opened to the general public in 1979.

Exercises

Useful words for exercises

画展	**huà zhǎn**	art exhibition
帮助	**bāngzhù**	help

按时	**ànshí**	on time
交	**jiāo**	to hand in
作业	**zuòyè**	homework, assignment
街道	**jiēdào**	street
宽	**kuān**	wide
直	**zhí**	straight
暑假	**shǔjià**	summer vacation
短	**duǎn**	short
绘画	**huìhuà**	painting

Exercise 4

Complete the following sentences using appropriate words or phrases in the vocabulary list for Dialogue 2:

a 昨天我_____了中国画展。
Zuótiān wǒ_____le Zhōngguó huà zhǎn.

b _____你的帮助，我明天可以按时交作业了。
_____nǐde bāngzhù, wǒ míngtiān kěyǐ ànshí jiāo zuòyè le.

c 他也不知道火车站在哪儿，因为他也是_____。
Tā yě bù zhīdào huǒchē zhàn zài nǎr, yīnwéi tā yě shì_____.

d 这个城市的街道很宽，_____也很直。
Zhè ge chéngshì de jiēdào hěn kuān, _____yě hěn zhí.

e 张老师经常和学生聊天，他对每个学生的情况都十分_____。
Zhāng lǎoshī jīngcháng hé xuéshēng liáotiān, tā duì měi ge xuéshēng de qíngkuàng dōu shífēn_____.

Exercise 5

Fill in the gaps using 的 (**de**) or 得 (**DE**), then translate the completed sentences into English (to distinguish between the two de's in *pinyin*, use capital letters for the second one):

a 在西安_____城墙上，可以骑自行车。
Zài Xī'ān_____chéng qiáng shàng, kěyǐ qí zìxíngchē.

b 他说中文说_____很好。
  Tā shuō Zhōngwén shuō_____hěn hǎo.

c 这趟火车开_____很慢。
  Zhè tàng huǒchē kāi_____hěn màn.

d 云南有许多美丽_____自然风景。
  Yúnnán yǒu xǔduō měilì_____zìrán fēngjǐng.

e 她暑假去了三峡，玩_____好极了。
  Tā shǔjià qù le Sānxiá, wán_____hǎojíle.

Exercise 6

Complete the following sentences using the phrase provided in brackets:

a 他在这么短的时间学会了这么多的汉字，_____(真让
  人...)。
  Tā zài zhème duǎn de shíjiān xué huì le zhème duō de hànzì, ____
  _____(zhēn ràng rén ...).

b 邮局_____(离...)，从我们家走路到邮局只需要五分钟。
  Yóujú_____(lí ...), cóng wǒmen jiā zǒulù dào yóujú zhǐ
  xūyào wǔ fēnzhōng.

c 我不怎么喜欢绘画，但_____(对...有...)。
  Wǒ bù zěnme xǐhuān huìhuà, dàn_____(duì ... yǒu ...).

Exercise 7 (CD 1; 9)

What do you say in the following situations?

a A Chinese person has just praised you, saying that you write
  Chinese characters very well. What do you say?
b A friend of yours would like to borrow some money from you, but
  unfortunately you haven't got any with you. What do you say?
c You try to find out if someone would like to visit the city wall
  with you.

Reading comprehension (CD 1; 10)

一篇日记 Yī piān rìjì
A diary

Bear the following questions in mind whilst reading the diary below. The diary is kept by Yingli (英丽, Yīnglì), an American Chinese who is visiting China for the first time. Answer the questions in Chinese after you have read the diary:

1 英丽现在在哪儿？
   Yīnglì xiànzài zài nǎr?

2 她怎么去重庆？
   Tā zěnme qù Chóngqìng?

3 西安从前叫什么？
   Xī'ān cóngqián jiào shénme?

4 西安有什么有意思的地方可以参观？
   Xī'ān yǒu shénme yǒuyìsi de dìfang kěyǐ cānguān?

5 城墙有几个入口处？
   Chéng qiáng yǒu jǐ gè rùkǒuchù?

Key words ♦

The following words may help you to understand the diary better:

重庆	Chóngqìng	(a city in China)
篇	piān	(measure word)
日记	rìjì	diary
古老的	gǔlǎo de	ancient
原名	yuán míng	original name
长安	Cháng'ān	(place name) (*lit.* forever peace)
著名	zhùmíng	well known; famous
规模	guīmó	scale
不敢相信	bù gǎn xiāngxìn	unbelievable
展出	zhǎnchū	to be on display
上千个	shàng qiān gè	over a thousand
面部表情	miànbù biǎoqíng	facial expression

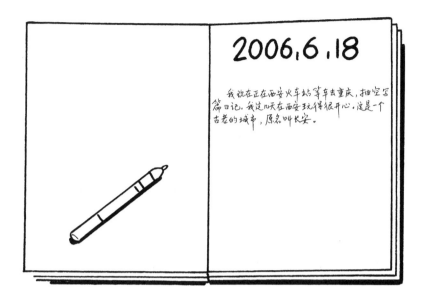

2006,6,18

我现在正在西安火车站等车去重庆,抽空写篇日记. 我这几天在西安玩得很开心. 这是一个古老的城市, 原名叫长安.

另外	**lìngwài**	besides
整整齐齐	**zhěng-zhěng-qí-qí**	orderly
中心	**zhōngxīn**	centre
钟楼	**Zhōng Lóu**	Bell Tower
保留	**bǎoliú**	to preserve
游人	**yóurén**	tourist

Diary in characters

2006, 6, 18   晴天
我现在正在西安火车站等车去重庆,抽空写篇日记。我这几天
在西安玩得很开心。这是一个古老的城市,原名叫长安。西安的
名胜古迹很多。今天上午我去了著名的兵马俑,规模那么大,
真让人不敢相信。展出的兵和马有上千个,可每个士兵的面部
表情都不一样。另外,这个城市看上去整整齐齐,一是因为全城
的中心是钟楼,四面有东、南、西、北四条大街,二是因为主要
街道都很直。西安还保留了古城墙,城墙有四个入口处:东门、
南门、西门和北门。游人可以到城墙上参观,还可以在上面骑
自行车呢!

Diary in pinyin

2006, 6, 18   Qíng tiān

Wǒ xiànzài zhèngzài Xī'ān huǒchē zhàn děng chē qù <u>Chóngqìng</u>, chōu kòng xiě <u>piān rìjì</u>. Wǒ zhè jǐ tiān zài Xī'ān wán de hěn kāixīn. Zhè shì yī gè <u>gǔlǎo de</u> chéngshì, <u>yuán míng</u> jiào <u>Cháng'ān</u>. Xī'ān de míng-shèng-gǔ-jī hěn duō. Jīntiān shàngwǔ wǒ qù le <u>zhùmíng</u> de Bīngmǎyǒng, <u>guīmó</u> nàme dà, zhēn ràng rén <u>bù gǎn xiāngxìn</u>. <u>Zhǎnchū</u> de bīng hé mǎ yǒu <u>shàng qiān gè</u>, kě měi gè shìbīng de <u>miànbù biǎoqíng</u> dōu bù yīyàng. Lìngwài, zhè ge chéngshì kànshàngqu <u>zhěng-zhěng-qí-qí</u>, yī shì yīnwéi quán chéng de <u>zhōngxīn</u> shì <u>Zhōng Lóu</u>, sì miàn yǒu dōng, nán, xī, běi sì tiáo dàjiē, èr shì yīnwéi zhǔyào jiēdào dōu hěn zhí. Xī'ān hái <u>bǎoliú</u> le gǔ chéng qiáng, chéng qiáng yǒu sì ge rùkǒuchù: dōng mén, nán mén, xī mén hé běi mén. <u>Yóurén</u> kěyǐ dào chéng qiáng shàng cānguān, hái kěyǐ zài shàng miàn qí zìxíngchē ne!

3 健康
Jiànkāng
Health

In this unit, you will learn about:

▶ some medical-related terms
▶ how to explain some health problems
▶ some sport-related terms
▶ using 什么 (**shénme**) in negative sentences
▶ using (**dé**) as a verb
▶ difference between 并且 (**bìngqiě**) and 和 (**hé**)
▶ noun clause signalled by 的 (**de**)

Dialogue 1 (CD 1; 11)

看医生　Kàn yīshēng
Seeing the doctor

Jane is teaching English in a northern city in China. She is not feeling very well today, so she has come to a health centre to see a doctor.

DOCTOR	你好！请坐。
JANE	你好！大夫。
DOCTOR	你哪儿不舒服？
JANE	我头疼，嗓子也疼。反正全身没劲。
DOCTOR	什么时候开始的？
JANE	两天前。
DOCTOR	发烧吗？
JANE	好像有点儿。
DOCTOR	给你量一下体温。

(having checked the thermometer)

At the health centre
Photographer: Zhang Ping

DOCTOR 你发烧了。三十八度五。
JANE 我得了什么病？
DOCTOR 重感冒。不要紧。我给你开一些退烧药。再吃几副中药。
JANE 熬中药太麻烦。您给我开一些中成药吧。
DOCTOR 没问题。你一定要按时吃药。多喝水，多休息。过两天就会好的。
JANE 大夫，您能给我开一张病假条吗？
DOCTOR 当然可以。我给你开三天。
JANE 谢谢，大夫。

Dialogue 1 in pinyin ♦

DOCTOR Nǐ hǎo. Qǐng zuò.
JANE Nǐ hǎo. <u>Dàifu</u>.
DOCTOR Nǐ nǎr <u>bù shūfu</u>?
JANE Wǒ <u>tóuténg</u>. <u>Sǎngzi</u> yě téng. <u>Fǎnzhèng</u> <u>quán shēn</u> <u>méi jìn</u>.
DOCTOR Shénme shíhòu kāishǐ de?

JANE   Liǎng tiān qián.
DOCTOR   <u>Fā shāo</u> ma?
JANE   <u>Hǎoxiàng</u> yǒu diǎnr.
DOCTOR   Gěi nǐ <u>liáng</u> yīxià <u>tǐwēn</u>.

(having checked the thermometer)

DOCTOR   Nǐ fā shāo le. Sānshí bā <u>dù</u> wǔ.
JANE   Wǒ <u>dé</u> le shénme <u>bìng</u>?
DOCTOR   <u>Zhòng gǎnmào</u>. <u>Bú yàojǐn</u>. Wǒ gěi nǐ kāi yīxiē <u>tuìshāo yào</u>. Zài chī jǐ <u>fù</u> <u>zhōng yào</u>.
JANE   <u>Áo</u> zhōng yào tài <u>máfán</u>. Nín gěi wǒ kāi yīxiē <u>zhōng chéng yào</u> ba.
DOCTOR   Méi wèntí. Nǐ yīdìng yào <u>àn shí</u> chī yào. <u>Duō</u> hē shuǐ, duō <u>xiūxi</u>. Guò liǎng tiān jiù huì hǎo de.
JANE   Dàifu, nín néng gěi wǒ kāi yī zhāng <u>bìngjià tiáo</u> ma?
DOCTOR   <u>Dāngrán</u> kěyǐ. Wǒ gěi nǐ kāi sān tiān.
JANE   Xièxiè, dàifu.

Vocabulary ◆

大夫	dàifū	doctor (informal)
不舒服	bù shūfu	unwell; not comfortable
头疼	tóuténg	headache
嗓子	sǎngzi	throat
反正	fǎnzhèng	anyway; in a word
全身	quán shēn	the whole body
没劲	méi jìn	no energy
发烧	fā shāo	to have a temperature
好像	hǎoxiàng	to seem; to appear; it seems
量体温	liáng . . . tǐwēn	to take the temperature
度	dù	degree
得 . . . 病	dé . . . bìng	to get/contract (illness)
重感冒	zhòng gǎnmào	bad cold
不要紧	bú yàojǐn	not serious
退烧药	tuìshāo yào	temperature relief medicine
副	fù	(measure word)
中药	zhōng yào	traditional Chinese medicine
熬	áo	to simmer
麻烦	máfán	trouble; troublesome
中成药	zhōng chéng yào	ready-made traditional Chinese medicine

按时	**àn shí**	at the prescribed intervals; according to time
多	**duō**	more
休息	**xiūxi**	to rest
病假条	**bìngjià tiáo**	sick note
当然	**dāngrán**	of course

Additional useful words

医务所	**yīwù suǒ**	clinic; health centre
高血压	**gāo xuè yā**	high blood pressure
咳嗽	**késòu**	to cough
鼻子不通	**bízi bù tōng**	blocked nose
耳朵疼	**ěrduoténg**	earache
牙疼	**yáténg**	toothache
背疼	**bèiténg**	backache
肚子疼	**dùziténg**	stomach ache
拉肚子	**lā dùzi**	diarrhoea
胃口不好	**wèikǒu bù hǎo**	no appetite
打针	**dǎzhēn**	to have an injection
急性	**jíxìng**	acute
阑尾炎	**lánwěiyán**	appendicitis

Language points ♦

3.1 你哪儿不舒服？(**Nǐ nǎr bù shūfu?**)

The literal translation of the question is 'you where uncomfortable/not well?'. What it really means is 'What is the matter with you?' In answering this question, you can say, for example:

我肚子不舒服。
Wǒ dùzi bù shūfu.
My tummy is not right.

3.2 Use of 得 · · · 病 (dé . . . bìng, 'to suffer from')

When 得 (**de**) is used to introduce a compliment of manner as in 你的中文说得很好 (**Nǐde Zhōngwén shuō de hěn hǎo**, You speak very good Chinese), '**de**' does not carry any tones. In Dialogue 1 above, 得 (**dé**) is a verb meaning 'to contract/get . . . (illness)' and it is pronounced with the second tone (**dé**). Let us see how it is used:

A 他得了什么病？
   Tā dé le shénme bìng?
lit. *he got what illness?*
   What is (medically) wrong with him?

B 高血压。
   Gāo xuè yā.
   High blood pressure.

Please note that adjectives such as 重 (**zhòng**) can be inserted between 得 (**dé**) and 病 (**bìng**). For example:

我父亲得了重病。
Wǒ fùqīn dé le zhòng bìng.
lit. *my father got serious illness*
   My father has been taken very ill.

3.3 Verb 开 (kāi, 'to prescribe/to write')

开 (**kāi**) is a multi-meaning word depending on what follows it. In the dialogue, 开退烧药 (**kāi tuìshāo yào**) means 'to prescribe temperature relief medicine' and 开病假条 (**kāi bìngjià tiáo**) means 'to write a sick note'.

3.4 吃药 (chī yào)

Please note that 'take medicine' is always 'eat medicine' in Chinese.

3.5 Use of 多 (duō)

When 多 (**duō**) is used as an adverb to mean 'to do more of something', it must be placed before the verb. For example: 多喝水 (**duō hē shuǐ**, drink more water); 多休息 (**duō xiūxi**, rest more). It can also be used in the construction: '多 (**duō**) + 和 (**hé**) + somebody + do something'. For example:

去一个国家旅游，应该多和当地人交流。
Qù yī ge guójiā lǚyóu, yìnggāi duō hé dāngdì rén jiāoliú.
When travelling in another country, one should communicate more with the locals.

3.6 疼 (téng) and 痛 (tòng)

Both of these verbs mean 'to hurt/ache'. 痛 (**tòng**) is used more by southern Chinese whilst 疼 (**téng**) is used more by northerners.

3.7　To express certainty

Use the pattern 会 ... 的 (huì ... de) to express the certainty of an event in the future. It is often used with expressions such as 一定 (yīdìng), 肯定 (kěndìng). For example:

我一定会按时吃药的。
Wǒ yīdìng huì àn shí chī yào de.
I'll definitely take the medicine at the prescribed intervals.

她肯定会来的。
Tā kěndìng huì lái de.
She'll definitely come.

Culture notes

Traditional Chinese medicine

Traditional Chinese medicine (中医 **zhōngyī**), with its unique theory and methods, has a history of thousands of years. Records of illnesses, medicines and treatment methods have been found inscribed on oracle bones from the Shang Dynasty (1766 to 1122 BC). In 1973, a number of medical treatises, written on silk banners and bamboo slips, were excavated from the No. 3 tomb at Mahuangdui in Changsha, Hunan Province. These treatises were transcribed in the time of the Qin and Han Dynasties (221 BC to 220 AD), and represent the oldest surviving Chinese medical literature.

Chinese medicine not only involves herbal preparations, it also embraces treatment methods such as acupuncture and moxibustion which have gained popularity all over the world. Both Chinese medicines and treatment methods have continued to develop and improve over time. According to the treatment selected for a certain disease, different methods of medicinal production are used. Ingredients may be processed by methods such as baking, simmering or roasting, all of which have benefited from modern technology. Therefore, you can get the dried herbs, prepare them yourself by simmering and then drink the resulting liquid or you may alternatively buy the medicines ready-made. The ready-made medicines come in different forms

– some are tablets, others liquid, some are in the shape of tiny balls, and some are in big, soft balls.

When consulting a traditional Chinese medicine doctor, he or she will feel your pulse and then ask you some questions. Based on this assessment of your condition, medicine may be prescribed. If the prescription is for raw dry herbs, it will consist of at least eight different ingredients, which you will need to prepare by simmering. People believe that these prescriptions are tailored to an individual's specific problem and are therefore more effective than the ready-made.

Seeing the doctor

Seeing the doctor in China is a different experience. Very often, two doctors share one consulting room. That is to say, you will not have the kind of privacy you are used to. Sometimes, other patients may come into the room and queue right next to you!

Exercises

Useful words for the following exercises

婚礼	hūnlǐ	wedding
黑云	hēi yún	black cloud
用功	yònggōng	hardworking (refer to academic work)
不管	bùguǎn	regardless
必须	bìxū	must
厉害	lìhai	serious, severe

Exercise 1

Fill in the gaps using appropriate words from the vocabulary list for Dialogue 1:

a 从昨天开始，我觉得全身_____，不想吃饭。
  Cóng zuótiān kāishǐ, wǒ juéde quán shēn_____, bù xiǎng chīfàn.

b 小李是我最好的朋友，她的婚礼我_____要去参加。
  Xiǎo Lǐ shì wǒ zuìhǎo de péngyǒu, tāde hūnlǐ wǒ_____yào qù cānjiā.

c   他这几天什么都不想吃，是不是_____了什么病？

Tā zhè jǐ tiān shénme dōu bù xiǎng chī, shì bú shì_____le shénme bìng?

d   你看，天上的黑云！_____快下大雨了。

Nǐ kàn, tiān shàng de hēi yún! _____kuài xià dà yǔ le.

e   他是个用功的学生，总是_____交作业。

Tā shì gè yònggōng de xuéshēng, zǒngshì_____jiāo zuòyè.

f   不管中药怎么好，我_____不喜欢吃。

Bùguǎn zhōng yào zěnme hǎo, wǒ_____bù xǐhuān chī.

g   你得了重感冒，应该_____睡觉。

Nǐ dé le zhòng gǎnmào, yìnggāi_____shuìjiào.

Exercise 2

Role-play: suppose you are the patient and have gone in to see the doctor. Fill in your part of the conversation:

DOCTOR   **你哪儿不舒服？**

Nǐ nǎr bù shūfu?

YOU   1 _____.

DOCTOR   **什么时候开始的？**

Shénme shíhòu kāishǐ de?

YOU   2 _____.

DOCTOR   **发烧吗？**

Fā shāo ma?

YOU   **烧得很高。**   3 _____?

Shāo de hěn gāo.

DOCTOR   **你得了急性阑尾炎。必须马上去医院。**

Nǐ dé le jíxìng lánwěi yán. Bìxū mǎshàng qù yīyuàn.

Exercise 3

Decide whether the 得 used in the following sentences is pronounced **dé** (with the second tone) or **de** (with the neutral tone); and then translate the sentences into English (**de** is deliberately left without the tone mark in the pinyin sentences):

a 他咳嗽得很厉害，晚上都睡不着觉。
Tā késòu de hěn lìhai, wǎnshàng dōu shuì bù zháo jiào.

b 我父亲得了急性阑尾炎。
Wǒ fùqīn de le jíxìng lánwěiyán.

c 我听说小王最近身体不好。他到底得了什么病？
Wǒ tīng shuō Xiǎo Wáng zuìjìn shēntǐ bù hǎo. Tā dàodǐ de le shénme bìng?

d 我们老师说话说得太快。我常常听不懂。
Wǒmen lǎoshī shuō huà shuō de tài kuài. Wǒ chángcháng tīng bù dǒng.

Exercise 4

Match the character(s) in the left-hand column with the appropriate character(s) in the right-hand column:

a	发	fā	没劲	méi jìn
b	量	liáng	条	tiáo
c	开	kāi	体温	tǐwēn
d	病假	bìng jià	烧	shāo
e	全身	quán shēn	退烧药	tuì shāo yào

Dialogue 2 (CD 1; 13)

谈论身体　Tánlùn shēntǐ
Talking about health

Xiao Li and Lao Wang are neighbours. They have bumped into each other on their way home from work.

XIAO LI　老王，您最近气色不错。有什么秘方？

LAO WANG　什么秘方都没有，小李。就是生活很有规律，比如早睡早起，而且每天慢跑半个小时。

XIAO LI　我应该向您学习。我最近总是头晕，晚上睡觉不好。

LAO WANG　看医生了吗？

XIAO LI　看了，可是没查出什么问题。

LAO WANG　你每天几点睡觉？

XIAO LI	大概十二点左右。
LAO WANG	锻炼身体吗？
XIAO LI	不锻炼。
LAO WANG	我觉得你应该改变你的生活习惯。晚上早些睡觉，并且做些运动。
XIAO LI	您说的对。我从明天就开始。

Dialogue 2 in pinyin ♦

XIAO LI	Lǎo Wáng, nín zuìjìn <u>qìsè</u> bú cuò. Yǒu shénme <u>mì fāng</u>?
LAO WANG	Shénme mìfāng dōu méi yǒu, Xiǎo Lǐ. Jiù shì shēnghuó hěn yǒu <u>guīlǜ</u>, <u>bǐ rú</u> zǎo shuì zǎo qǐ. <u>Érqiě</u>, měi tiān màn pǎo bàn gè xiǎoshí.
XIAO LI	Wǒ <u>yìnggāi xiàng</u> nín <u>xuéxí</u>. Wǒ zuìjìn zǒngshì <u>tóu yūn</u>, wǎnshang shuìjiào bù hǎo.
LAO WANG	Kàn yīshēng le ma?
XIAO LI	Kàn le, kěshì méi <u>chá chū</u> shénme wèntí.

LAO WANG	Nǐ měi tiān jǐ diǎn shuìjiào?
XIAO LI	<u>Dàgài</u> shí'èr diǎn zuǒyòu.
LAO WANG	<u>Duànliàn shēntǐ</u> ma?
XIAO LI	Bù duànliàn.
LAO WANG	Wǒ juéde nǐ yìnggāi <u>gǎibiàn</u> nǐde <u>shēnghuó xíguàn</u>.
	Wǎnshang zǎo xiē shuìjiào, <u>bìngqiě</u> zuò xiē <u>yùndòng</u>.
XIAO LI	Nín shuō de duì. Wǒ <u>cóng</u> míngtiān jiù <u>kāishǐ</u>.

Vocabulary ♦

气色	qìsè	complexion, colour
秘方	mì fāng	secret recipe
规律	guīlǜ	routine
比如	bǐrú	for example
而且	érqiě	furthermore
应该	yìnggāi	should
向...学习	xiàng . . . xuéxí	to learn from . . .
头晕	tóu yūn	to feel dizzy (*lit.* head dizzy)
查出	chá chū	to have found out
大概	dàgài	approximately
锻炼	duànliàn	to exercise
身体	shēntǐ	body
改变	gǎi biàn	to change
生活习惯	shēnghuó xíguàn	daily routine (*lit.* living habit)
并且	bìngqiě	and
运动	yùndòng	exercise; sport
从...开始	cóng . . . kāishǐ	to start from

Additional useful words

乒乓球	pīng pāng qiú	table-tennis
羽毛球	yǔmáo qiú	badminton (*lit.* feather ball)
足球	zú qiú	football
篮球	lán qiú	basketball
网球	wǎng qiú	tennis
气功	qì gōng	Chi Kung
长跑	cháng pǎo	jogging
游泳	yóu yǒng	swimming
太极拳	tài jí quán	Tai-chi

Language points ♦

3.8   气色 (qìsè)

If you want to say 'You look well' in Chinese, you say 你的气色不错 (**Nǐde qìsè bú cuò**) or 你的气色很好 (**Nǐde qìsè hěn hǎo**). Culturally, it is acceptable to say to someone you know fairly well that they don't look too good. So you may hear a Chinese friend telling you 你的气色不怎么好 (**Nǐde qìsè bù zěnme hǎo**, You don't look very well). Literally, it means 'Your complexion is not too good.'

3.9   什么 (shénme) used in negative sentences

In Dialogue 2, 什么 (**shénme**) is not the question word but an adjective meaning 'any'. Please see more examples:

我没有什么好衣服。
Wǒ méi yǒu shénme hǎo yīfu.
I haven't got any good clothes.

他说不出什么有意思的话。
Tā shuō bù chū shénme yǒu yìsi de huà.
He never comes up with anything interesting.

3.10   Difference between 并且 (bìngqiě) and 和 (hé)

和 (**hé**) can only be used to link two nouns or short noun-like phrases, but not sentences. If you want to link two sentences together with a conjunction, then use 并且 (**bìng qiě**). For example:

我喜欢打乒乓球和游泳。
Wǒ xǐhuān dǎ pīngpāng qiú hé yóuyǒng.
I like playing table-tennis and swimming.

他每天睡觉睡得很晚，并且只睡五、六个小时。
Tā měitiān shuìjiào shuì de hěn wǎn, bìngqiě zhǐ shuì wǔ, liù gè xiǎoshí.
He goes to bed very late each night, and sleeps for five or six hours only.

Please note that both sentences linked by 并且 (**bìngqiě**) normally share the same subject (e.g. 他, **tā** in the example above).

3.11   More on noun clauses signalled by 的 (de)

In Language point 1.11 of Unit 1, we saw the use of 的 (de) to introduce a noun clause. The examples given there were noun clauses used as subjects and that 的 (de) is followed by 是 . . . (shì . . .). For example:

我应该改变的   是我的生活习惯。
<u>**Wǒ yìnggāi gǎibiàn** *de*</u>   <u>**shì** wǒde shēnghuó xíguàn.</u>
[subject]   [be]
What I should change is my daily routine.

When a noun clause functions as the subject, it can also be followed by verbs other than 是 . . . (shì . . .). Take the last sentence in Dialogue 2 above:

您说的   对。
<u>**Nín shuō** *de*</u>   **duì.**
[subject]   [verb]
What you said is right.

Noun clauses can also function as object. For example:

这些正是他最喜欢的。
Zhèxiē zhèng shì tā zuì xǐhuān *de*.
              [object]
These are exactly what he likes most.

Exercises

Exercise 5

Fill in the gaps using appropriate words from the vocabulary list for Dialogue 2:

a   他生活没有_____，有时候睡得早，有时候睡得特别晚。
    Tā shēnghuó méi yǒu_____, yǒu shíhòu shuì de zǎo, yǒu shíhòu shuì de tèbié wǎn.

b   您这么大年纪了，身体还这么好。有什么_____？
    Nín zhème dà niánjì le, shēntǐ hái zhème hǎo. Yǒu shénme
    _____?

c 王老师今天＿＿＿＿＿＿不太好。她是不是不舒服？
Wáng lǎoshī jīntiān＿＿＿＿＿＿bú tài hǎo. Tā shì bú shì bù shūfu?

d 我应该向我妹妹＿＿＿＿＿＿，早睡早起。
Wǒ yìnggāi xiàng wǒ mèimei＿＿＿＿＿＿, zǎo shuì zǎo qǐ.

e 我爸爸每天早上六点起床，去公园＿＿＿＿＿＿身体。
Wǒ bàba měi tiān zǎoshàng liù diǎn qǐchuáng, qù gōngyuán
＿＿＿＿＿＿shēntǐ.

Exercise 6

There is one word in each of the following columns which does not
belong to the same category. Find it:

A		B		C	
中药	zhōng yào	头疼	tóu téng	长跑	cháng pǎo
病假条	bìngjià tiáo	嗓子疼	sǒngzi téng	游泳	yóuyǒng
退烧药	tuì shāo yào	大夫	dàifu	头晕	tóuyūn
中成药	zhōng chéng yào	发烧	fā shāo	太极拳	tàijí quán

Exercise 7

Translate the following into Chinese:

a You should eat more vegetables, and also start doing exercises.
b He follows a routine in his life, and also exercises every morning.
c What he told you is not true.
d Starting from tomorrow, I'm going to get up early.

Listening comprehension (CD 1; 14)

锻炼身体　Duànliàn shēntǐ
Doing exercises

Listen to the following passage. Try not to read the script. Bear the
following questions in mind whilst listening to the passage and try to
answer them afterwards:

Doing morning exercises

1 说话人今年多大了？   **Shuōhuàrén jīnnián duō dà le?**
2 他的身体怎么样？   **Tāde shēntǐ zěnme yàng?**
3 他有什么秘方？   **Tā yǒu shénme mìfāng?**
4 他每天早上去公园干什么？   **Tā měitiān zǎoshang qù gōngyuán gàn shénme?**
5 公园里，其他人在做什么？   **Gōngyuán lǐ, qítā rén zài zuò shénme?**

Key words ♦

You may find the following words useful to understand the passage better:

说话人	**shuōhuàrén**	the speaker
热闹	**rènao**	lively; bustling with noise and excitement
在 . . . 的伴奏下	**zài . . . de bànzòu xià**	to be accompanied by (musical instrument)
跳舞	**tiàowǔ**	to dance
退休	**tuìxiū**	retired
拿 . . . 来说	**ná . . . lái shuō**	to take . . . as example

健美操	**jiànměi cāo**	keep-fit exercises
孙子	**sūnzi**	grandson
老伴	**lǎobàn**	spouse (used among elderly people)
散步	**sànbù**	to stroll

Script in characters ♦

在中国，你应该早上去公园看看，那儿特别热闹。有打太极拳的，有做健美操的，也有在音乐的伴奏下跳舞的。你如果有兴趣的话，也可以跟着一起学。大多数在公园运动的人是退休的老人。就拿我来说吧，今年已经六十八岁了，可我很少感冒生病。你看我的气色不错吧。那是因为我每天早上都去公园锻炼身体。有时候我打太极拳，有时候我跳健美操。如果我孙子和我一起去公园，我们还打打羽毛球。另外，每天吃完晚饭后，我和老伴常常一起出去散步。

Script in pinyin ♦

Zài Zhōngguó, nǐ yìnggāi zǎoshang qù gōngyuán kànkan, nàr tèbié rènao. Yǒu dǎ tàijíquán de, yǒu zuò jiànměi cāo de, yě yǒu zài yīnyuè de bànzòu xià tiàowǔ de. Nǐ rúguǒ yǒu xìngqù de huà, yě kěyǐ gēn zhe yīqǐ xué. Dàduōshù zài gōngyuán yùndòng de rén shì tuìxiū de lǎo rén. Jiù ná wǒ lái shuō ba, jīnnián yǐjīng liùshí bā suì le, kě wǒ hěn shǎo gǎnmào shēngbìng. Nǐ kàn wǒde qìsè bú cuò ba. Nà shì yīnwéi wǒ měitiān zǎoshang dōu qù gōngyuán duànliàn shēntǐ. Yǒushíhòu wǒ dǎ tàijíquán, yǒushíhòu wǒ tiào jiànměicāo. Rúguǒ wǒ sūnzi hé wǒ yīqǐ qù gōngyuán, wǒmen hái dǎda yǔmáoqiú. Lìngwài, měi tiān chī wán wǎnfàn hòu, wǒ hé lǎobàn chángcháng yīqǐ chūqu sànbù.

4 聚会和饮食
Jùhuì hé yǐnshí
Get-togethers and food

In this unit, you will learn about:

▶ 去 (**qu**) as a direction indicator
▶ 什么 (**shénme**) as an indefinite pronoun
▶ 把 (**bǎ**) sentence
▶ words indicating procedures and sequences
▶ some very useful expressions such as 有什么不同的地方？ (. . . **yǒu shénme bùtóng de dìfāng**); 以 . . . 为主 (**yǐ . . . wéi zhǔ**); etc.

Dialogue 1 (CD 1; 15)

聚会 Jùhuì
Get-togethers

Jane is working in Beijing, and she wants to invite Lili and some other Chinese friends around for a meal . . .

JANE 丽丽，这个周日，我要请几个朋友来吃饭。你能来吗？
LILI 吃午饭还是晚饭？
JANE 晚饭，七点左右。
LILI 那，我能来。
JANE 太好了。这样，我们可以包饺子吃。
LILI 包饺子很费时间。你最好叫几个朋友早些到，帮我们一起包。我五点左右可以到你那儿。
JANE 我需要买些什么？
LILI 买几斤猪肉末，一棵大白菜，几根葱，还有面粉。
JANE 需要什么调料？
LILI 酱油，盐，香油，五香粉和鸡蛋。

Get-together
Photographer: Kan Jia

JANE	这些我都有。
LILI	你会调馅吗？
JANE	不会，你告诉我怎么调。
LILI	比较复杂，说不清。还是等我到了你家后，咱们再调馅、和面。
JANE	好吧。周日五点见。
LILI	需要我带一些什么去？
JANE	什么都不要带。你帮我包饺子就是最好的礼物。

Dialogue 1 in pinyin ◆

JANE	Lìlì, zhègè <u>zhōurì</u> wǒ yào qǐng jǐ gè péngyǒu lái chīfàn. Nǐ néng lái ma?
LILI	Chī wǔfàn háishì wǎnfàn?
JANE	Wǎnfàn, qī diǎn zuǒyòu.
LILI	Nà, wǒ néng lái.
JANE	Tài hǎo le. Zhè yàng, wǒmen kěyǐ <u>bāo jiǎozi</u> chī.
LILI	Bāo jiǎozi hěn <u>fèishíjiān</u>. Nǐ zuìhǎo jiào jǐ gè péngyou zǎoxiē dào, bāng wǒmen yīqǐ bāo. Wǒ wǔ diǎn zuǒyòu kěyǐ dào <u>nǐ nàr</u>.

JANE	Wǒ xūyào mǎi xiē shénme?
LILI	Mǎi jǐ jīn <u>zhūròu mò</u>, yī <u>kē</u> dà <u>báicài</u>, jǐ <u>gēn</u> <u>cōng</u>, háiyǒu <u>miànfěn</u>.
JANE	Xūyào shénme <u>tiáoliào</u>?
LILI	<u>Jiàngyóu</u>, <u>yán</u>, <u>xiāng yóu</u>, <u>wǔ xiāng fěn</u> he jī dàn.
JANE	Zhèxiē wǒ dōu yǒu.
LILI	Nǐ huì <u>tiáo xiàn</u> ma?
JANE	Bú huì. Nǐ gàosù wǒ zěnme tiáo.
LILI	<u>Bǐjiào</u> <u>fùzá</u>, <u>shuō bu qīng</u>. Háishì děng wǒ dào le nǐ jiā hòu, zánmen zài tiáo xiàn, <u>hé miàn</u>.
JANE	Hǎo ba. Zhōurì wǔ diǎn jiàn.
LILI	Xūyào wǒ dài yīxiē shénme qu?
JANE	Shénme dōu bú yào dài. Nǐ bāng wǒ bāo jiǎozi jiù shì zuìhǎode lǐwù.

Vocabulary ◆

聚会	**jù huì**	a get-together; party
饮食	**yǐnshí**	food; cuisine
周日	**zhōu rì**	Sunday
包饺子	**bāo jiǎozi**	to make dumplings
费时间	**fèishíjiān**	time-consuming
你那儿	**nǐ nàr**	your place
猪肉末	**zhūròu mò**	pork mince
棵	**kē**	(measure word for plants and vegetables)
白菜	**báicài**	Chinese leaves
根	**gēn**	(measure word for long and slim things)
葱	**cōng**	spring onion
面粉	**miànfěn**	flour
调料	**tiáo liào**	seasoning; condiment
酱油	**jiàng yóu**	soya sauce
盐	**yán**	salt
香油	**xiāng yóu**	sesame oil
五香粉	**wǔ xiāng fěn**	Chinese five-spice powder
调馅	**tiáo xiàn**	to make the filling
比较	**bǐjiào**	rather
复杂	**fùzá**	complicated; complex
说不清	**shuō bu qīng**	cannot be explained easily
和面	**hé miàn**	to make the dough

Language points ♦

4.1 Use of 要 (yào)

Here, 要 (yào) is used to indicate that the matter under discussion is definitely going to happen. For example:

这个周末，我要给我妈妈打电话。
Zhège zhōumò, wǒ yào gěi wǒ māma dǎ diànhuà.
This weekend, I'm going to call my mother.

When 一定 (yīdìng, definitely) is used with 要 (yào), it means 'must'. For example:

你一定要来帮我包饺子。
Nǐ yīdìng yào lái bāng wǒ bāo jiǎozi.
You must come and help me make the dumplings.

4.2 Use of 费时间 (fèishíjiān)

Please note the difference between 浪费时间 (làngfèi shíjiān) and 费时间 (fèishíjiān). 浪费时间 (làngfèi shíjiān) is a verb + noun construction, which means 'to waste time' or 'a waste of time'; whilst 费时间 (fèishíjiān) means 'time-consuming' and it can function as a predicate. For example:

昨天晚上的电影太没意思了，简直是浪费时间。
Zuótiān wǎnshang de diànyǐng tài méi yìsī le, jiǎnzhí shì làngfèi shíjiān.
Last night's film was too boring. It was a real waste of time.

自己做蛋糕太费时间了。
Zìjǐ zuò dàngāo tài fèishíjiān le.
Making a cake is very time-consuming.

4.3 去 (qu) as a direction indicator

去 (qu) in 需要我带一些什么去？ (**Xūyào wǒ dài yīxiē shénme qu?**) functions as a direction indicator to indicate the direction away from the speaker. 去 (qu) can directly follow a verb of movement or come after the object of that verb. For example:

你妈妈不在家，我就不进去了。
Nǐ māma bù zài jiā wǒ jiù bù jìn qu le.
lit. *your mum not at home, I then won't enter* [direction indicator]
As your mum is not at home, I won't come in.

请给她带几本书去。
Qǐng gěi tā dài jǐ běn shū qu.
Please take a few books to her.

Please note the word 来 (**lai**) can also be used as a direction indicator, and has similar usage, but indicating direction towards the speaker. Both, when functioning as direction indicators, are normally pronounced with a neutral tone.

4.4 什么 (shénme)

Here, 什么 (**shénme**) is used as an indefinite pronoun, meaning 'anything' or 'whatever', and it is always used in conjunction with 都 (**dōu**). The word order must be 'subject + 什么 (**shénme**) + 都 (**dōu**) + verb'. For example:

他什么都吃。
Tā shénme dōu chī.
lit. *he anything all eat*
He would eat anything.

A noun can be put after 什么 (**shénme**). For example:

我妹妹是个电影迷。她什么电影都看。
Wǒ mèimei shì ge diànyǐng mí. Tā shénme diànyǐng dōu kàn.
My sister is a film fan. She would watch anything.

If you wish to say 'she doesn't like anything', simply put 不 (**bù**) in front of the verb: 她什么都不喜欢 (**Tā shénme dōu bù xǐhuān**).

Culture notes

Noodles

The dish of noodles in Chinese culture symbolises longevity. Traditionally, it is a must dish to mark a birthday. Some Chinese people take pains to ensure that each celebrant's full bowl contains a single unbroken noodle of considerable length.

www.istock.com

Dumplings

Dumplings (with fillings such as meat, seafood, or vegetables) are very popular in the north of China. They symbolise reunion as everything is wrapped in the middle. Therefore, when families and friends have meals together, dumplings are often on the table.

Exercises

Exercise 1

Fill in the gaps using an appropriate word from the vocabulary list for Dialogue 1:

a   今天是小明的生日。我们今晚在他家_____。
    Jītiān shì Xiǎomíng de shēngrì. Wǒmen jīnwǎn zài tā jiā_____.

b   包六个人吃的饺子最少需要三个小时，比较_____。
    Bāo liù gè rén chī de jiǎozi zuìshǎo xūyào sān ge xiǎoshí, bǐjiào
    _____.

c   这件事太复杂了，用几句话_____。
    Zhè jiàn shì tài fùzá le, yòng jǐ jù huà_____.

d 我想请你这个_____去看电影。你有空吗？
Wǒ xiǎng qǐng nǐ zhè ge_____qù kàn diànyǐng. Nǐ yǒu kòng ma?

Exercise 2 (CD 1; 16)

Decide whether 去 (qu) in the following sentences is a verb or a direction indicator (qu is deliberately not marked with a tone):

a 我要去医院看一个朋友。
Wǒ yào qu yīyuàn kàn yī ge péngyou.

b 奶奶想到公园散步去。
Nǎinai xiǎng dào gōngyuán sànbù qu.

c 他们带去了一个特别大的蛋糕。
Tāmen dài qu le yī ge tèbié dà de dàngāo.

d 听说桂林的风景很美，咱们去那儿度假吧。
Tīngshuō Guìlín de fēngjǐng hěn měi, zánmen qu nàr dù jiǎ ba.

Exercise 3

Fill in the gaps with an appropriate measure word:

a 这_____事很复杂，我慢慢给你说。
Zhè_____shì hěn fùzá, wǒ mànmàn gěi nǐ shuō.

b 我们家的花园里有两_____苹果树。
Wǒmen jiā de huāyuán lǐ yǒu liǎng_____píngguǒ shù.

c 他认识五百_____汉字。
Tā rènshí wǔ bǎi_____hànzì.

d 你看，这_____面条这么长！
Nǐ kàn, zhè_____miàntiáo zhème cháng!

Exercise 4

Translate the following into Chinese:

a My younger brother loves football. He would watch any game.
b You are my best friend. You must come to my wedding.

c When you come here next Saturday, can you bring some Chinese music?

d Please don't worry. Wait until I get to your place and then we'll start making the dumplings.

Dialogue 2  (CD 1; 17)

中餐和西餐 Zhōng cān hé xī cān
Chinese food and Western food

Below is a dialogue between a Chinese teacher and her students in a Chinese conversation class. Today's topic is Chinese food and Western food ...

TEACHER	你喜欢吃中餐还是西餐？
JOHN	'中餐' 是什么意思？
TEACHER	就是 '中国饭'。
JOHN	我十分喜欢中餐，不过早饭，我喜欢吃西式的。
TEACHER	你能不能告诉大家 '中餐' 和 '西餐' 有什么不同的地方？

Group work at a Chinese class

JOHN	我试试。中餐的主食主要是米饭和面条，而西餐以土豆和面包为主。
TEACHER	很好，其他同学有什么需要补充吗？
ANNE	我有。中国饭每顿饭有好几个菜，西餐一般只有一个菜。
JAMES	我想补充一点。做中国菜准备的时间比较长，比如，要把肉和菜先切成小块，然后再做。
TEACHER	谁能说说中国菜的做法和西餐有什么不同？
JOHN	中国菜主要是炒，蒸，炖；而西餐主要是用烤箱烤或者煮。
TEACHER	大家都说得很好。最后，在吃的方法上，中西餐有什么不同？
JAMES	老师，这个问题太简单了。中国人吃饭用筷子，而西方人用刀叉。

Dialogue 2 in pinyin ♦

TEACHER	Nǐ xǐhuān chī <u>zhōng cān</u> háishì <u>xī cān</u>?
JOHN	'Zhōng cān' shì shénme <u>yìsi</u>?
TEACHER	Jiù shì 'Zhōngguó fàn'.
JOHN	Wǒ shífēn xǐhuān zhōng cān, búguò zǎofàn, wǒ xǐhuān chī <u>xī shì</u> de.
TEACHER	Nǐ néng bù néng gàosu dàjiā zhōng cān hé xī cān yǒu shénme <u>bùtóng</u> de dìfāng?
JOHN	Wǒ shìshi. Zhōng cān de <u>zhǔshí</u> <u>zhǔyào</u> shì <u>mǐfàn</u> hé miàntiáo, ér xī cān <u>yǐ</u> <u>tǔdòu</u> hé <u>miànbāo</u> <u>wéi zhǔ</u>.
TEACHER	Hěn hǎo. Qítā <u>tóngxué</u> yǒu shénme xuyào <u>bǔchōng</u> ma?
ANNE	Wǒ yǒu. Zhōngguó fàn měi <u>dùn</u> fàn yǒu <u>hǎo jǐ ge cài</u>, xī cān <u>yìbān</u> zhǐ yǒu yī ge cài.
JAMES	Wǒ xiǎng bǔchōng yī diǎn. Zuò Zhōngguó cài zhǔnbèi de shíjiān bǐjiào cháng, bǐrú yào <u>bǎ</u> <u>ròu</u> hé <u>cài</u> xiān <u>qiē chéng xiǎo kuài</u>, ránhòu zài zuò.
TEACHER	Shéi néng shuōshuo Zhōngguó cài de <u>zuòfǎ</u> hé xī cān yǒu shénme bùtóng?
JOHN	Zhōngguó cài zhǔyào shì <u>chǎo</u>, <u>zhēng</u>, <u>dùn</u>, ér xī cān zhǔyào shì yòng <u>kǎoxiāng</u> kǎo, huòzhě <u>zhǔ</u>.
TEACHER	Dàjiā dōu shuō de hěn hǎo. Zuìhòu, <u>zài</u> chī de <u>fāngfǎ</u> <u>shàng</u>, zhōng xī cān yǒu shénme bùtóng?
JAMES	Lǎoshī, zhè ge wèntí tài <u>jiǎndān</u> le. Zhōngguórén chīfàn yòng <u>kuàizi</u>, ér xīfāngrén yòng <u>dāo chā</u>.

Vocabulary ♦

中餐	**zhōng cān**	Chinese cuisine; Chinese food
西餐	**xī cān**	Western cuisine; Western food
意思	**yìsi**	meaning
西式	**xī shì**	Western style
不同	**bùtóng**	difference
主食	**zhǔ shí**	staple food
主要	**zhǔyào**	mainly
米饭	**mǐfàn**	(cooked) rice
以...为主	**yǐ...wéi zhǔ**	be mainly; to mainly consist of
土豆	**tǔdòu**	potato
面包	**miànbāo**	bread
同学	**tóngxué**	student (when a teacher addresses a class and means 'any one of you')
补充	**bǔ chōng**	to add
顿	**dùn**	(measure word for a meal)
好几个菜	**hǎo jǐ ge cài**	quite a few dishes
一般	**yībān**	normally
把...切成	**bǎ...qiē chéng**	to cut...into
肉	**ròu**	meat
菜	**cài**	vegetables
小块	**xiǎo kuài**	small pieces
做法	**zuò fǎ**	method of cooking
炒	**chǎo**	to stir-fry
蒸	**zhēng**	to steam
炖	**dùn**	to stew
烤箱	**kǎoxiāng**	oven
或者	**huòzhě**	or
煮	**zhǔ**	to boil
在...上	**zài...shàng**	in terms of...; regarding...
方法	**fāngfǎ**	method
简单	**jiǎndān**	simple
筷子	**kuàizi**	chopsticks
刀叉	**dāo chā**	knife and fork

Language points ♦

4.5   To emphasise

In the sentence 不过早饭，我喜欢吃西式的 (**búguò zǎofàn, wǒ xǐhuān chī xī shì de**), 早饭 (**zǎofàn**) is brought forward. It should follow

西式的 (**xī shì de**) in a normal sentence order. But here, the speaker wants to emphasise that when it comes to breakfast, he likes Western food.

4.6 Question: '… 有什么不同的地方？' (… **yǒu shénme bùtóng de dìfāng**)

Literally, this means 'have what different places' (What are the differences between … ?). The order of the question is 'A and B + 有什么不同的地方？' (… **yǒu shénme bùtóng de dìfāng**). For example:

北京和上海有什么不同的地方？
Běijīng hé Shànghǎi yǒu shénme bùtóng de dìfāng?
What are the differences between Beijing and Shanghai?

A more formal way of saying 不同的地方 (**bùtóng de dìfāng**) is 不同之处 (**bùtóng zhī chù**).

4.7 Pattern: 以 … 为主 (**yǐ … wéi zhǔ**, 'mainly')

Literally, it means 'take … as the main thing'. This construction has the following elements: 'subject + 以 (**yǐ**) + something/somebody + 为主 (**wéi zhǔ**)', which has the basic meaning of 'A consists mainly of B' or 'A is mainly B'. For example:

这个旅游团以英国人为主。
Zhè ge lǚyóu tuán yǐ Yīngguórén wéi zhǔ.
This tourist group consists mainly of British people.

今晚的晚餐以海鲜为主。
Jīnwǎn de wǎncān yǐ hǎixiān wéi zhǔ.
Tonight's dinner is mainly seafood.

4.8 好 (**hǎo**) as adverb

When 好 (**hǎo**) is placed before adjectives, it means 'very' or 'quite'. So 好几个菜 (**hǎo jǐ ge cài**) in the dialogue above means 'quite a few dishes'. It is often used in spoken language. For example: 好冷 (**hǎo lěng**, very cold), 好棒 (**hǎo bàng**, extremely good), 好简单 (**hǎo jiǎndān**, terribly simple).

4.9 把 (**bǎ**) sentence

The 把 (**bǎ**) construction is a unique feature in Chinese and is rather complex. The basic structure is:

'把 + something/somebody + verb + the result of an action'. For example:

我 已经 把 衣服 洗 干净 了。
Wǒ yǐjing bǎ yīfu xǐ gānjìng le.
lit. *I already* [ba] *clothes wash clean* [le]
I've already washed the clothes clean.

From the above example, we can summarise three rules for the 把 (**bǎ**) sentence:

i whatever follows 把 (**bǎ**) must have definite reference (i.e. 衣服 **yīfu** refers to certain clothes);
ii the main verb must be an action verb (洗 **xǐ**); and
iii the main verb must be followed by a word/phrase indicating the result of the verb (干净 **gānjìng**).

Please note that the 把 (**bǎ**) construction is very often used in giving instructions (i.e. in imperative sentences). For example:

请 把 肉 切 成 片。
Qǐng bǎ ròu qiē chéng piàn.
lit. *please* [ba] *meat cut into slice*
Please cut the meat into slices.

4.10 Use of 而 (ér)

而 (**ér**, whilst/but) is mostly used in between two sentences to indicate some degree of contrast. For example:

南方人喜欢吃米饭，而北方人喜欢吃面食。
Nánfāngrén xǐhuān chī mǐfàn, ér běifāngrén xǐhuān chī miànshí.
Southerners like to eat rice, whilst northerners like flour-based food.

4.11 Words of sequence

When giving instructions, or when describing procedures and processes, the following expressions are often used:

首先 (**shǒuxiān**, first of all)
先 (**xiān**, first of all; first)
再 (**zài**, then)
接下来 (**jiē xiàlai**, following that)

过 . . . 分钟 (**guò . . . fēnzhōng**, after . . . minutes)
然后，随后 (**ránhòu, suíhòu**, then; after that; afterwards)
最后 (**zuìhòu**, finally)

4.12　Shortened form

When the second character in the two words is the same, the second character in the first word can sometimes be omitted. For example:

中餐 (**zhōng cān**), 西餐 (**xī cān**) = 中西餐 (**zhōng xī cān**, Chinese and Western food)
中文 (**zhōngwén**), 英文 (**yīngwén**) = 中英文 (**zhōng yīng wén**, Chinese and English languages)

4.13　Difference between 还是 (**háishì**) and 或者 (**huòzhě**)

还是 (**háishì**, or) is only used in asking alternative questions whilst 或者 (**huòzhě**, or) is used in normal sentences. For example:

你喜欢中餐还是西餐？
Nǐ xǐhuān zhōng cān háishì xī cān?
Do you like Chinese cuisine or Western cuisine?

去参加聚会时，你可以带一瓶酒或者一些水果。
Qù cānjiā jùhuì shí, nǐ kěyǐ dài yī píng jiǔ huòzhě yīxiē shuǐguǒ.
When going to a party, you can bring a bottle of wine or some fruit.

Culture note

Traditional Chinese breakfast

Traditional Chinese breakfast is mostly savoury and filling, consisting of rice or corn porridge and steamed bread. These staples are often accompanied by salted duck eggs and any one of a wide variety of pickles. Sweet soya milk and deep-fried dough sticks are also very popular. In cities, many people buy their breakfast from street stalls and eat it on the way to work. Nowadays, many young people have adopted Western-style breakfast – coffee and toast. In most big hotels in China, breakfast is served in both Chinese and Western styles.

Exercises

Exercise 5

Fill in the gaps using appropriate words from the vocabulary list for Dialogue 2:

a 你能告诉我这句话是什么_____吗？
　 Nǐ néng gàosù wǒ zhè jù huà shì shénme_____ma?

b 连这么_____的问题她也不会回答！太奇怪了。
　 Lián zhème_____de wèntí tā yě bú huì huídá! Tài qíguài le.

c 他们两个虽然是姐妹，但在性格上有许多_____的地方。
　 Tāmen liǎng gè suīrán shì jiěmèi, dàn zài xìnggé shàng yǒu xǔduō_____de dìfang.

d 我喜欢王老师。他的教学_____很特别。
　 Wǒ xǐhuān Wáng lǎoshī. Tāde jiàoxué_____hěn tèbié.

e 早上在公园锻炼的人_____是老年人。
　 Zǎoshang zài gōngyuán duànliàn de rén_____shì lǎonián rén.

Exercise 6

Fill in the gaps using words of sequence (refer to Language point 4.11 above):

a 南方人一般喜欢_____喝汤，_____吃饭和炒菜，_____吃水果。
　 Nánfāngrén yībān xǐhuān_____hē tāng, _____chī fàn hé chǎo cài, _____chī shuǐguǒ.

b 小明，你能不能_____把房间打扫干净_____出去玩？
　 Xiǎomíng, nǐ néng bù néng_____bǎ fángjiān dǎsǎo gānjìng _____chūqu wánr?

Exercise 7　 (CD 1; 18)

Fill in the gaps using either 还是 (háishì) or 或者 (huòzhě):

a 你想吃饺子_____面条？
　 Nǐ xiǎng chī jiǎozi_____miàntiáo?

b 我可以用筷子_____刀叉。
   Wǒ kěyǐ yòng kuàizi_____dāo chā.

c 我今天晚上_____明天晚上都有空。
   Wǒ jīntiān wǎnshang_____míngtiān wǎnshang dōu yǒu kòng.

d 你喜欢咖啡_____茶？
   Nǐ xǐhuān kāfēi_____chá?

Exercise 8

Translate into Chinese:

a Southerners like to eat spring rolls but northerners like to eat dumplings.
b Last night's concert was mainly Chinese music.
c As for chopsticks, I'm not good at using them.
d Please wash those knives and forks clean.
e Please will you wake me up at 7 o'clock.

Exercise 9

Describe orally the differences between Chinese and Western foods. Try to use the following expressions in your description:

中餐 zhōng cān, 西餐 xī cān, 比较 bǐjiào, 不同的地方 bùtóng de dìfāng, 以...为主 yǐ...wéi zhǔ, 做法 zuò fǎ

Listening comprehension (CD 1; 19)

做蛋炒饭 Zuò dàn chǎo fàn
Making egg-fried rice

Listen to the following dialogue between Wang Li and Liping. Try not to read the script. Bear the following questions in mind whilst listening to the dialogue and try to answer them afterwards:

1 做蛋炒饭需要什么作料？
   Zuò dàn chǎo fàn xūyào shénme zuòliào?

2 做蛋炒饭需要什么调料呢？
Zuò dàn chǎo fàn xūyào shénme tiáoliào ne?

3 需要做什么准备工作？
Xūyào zuò shénme zhǔnbèi gōngzuò?

4 等油热了后，你先把什么倒进炒锅？然后倒什么？最后倒什么？
Děng yóu rè le hòu, nǐ xiān bǎ shénme dàojìn chǎoguō, ránhòu
dào shénme? Zuìhòu dào shénme?

Key words ♦

You may find the following words useful in understanding
the dialogue:

蛋炒饭	**dàn chǎo fàn**	egg-fried rice
作料	**zuòliào**	ingredient
剩米饭	**shèng mǐfàn**	left-over rice

菜油	**cài yóu**	cooking oil
打碎	**dǎ suì**	to beat it up; to whisk it
加点儿	**jiādiǎnr**	to add a little
记住	**jìzhù**	to remember
倒	**dào**	to pour
炒锅	**chǎoguō**	wok
稍微	**shāowéi**	a little
容易	**róngyì**	easy
试试	**shìshi**	to give it a try; to have a go

Script in characters ♦

WANG LI	丽萍，我特别喜欢吃蛋炒饭。你会做吗？
LIPING	会，非常简单。
WANG LI	需要什么作料？
LIPING	剩米饭，鸡蛋和葱。
WANG LI	调料呢？
LIPING	菜油，盐和五香粉。
WANG LI	这些我都有。
LIPING	太好了。准备工作只需要做两件事，第一：把鸡蛋打碎，加点儿盐一起打。第二：把葱切碎。
WANG LI	我记住了。然后呢？
LIPING	倒一些菜油在炒锅里，等油热了后，先把葱倒进去炒几下，再把打碎的鸡蛋倒进去，炒一分钟左右，最后把剩饭倒进去，炒两三分钟后，加一点儿盐和五香粉，稍微再炒几下，就可以吃了。
WANG LI	听上去很容易。今天晚上我就试试。

Script in pinyin ♦

WANG LI	Lìpíng, wǒ tèbié xǐhuān chī <u>dàn chǎo fàn</u>. Nǐ huì zuò ma?
LIPING	Huì, fēicháng jiǎndān.
WANG LI	Xūyào shénme <u>zuòliào</u>?
LIPING	<u>Shèng mǐfàn</u>, jīdàn hé cōng.
WANG LI	Tiáoliào ne?
LIPING	<u>Cài yóu</u>, yán hé wǔ xiāngfěn.

WANG LI   Zhèxiē wǒ dōu yǒu.

LIPING   Tài hǎo le. Zhǔnbèi gōngzuò zhǐ xūyào zuò liǎng jiàn shì.
Dì yī, bǎ jīdàn dǎ suì, jiā diǎnr yán yīqǐ dǎ. Dì èr, bǎ cōng
qiē suì.

WANG LI   Wǒ jìzhù le. Ránhòu ne?

LIPING   Dào yīxiē cài yóu zài chǎoguō lǐ. Děng yóu rè le hòu, xiān
bǎ cōng dào jìnqu, chǎo jǐ xià, zài bǎ dǎsuì de jīdàn dào
jìnqu chǎo yī fēn zhōng zuǒyòu, zuìhòu bǎ shèng fàn dào
jìnqu, chǎo liǎng sān fēnzhōng hòu, jiā yīdiǎnr yán hé wǔ
xiāngfěn, shāowéi zài chǎo jǐ xià jiù kěyǐ chī le.

WANG LI   Tīng shàngqu hěn róngyì, jīntiān wǎnshang wǒ jiù shìshi.

5 过年
Guò nián
Celebrate Chinese New Year

In this unit, you will learn about:

- useful expressions about Chinese New Year
- using 才 (**cái**) and 就 (**jiù**)
- plural 们 (**men**)

Text 1 (CD 1; 20)

怎么过年　Zěnme guò nián
How to celebrate Chinese New Year

在中国的传统节日里，最重要的就是春节。春节是农历的新年。很多中国人把它叫'过年'，而西方人把它称为'中国新年'。

春节通常是在一月底或者二月初。中国人是怎么过年的呢？和西方人过圣诞节差不多，这是一个全家团聚的节日。除夕晚上全家人要吃团圆饭(也叫'年夜饭')，北方人的饭桌上一定有饺子，南方人一定有春卷。全家人一边吃一边看电视，一直看到午夜，然后放鞭炮，欢迎新的一年的到来。有些人家按照老习惯'守夜'，整晚上不睡觉。第二天一大早，也就是大年初一，邻居朋友和亲戚互相拜年，祝贺新年。人们从初二开始走亲戚，也就是去亲戚家拜年，吃饭。比如，去看奶奶，爷爷；也可以跟朋友，同学，同事聚会。在农村，正月十五的元宵节后，春节才算过完。

Text in pinyin ♦

Zài Zhōngguó de chuántǒng jiérì lǐ, zuì zhòngyào de jiù shì Chūn Jié. Chūn Jié shì nónglì de xīn nián. Hěnduō Zhōngguórén bǎ tā jiào 'guò nián', ér xīfāngrén bǎ tā chēng wéi 'Zhōngguó xīnnián'.

Celebrating Chinese New Year
www.istock.com

Chūnjié tōngcháng shì zài yīyuè dǐ huòzhě èryuè chū. Zhōngguórén shì zěnme guò nián de ne? Hé xīfāngrén guò Shèngdànjié chā bù duō, zhè shì yī gè quánjiā tuánjù de jiérì. Chú xī wǎnshang, quánjiārén yào chī tuányuán fàn (yě jiào 'nián yè fàn'), běifāngrén de fàn zhuō shàng yīdìng yǒu jiǎozi, nánfāng rén yīdìng yǒu chūnjuǎn. Quánjiārén yībiān chī yībiān kàn diànshì, yīzhí kàn dào wǔyè, ránhòu fàng biānpào, huānyíng xīn de yī nián de dàolái. Yǒuxiē rén jiā ànzhào lǎo xíguàn 'shǒu yè', zhěng wǎnshang bú shuìjiào. Dì èr tiān yī dà zǎo, yějiùshì dànián chū yī, línjū, péngyou hé qīnqī hùxiāng bàinián, zhùhè xīn nián. Cóng chū èr káishǐ zǒu qīnqī, yějiùshì qù qīnqī jiā bàinián, chī fàn, bǐrú, qù kàn nǎinai, yéye; yě kěyǐ gēn péngyou, tóngxué, tóngshì jùhuì. Zài nóngcūn, zhèngyuè shíwǔ de yuánxiāojié hòu, Chūn Jié cái suàn guò wán.

Vocabulary ◆

传统	chuántǒng	tradition; traditional
节日	jiérì	festival
重要	zhòngyào	important
春节	Chūn Jié	Spring Festival
过年	guò nián	to celebrate the New Year; to spend the New Year
西方人	xīfāngrén	Westerner
称为	chēng wéi	to call something as
新年	xīn nián	New Year
通常	tōngcháng	usually
农历	nóng lì	lunar calendar
底	dǐ	the end (of a month, year)
初	chū	the beginning (of a month, year)
圣诞节	Shèngdànjié	Christmas
全家	quán jiā	whole family
团聚	tuánjù	to get together
除夕	chú xī	Chinese New Year's Eve (*lit.* to get rid of the past)
团圆饭	tuányuán fàn	reunion meal
年夜饭	nián yè fàn	Chinese New Year's Eve meal
饭桌	fàn zhuō	dining table
春卷	chūn juǎn	spring roll

午夜	**wǔyè**	midnight
放鞭炮	**fàng biānpào**	to set off fireworks
按照	**àn zhào**	according to
守夜	**shǒu yè**	to stay awake for the whole night
大年初一	**dànián chū yī**	Chinese New Year's Day (*lit.* first day of the new year)
邻居	**línjū**	neighbour
亲戚	**qīnqi**	relative
拜年	**bài nián**	to exchange New Year's greetings; to wish somebody Happy New Year
互相	**hùxiāng**	each other
祝贺	**zhùhè**	to congratulate
走亲戚	**zǒu qīnqi**	to visit family and relatives
同事	**tóngshì**	colleague
正月	**zhèng yuè**	first month of lunar calendar
元宵节	**yuánxiāo jié**	Lantern Festival
算	**suàn**	to count as

Language points ♦

5.1 Use of 拜年 (bài nián)

On Chinese New Year's Day, families and friends go to each other's houses to say 'Happy New Year', and this ritual is called 拜年 (**bài nián**). The phrase is used to mean 'to wish someone Happy New Year' (please note that this phrase itself is not a new year's greeting) or 'to exchange New Year's greetings'. For example:

奶奶，我来给您拜年。
Nǎinai, wǒ lái gěi nín bài nián.
Grandma, I've come to wish you a Happy New Year!

大年初一，中国人都要互相拜年。
Dànián chū yī, Zhōngguórén dōu yào hùxiāng bài nián.
On Chinese New Year's Day, Chinese people exchange seasonal greetings with each other.

5.2 Use of 叫 (jiào, 'to call') and 称 (chēng, 'to call')

叫 (**jiào**) is informal and 称 (**chēng**) is more formal. Also, 称 (**chēng**) is usually followed by 为 (**wéi**) or 作 (**zuò**). For example:

我把她叫 '小李'，因为她比我小。

Wǒ bǎ tā jiào 'Xiǎo Lǐ', yīnwéi tā bǐ wǒ xiǎo.

I call her 'Little Li' as she is younger than me.

人们都称他为 '中国通'。

Rénmen dōu chēng tā wéi 'Zhōngguó tōng'.

Everyone calls him 'a China expert'.

5.3 走亲戚 (zǒu qīnqī)

This is a very informal and colloquial expression, meaning 'to visit families and relatives'.

5.4 Use of 才 (cái)

才 (**cái**) is an adverb that is used to indicate that the speaker thinks that something happens too late, too slowly or takes too long. For example:

这顿晚饭怎么才吃完？

Zhè dùn wǎnfàn zěnme cái chī wán?

How come (you've) only just finished dinner?

他七点半才来。

Tā qī diǎn bàn cái lái.

He turned up (as late as) half past seven.

Culture notes

Terms associated with Chinese New Year

The first month of the Chinese lunar calendar is 正月 (**zhèng yuè**). The first day of the first month is 初一 (**chū yī**), the second day is 初二 (**chū èr**), and so on and so forth. Normally, after the tenth day, the term 初 (**chū**) is omitted. 春节 (**Chūn Jié**) is a general term used to refer to the festival season. Strictly speaking, 过年 (**guò nián**) means 'to celebrate the New Year'. However, the term is also loosely used to refer to the Chinese New Year season. For Chinese New Year's Day, the most commonly used terms are: 大年初一 (**dànián chū yī**), 正月初一 (**zhèng yuè chū yī**), 年初一 (**nián chū yī**), 初一 (**chū yī**). The last day of the previous year is 除夕 (**chú xī**) or 年三十 (**nián sān shí**).

Chinese New Year customs

On Chinese New Year's Eve, most families have a meal together. After the meal, they make dumplings or prepare other food for New Year's Day while watching spectacular singing and dancing shows on TV. When the clock strikes midnight, fireworks are set off to send the old year out and to welcome the new year in (the traditional belief is that the noise scares the evil spirits and ghosts away). On New Year's Day, one is not supposed to do any work, not even cooking. It is believed that if you work on this day, you will have to work very hard for the rest of the year! Children wear brand new clothes on this day and receive money wrapped in red paper, known as 红包 (**hóng bāo**), from their parents and grandparents.

Exercises

Exercise 1

Fill in the gaps using an appropriate word from the vocabulary list for Text 1:

a 东方人吃饭时用筷子，而＿＿＿＿＿＿用刀叉。
   Dōngfāngrén chī fàn shí yòng kuàizi, ér＿＿＿＿＿＿yòng dāo chā.

b 我们家总是在除夕晚上吃＿＿＿＿＿＿。
   Wǒmen jiā zǒngshì zài chúxī wǎnshang chī＿＿＿＿＿＿.

c 春节是中国最重要的＿＿＿＿＿＿节日。
   Chūnjié shì Zhōngguó zuì zhòngyào de＿＿＿＿＿＿jiérì.

d ＿＿＿＿＿＿农历，正月十五是元宵节。
   ＿＿＿＿＿＿nóng lì, zhèngyuè shíwǔ shì yuánxiāo jié.

e 王林和我在一个学校工作，所以我们是＿＿＿＿＿＿。
   Wáng Lín hé wǒ zài yī gè xuéxiào gōngzuò, suǒyǐ wǒmen shì
   ＿＿＿＿＿＿.

Exercise 2 **(CD 1; 22)**

Answer the following questions orally in Chinese based on Text 1:

a 除夕晚上，许多中国人家做什么？
Chúxī wǎnshang, xǔduō Zhōngguó rénjiā zuò shénme?

b 什么是 '守夜'？
Shénme shì 'shǒu yè'?

c 大年初一，大家做什么？
Dànián chū yī, dàjiā zuò shenme?

d 什么时候开始 '走亲戚'？
Shénme shíhòu kāishǐ 'zǒu qīnqi'?

e 在农村，过年要过多长时间？
Zài nóngcūn, guò nián yào guò duō cháng shíjiān?

Exercise 3

Translate the following into Chinese:

a This is the first time I have spent Chinese New Year in China.
b On New Year's Day, we went to our teacher's to wish him Happy New Year.
c We agreed to have our family reunion meal at 8 o'clock, but my elder brother turned up at 9!
d I know Xiao Ming is your relative. How do you address him?

Dialogue 1 (CD 1; 23)

过年好　Guò nián hǎo
Happy New Year

On Chinese New Year's Day, Lao Li knocks on neighbour Lao Wang's door ...

LAO LI　老王，过年好！

LAO WANG　老李，过年好！这么早就来拜年了。你的孩子们都回来了吗？

LAO LI	今年我们家可热闹了，两个儿子和他们的媳妇，还有孙女都回来了。你家呢？
LAO WANG	我家老大今年没回来，轮到他值班，两个女儿回来了。
LAO LI	初三你们有空吗？到我家去吃饺子吧。
LAO WANG	有空。我正要请你们全家过来呢！这样吧，我们带几个菜去。
LAO LI	那太好了！你夫人的菜是出了名的好吃。
LAO WANG	几点？
LAO LI	六点怎么样？
LAO WANG	行。

Dialogue 1 in pinyin

LAO LI	Lǎo Wáng, guò nián hǎo!
LAO WANG	Lǎo Lǐ, guò nián hǎo! Zhème zǎo jiù lái bài nián le. Nǐde háizimen dōu huílai le ma?

LAO LI	Jīnnián wǒmen jiā kě rènào le. Liǎng gè érzi hé tāmen de xífù, háiyǒu sūnnǚ dōu huílai le. Nǐ jiā ne?
LAO WANG	Wǒ jiā lǎodà jīnnián méi huílai, lúndào tā zhíbān, liǎng gè nǚ'ér huílai le.
LAO LI	Chū sān nǐmen yǒu kòng ma? Dào wǒ jiā qù chī jiǎozi ba.
LAO WANG	Yǒu kòng, wǒ zhèngyào qǐng nǐmen quán jiā guòlai ne! Zhè yàng ba, wǒmen dài jǐ gè cài qu.
LAO LI	Nà tài hǎo le! Nǐ fūrén de cài shì chūlemíng de hǎochī.
LAO WANG	Jǐ diǎn?
LAO LI	Liù diǎn zěnme yàng?
LAO WANG	Xíng.

Vocabulary ◆

过年好	guò nián hǎo	Happy New Year
可	kě	very; really
媳妇	xífù	wife
孙女	sūnnǚ	grand-daughter
老大	lǎodà	the eldest child
值班	zhí bān	be on duty
初三	chū sān	the third day of the first month
正要	zhèngyào	just about to; just going to
这样吧	zhè yàng ba	let's do this
夫人	fūrén	wife
出了名	chūlemíng	famously

Language points ◆

5.5   New Year greetings   🔊   (CD 1; 24)

The most often used New Year's greetings are: 过年好! (**guò nián hǎo!**), 新年好! (**xīn nián hǎo!**) and 恭喜发财! (**gōng xǐ fā cái!**). The first two expressions mean 'Happy New Year' whilst the last one means 'wishing you a Prosperous New Year' and it is mostly used in Cantonese-speaking communities and in business circles.

5.6 Use of 可 (kě)

可 (kě) is an adverb meaning 'very' or 'terribly'. It is almost always used in spoken and informal language. It is often used with 了 (le) at the end of the sentence. For example:

我爸爸可喜欢锻炼身体了。
Wǒ bàba kě xǐhuān duànliàn shēntǐ le.
My father really likes to do exercises.

Dialogue 2 (CD 1; 25)

看朋友 **Kàn péngyou**
Visiting a friend

A week after New Year's Day, Liping is cooking for Meili who turns up late . . .

LIPING 你怎么才来？我还以为你不来了。
MEILI 真对不起。这几天我都忙晕了。
LIPING 为什么？你们家有妈妈做饭，又不用你忙。
MEILI 嗨，别提了。我姐姐把他们三岁的女孩带来了。这两天，她和我姐夫出去看朋友，我留在家看外甥女。累死我了！
LIPING 今天你可以休息休息了。你不用做饭，也不用看孩子！
MEILI 今天吃什么好吃的？
LIPING 春卷，还有别的菜。马上就可以吃饭。
MEILI 这么快就做好了。你太伟大了！

Dialogue 2 in pinyin ♦

LIPING Nǐ zěnme cái lái? Wǒ hái yǐwéi nǐ bù lái le.
MEILI Zhēn duìbùqǐ. Zhè jǐ tiān wǒ dōu máng yūn le.
LIPING Wèishénme? Nǐmen jiā yǒu māma zuòfàn, yòu bùyòng nǐ máng.
MEILI Hāi, bié tí le. Wǒ jiějie bǎ tāmen sān suì de nǚhái dàilai le. Zhè liǎng tiān tā hé wǒ jiěfū chūqu kàn péngyou, wǒ liú zài jiā kān wàishēnǚ. Lèi sǐ wǒ le!

LIPING	Jīntiān nǐ kěyǐ xiūxi xiūxi le. Nǐ bùyòng zuòfàn, yě bùyòng kān háizi!
MEILI	Jīntiān chī shénme hǎochī de?
LIPING	Chūn juǎn, háiyǒu biéde cài. Mǎshàng jiù kěyǐ chī fàn.
MEILI	Zhème kuài jiù zuò hǎo le. Nǐ tài wěidà le!

Vocabulary ♦

以为	**yǐwéi**	thought
晕	**yūn**	dizzy
不用	**bú yòng**	do not have to
嗨	**hāi**	(exclamation word)
别提了	**bié tí le**	Don't mention it!; You can well imagine
留	**liú**	to be left behind
看	**kān**	to look after
外甥女	**wàishēngnǚ**	niece
马上	**mǎshàng**	immediately
伟大	**wěidà**	great

Language points

5.7   Use of 就 (**jiù**)

Unlike 才 (**cái**) we saw in 5.4 above, 就 (**jiù**) is used to indicate that the speaker thinks that something happens fast, early, smoothly or takes a short time.

你这么快就吃完饭了!
Nǐ zhème kuài jiù chī wán fàn le!
You've finished your meal so quickly!

还不到十点，他就睡觉了.
Hái bù dào shí diǎn, tā jiù shuìjiào le.
It was not even 10 o'clock and he had gone to bed.

5.8   Plural 们 (men)

In Chinese, there is no distinction between singular and plural. However, there is one exception and it is the use of 们 (**men**). 们 (**men**) can be attached to some people-related nouns. For example:

老师们	**lǎoshīmen**	teachers
同学们	**tóngxuémen**	students; fellow-students
朋友们	**péngyoumen**	friends
孩子们	**háizimen**	children
运动员们	**yùndòngyuánmen**	athletes

5.9 看 (kàn) and 看 (kān)

As you all know, when 看 (kàn) is pronounced with the fourth tone, it means 'to see, to watch, to look at'. In Dialogue 2, it is pronounced with the first tone (kān) and it means 'to look after'. For example:

你想去看放鞭炮吗？
Nǐ xiǎng qù kàn fàng biānpào ma?
Would you like to go and watch the fireworks?

我姐姐让我帮她看小孩。
Wǒ jiějie ràng wǒ bāng tā kān xiǎohái.
My elder sister asked me to help her look after the children.

5.10 Expressions of exaggeration

When exaggerating things, you can add 死了 (sǐ le, to have died) after an adjective. For example, 饿死了 (è sǐ le, starving) and 热死了 (rè sǐ le, extremely hot) literally mean 'hungry to death' and 'hot to death'. The phrase 晕了 (yūn le, to have passed out) is similar in its meaning and usage. So you can say 饿晕了 (è yūn le) and 热晕了 (rè yūn le), literally meaning 'so hungry/hot that one is going to pass out'.

Culture note

Animal signs

According to the Chinese lunar calendar, each year is associated with an animal sign. Altogether there are 12 animal signs and they come round every 12 years. The dragon is generally regarded as the most popular sign, and 'the Year of the Dragon' is 龙年, **lóng nián** in Chinese. If we take the following 12 years as an example, below is a table illustrating the 12 animal signs corresponding to those years:

Year	Sign	Character	Pinyin
1996	Rat	鼠	shǔ
1997	Ox	牛	niú
1998	Tiger	虎	hǔ
1999	Rabbit	兔	tù
2000	Dragon	龙	lóng
2001	Snake (small dragon)	蛇(小龙)	shé (xiǎo lóng)
2002	Horse	马	mǎ
2003	Sheep	羊	yáng
2004	Monkey	猴	hóu
2005	Rooster	鸡	jī
2006	Dog	狗	gǒu
2007	Pig	猪	zhū

Exercises

Exercise 4

Fill in the gaps using an appropriate word from the vocabulary list for Dialogue 1 and Dialogue 2:

a 我们家一共有三个孩子。_____是男孩，另外两个是女孩。
Wǒmen jiā yīgòng yǒu sān ge háizi. _____shì nánhái, lìngwài liǎng gè shì nǚhái.

b 你能不能晚一点走，_____下来帮我包饺子？
Nǐ néng bù néng wǎn yīdiǎn zǒu, _____xiàlái bāng wǒ bāo jiǎozi?

c 我明天晚上不能回家吃年夜饭，因为轮到我_____。
Wǒ míngtiān wǎnshang bù néng huíjiā chī nián yè fàn, yīnwéi lúndào wǒ _____.

d 我奶奶是上海人，她可爱吃_____了。
Wǒ nǎinai shì Shànghǎirén, tā kě ài chī_____le.

e 我还_____他是北京人！一点儿都没听出他的上海口音！
Wǒ hái_____tā shì Běijīngrén! Yīdiǎnr dōu méi tīng chū tāde Shànghǎi kǒuyīn!

Exercise 5

Fill in the gaps using 才 (**cái**) or 就 (**jiù**):

a 他刚学了两个星期汉语，_____认识五十个汉字了。
Tā gāng xué le liǎng gè xīngqī hànyǔ, _____rènshí wǔshí gè hànzì le.

b 今年春节怎么这么快_____过完了。
Jīnnián Chūn Jié zěnme zhème kuài_____guò wán le.

c 都十二点了，你怎么_____来？
Dōu shí'èr diǎn le, nǐ zěnme_____lái?

d 我妈妈最近不忙。昨天晚上她六点_____回家了。
Wǒ māma zuìjìn bù máng. Zuótiān wǎnshang tā liù diǎn_____huí jiā le.

e 小明最近气色不好。我早就让他去看大夫，可是他昨天_____去。
Xiǎo Míng zuìjìn qìsè bù hǎo. Wǒ zǎo jiù ràng tā qù kàn dàifū, kěshì tā zuótiān_____qù.

Exercise 6

Match the words on the left with the words on the right:

a	看	kān		A	做饭	zuòfàn
b	互相	hùxiāng		B	电视	diànshì
c	轮到我	lún dào wǒ		C	晕了	yūn le
d	看	kàn		D	孩子	háizi
e	累	lèi		E	拜年	bài nián

Exercise 7

Translate the following into Chinese:

a   Where are you going to spend the Chinese New Year this year?
b   I thought you didn't know how to make dumplings.
c   Don't mention it. It's terribly tiring looking after a child.
d   You don't have to bring any presents with you.
e   I was just about to telephone you.

Reading comprehension

全家团聚   Quán jiā tuānjù   (CD 1; 26)
Family reunion

Bear the following questions in mind while reading the passage below and try to answer them afterwards:

1   王强是干什么工作的？
    Wáng Qiáng shì gàn shénme gōngzuò de?

2   王强是在什么地方过的大年初一？
    Wáng Qiáng shì zài shénme dìfāng guò de dànián chū yī?

3   他们为什么去了北京？
    Tāmen wèishénme qù le Běijīng?

Key words ◆

The following words may help you to understand the passage better:

天津	**Tiānjīn**	(a city near Beijing)
家	**jiā**	(measure word for an organisation)
医院	**yīyuàn**	hospital
医生	**yīshēng**	doctor
妻子	**qīzi**	wife
激动	**jīdòng**	excited; excitedly
这下	**zhèxià**	this way; now

Passage in characters ♦

老王的大儿子王强是天津一家医院的医生。今年轮到他大年初一值班，所以他不能回北京的父母家。初一早上，他打电话给父母拜了年，然后就去了医院。一直到晚上七点王强才回家。回家后，他五岁的女儿说：'爸爸，我想去看奶奶，爷爷，给他们拜年。' 王强和妻子商量了一下，决定初三去北京住几天。女儿听说后，高兴极了！

初三他们三个人坐火车到了北京。王强的父母看到大儿子，大儿媳，还有孙女都来了，高兴地说 '我们还以为今年春节见不到你们了'！王强的两个妹妹也激动地说：'这下，我们家也热闹了！'

Passage in pinyin ♦

Lǎo Wáng de dà érzi Wáng Qiáng shì Tiānjīn yī jiā yīyuàn de yīshēng. Jīnnián lúndào tā dànián chū yī zhí bān, suǒyǐ tā bù néng huí Běijīng de fùmǔ jiā. Chū yī zǎoshang, tā dǎ diànhuà gěi fùmǔ bài le nián, ránhòu jiù qù le yīyuàn. Yī zhí dào wǎnshang qī diǎn Wáng Qiáng cái huí jiā. Huí jiā hòu, tā wǔ suì de nǚ'ér shuō: 'Bàba, wǒ xiǎng qù kàn nǎinai, yéye, gěi tāmen bài nián'. Wáng Qiáng hé qīzi shāngliàng le yīxià, juédìng chū sān qù Běijīng zhù jǐ tiān. Nǚ'ér tīng shuō hòu, gāoxìng jí le!

Chū sān tāmen sān gè rén zuò huǒchē dào le Běijīng. Wáng Qiáng de fùmǔ kàndao dà érzi, dà érxí, háiyǒu sūnnǚ dōu lái le, gāoxìng de shuō: 'wǒmen hái yǐwéi jīnnián Chūn Jié jiàn bù dào nǐmen le! Wáng Qiáng de liǎng gè mèimei yě jīdòng de shuō 'Zhèxià, wǒmen jiā yě rènào le!'

6 兴趣和爱好
Xìngqù hé àihào
Interests and hobbies

In this unit, you will learn about:

▶ expressing preferences
▶ expressing the result or potential result of an action
▶ using the continuous particle 正在 (**zhèngzài**)
▶ end-of-sentence 了 (**le**)

Text 1 〔🎧〕 (CD 1; 27)

中国文学　**Zhōngguó wénxué**
Chinese literature

在我们家，我父母喜欢音乐，我哥哥爱好足球，我奶奶特别喜欢
养花，我爷爷是个电影迷。至于我呢，我也喜欢电影，但我
更喜欢文学。自从学中文以来，我对中国文学越来越感兴趣。
我已经读过了一些中国文学作品的英文翻译，比如《红楼梦》和
《家》。《红楼梦》是一部古典长篇小说，里面的人物特别多。
刚开始读的时候，总是记不住有些人的名字。《家》是一部现代
小说，里面的人物不多，比较容易读。这两部作品都很有意思。
最近，我正在读老舍的名著《骆驼祥子》。这一次，我读的是
中文的原著！这是我第一次读原著，困难可真不小。我不得不
一边查字典，一边看。有时候，一句话要看好几遍。但是，看懂
了后心里特别高兴。

Text 1 in pinyin ♦

Zài wǒmen jiā, wǒ fùmǔ xǐhuān yīnyuè, wǒ gēge àihào zúqiú, wǒ
nǎinai tèbié xǐhuān yǎng huā, wǒ yéye shì gè diànyǐng mí. Zhìyú

Chinese novels

wǒ ne, wǒ yě xǐhuān diànyǐng, dàn wǒ gèng xǐhuān wénxué.
Zìcóng xué Zhōngwén yǐlái, wǒ duì Zhōngguó wénxué yuè lái yuè
gǎn xìngqu. Wǒ yǐjīng dú guò le yīxiē Zhōngguó wénxué zuòpǐn
de Yīngwén fānyì, bǐ rú 《Hóng Lóu Mèng》 hé 《Jiā》. 《Hóng Lóu
Mèng》 shì yī bù gǔdiǎn chángpiān xiǎoshuō, lǐmiàn de rénwù
tèbié duō. Gāng kāishǐ dú de shíhou, zǒngshì jì bú zhù yǒuxiē rén
de míngzì. 《Jiā》 shì yī bù xiàndài xiǎoshuō. Lǐmiàn de rénwù bù
duō, bǐjiào róngyì dú. Zhè liǎng bù zuòpǐn dōu hěn yǒuyìsi. Zuìjìn,
wǒ zhèngzài dú Lǎo Shě de míng zhù 《Luòtuó Xiángzi》. Zhè yīcì,
wǒ dú de shì Zhōngwén de yuán zhù! Zhè shì wǒ dì yī cì dú
yuánzhù, kùnnán kě zhēn bù xiǎo. Wǒ bù dé bù yībiān chá zìdiǎn,
yībiān kàn. Yǒu shí hòu, yī jù huà yào kàn hǎo jǐ biàn. Dànshì,
kàn dǒng le hòu xīn lǐ tèbié gāoxìng.

Vocabulary ♦

音乐	**yīnyuè**	music
爱好	**àihào**	to like something as a hobby; hobby
养花	**yǎng huā**	to grow flowers

电影迷	**diànyǐng mí**	film fan
至于	**zhì yú**	as for
更	**gèng**	even more
文学	**wénxué**	literature
自从 . . . 以来	**zìcóng . . . yǐlái**	since
越来越	**yuè lái yuè**	more and more
对 . . . 感兴趣	**duì . . . gǎn xìngqu**	be interested in . . .
读	**dú**	to read
作品	**zuòpǐn**	a work (as in literature or art)
翻译	**fānyì**	translation
红楼梦	**Hóng Lóu Mèng**	*A Dream of Red Mansions*
部	**bù**	(measure word for a literary work or film)
古典	**gǔdiǎn**	classical
长篇	**cháng piān**	long; major (e.g. a major work of fiction)
小说	**xiǎoshuō**	novel; story
人物	**rénwù**	character
记不住	**jì bú zhù**	cannot remember
有些	**yǒuxiē**	some
正在	**zhèngzài**	(continuous particle)
老舍	**Lǎo Shě**	(name of a famous author)
名著	**míng zhù**	a famous work
骆驼祥子	**Luòtuó Xiángzi**	*Camel Xiangzi* (a famous novel)
原著	**yuán zhù**	original work
困难	**kùnnán**	difficulty
不得不	**bù dé bù**	to have to
查字典	**chá zìdiǎn**	to look it up in the dictionary
有时候	**yǒu shíhou**	sometimes
好几遍	**hǎo jǐ biàn**	several times

Language points ♦

6.1 Use of 更 (gèng)

更 (**gèng**), meaning 'even more' is always placed before the verb or adjective. For example:

我喜欢吃法国菜，更喜欢吃中国菜。
Wǒ xǐhuān chī Fǎguó cài, gèng xǐhuān chī Zhōngguó cài.
I like French cuisine, but I like Chinese even better.

6.2 Use of 自从 . . . 以来 (zìcóng . . . yǐlái, 'since')

Put the time expression in between 自从 (zìcóng) and 以来 (yǐlái). For example:

自从六月份以来，旅游的人越来越多。
Zìcóng liùyuè fèn yǐlái, lǚyóu de rén yuè lái yuè duō.
Since June, the number of tourists has been increasing.

以来 (yǐlái) is very often omitted. For example:

自从上大学(以来)，我一直坚持锻炼身体。
Zìcóng shàng dàxué (yǐlái), wǒ yīzhí jiānchí duànliàn shēntǐ.
Since starting university, I've been doing exercises persistently.

Please note that 我 (wǒ) is omitted from the first half of the above sentence as both parts share the same subject. If different subjects are used, then it cannot be omitted. For example:

自从我父母去中国工作(以来)，我对中国文化越来越感兴趣。
Zìcóng wǒ fùmǔ qù Zhōngguó gōngzuò (yǐlái), wǒ duì Zhōngguó wénhuà yuè lái yuè gǎn xìngqu.
Since my parents went to work in China, I've become more and more interested in Chinese culture.

6.3 Result or potential result of an action

When an adjective follows a verb directly, it shows the result of that verb as explained in the 把 (bǎ) sentence in 4.9 of Unit 4. In grammatical terms, the adjective is known as the 'resultative complement'. Most adjectives can function as resultative complements. For example:

我洗　干净了　你的衣服。
Wǒ xǐ gānjìng le nǐde yīfú.
lit. *I wash clean* [le] *your clothes*
I washed your clothes and they were all clean.

There are also sets of verbs in Chinese which indicate the result of an action such as 懂 (dǒng) in 看懂 (kàn dǒng, read and understand) and 听懂 (tīng dǒng, listen and understand), 着 (zháo) in 睡着 (shuì zháo, to go to bed and fall asleep), and 住 (zhù) in 记住 (jì zhù, remember).

These special sets of verbs can function as resultative complements. For example:

我看懂了这封信后心里特别高兴。

Wǒ kàn dǒng le zhè fēng xìn hòu xīn lǐ tèbié gāoxìng.

I was extremely pleased once I understood the letter.

To express that something is potentially possible or impossible, place 得 (**de**) in between the verb and the resultative complement for positive potential, and 不 (**bù**) in between for negative potential. Please note that 不 is often pronounced with a neutral tone here. For example:

你的汉语这么好，一定看得懂这部小说。

Nǐde hànyǔ zhème hǎo, yīdìng kàn de dǒng zhè bù xiǎoshuō.

Your Chinese is so good. You'll definitely be able to understand this book.

他的名字太复杂了，我记不住。

Tā de míngzi tài fùzá le, wǒ jì bu zhù.

His name is too complicated. I can't remember.

6.4 Differences between 一些 (yīxiē) and 有些 (yǒuxiē)

Although both of these mean 'some', they are used in different positions in a sentence. First, 一些 (**yīxiē**) can follow a verb, but 有些 (**yǒuxiē**) normally appears in the subject position. For example:

老舍的作品，我读过一些。

Lǎo Shě de zuòpǐn, wǒ dú guò yīxiē.

I've read some of Lao She's work.

It is inappropriate to use 有些 (**yǒuxiē**) in the above sentence. Second, 一些 (**yīxiē**) can be of general reference, but 有些 (**yǒuxiē**) normally refers to people or things that are specific. For example:

我有一些中国朋友。

Wǒ yǒu yīxiē Zhōngguó péngyǒu.

I have some Chinese friends.

在我的中国朋友中，有些是从大陆来的，有些是从台湾来的。

Zài wǒde Zhōngguó péngyou zhōng, yǒuxiē shì cóng dàlù lái de, yǒuxiē shì cóng Táiwān lái de.

Among my Chinese friends, some come from the mainland, and some from Taiwan.

6.5 Use of 正在 (zhèngzài)

Place 正在 (zhèngzài) in front of the verb to indicate that something is, was, or will be happening. For example:

妈妈，我正在吃饭，快坐下来和我一起吃吧。
Māma, wǒ zhèngzài chīfàn, kuài zuò xialái hé wǒ yīqǐ chī ba.
Mum, I'm having my meal now. Please sit down and join me.

Very often, 正 (**zhèng**) can be omitted. For example:

昨天我去接他的时候，他在打太极拳。
Zuótiān wǒ qù jiē tā de shíhou, tā zài dǎ tàijíquán.
Yesterday when I went to collect him, he was practising his Tai-chi.

Culture notes

A Dream of Red Mansions

A Dream of Red Mansions (Hong Luo Meng) is a celebrated Chinese literary novel (three volumes) written by Cao Xueqin during the Qing Dynasty. This Eastern version of *Romeo and Juliet* concentrates more on the inevitable law of change rather than just teenage love. The story is set in Beijing under an unknown dynasty, which we assume to be the Ming. The novel tells the story of two star-crossed lovers: Jia Baoyu and Lin Daiyu, who are first cousins. It also tells the story of the downfall of the powerful and prosperous Jia family, which in a way symbolises the downfall of the Ming Dynasty.

The Family

The Family (*Jia*) was written by Ba Jin and published in 1933 as the first of his epic trilogy *The Torrent* (*Jiliu*). The novel is a vivid portrayal of the young people whose aspirations and love were crushed in an old family of three generations under the reign of the patriarch, grandfather Gao. They had to succumb to the centuries-old feudal family rules, even at a time when China, then already a republic, was absorbing new Western ideas. When Ba Jin published the novel in the 1930s it inspired a lot of educated young people to examine and rebel against the old feudal society of China. *The Family* was adapted into a four-act play by Cao Yu (1942).

Exercises

Useful words for the following exercises

作者	**zuòzhě**	author; writer
家人	**jiārén**	family members; family
解释	**jiěshì**	explanation; to explain

Exercise 1

Fill in the gaps using an appropriate word from the vocabulary list for Text 1:

a 这部小说里的_____太多，我记不住他们的名字。
　Zhè bù xiǎoshuō lǐ de_____tài duō, wǒ jì bú zhù tāmen de míngzi.

b 我爷爷特别喜欢看电影。大家都叫他 '_____'。
　Wǒ yéye tèbié xǐhuān kàn diànyǐng. Dàjiā dōu jiào tā '_____'.

c 这个月我买了许多中国文学_____，花了不少钱。
　Zhè gè yuè wǒ mǎi le xǔduō Zhōngguó wénxué_____, huā le bù shǎo qián.

d 今天我发烧了，_____在家休息一天。
　Jīntiān wǒ fāshāo le, _____zài jiā xiūxi yī tiān.

e 这部电影我已经看过_____了，可是我还想再看一遍。
　Zhè bù diànyǐng wǒ yǐjīng kàn guò_____le, kěshì wǒ hái xiǎng zài kàn yī biàn.

f 开始学中文的时候，有许多_____。现在，我觉得容易多了。
　Kāishǐ xué Zhōngwén de shíhou, yǒu xǔduō_____. Xiànzài, wǒ juéde róngyì duō le.

Exercise 2

Answer the following questions orally in Chinese based on Text 1 above:

a 作者的家人有什么爱好？
  Zuòzhě de jiārén yǒu shénme àihào?

b 作者自己对什么最有兴趣？
  Zuòzhě zìjǐ duì shénme zuì yǒu xìngqù?

c 作者读过什么中国文学作品？
  Zuòzhě dú guò shénme Zhōngguó wénxué zuòpǐn?

d 《红楼梦》是一部什么样的小说？
  《Hóng Lóu Mèng》shì yī bù shénme yàng de xiǎoshuō?

Exercise 3

Fill in the gaps using 一些 (yīxiē) or 有些 (yǒuxiē):

a 我有不少中文的小说，_____有英文解释，_____没有。
  Wǒ yǒu bù shǎo Zhōngwén de xiǎoshuō, _____yǒu Yīngwén
  jiěshì, _____méi yǒu.

b 绿茶都喝完了，我还有_____红茶。
  Lǜ chá dōu hē wán le, wǒ hái yǒu_____hóng chá.

c 你今天晚上在家吗？我想给你送_____书去。
  Nǐ jīntiān wǎnshang zài jiā ma? Wǒ xiǎng gěi nǐ sòng_____
  ____shū qu.

d 我妈妈做的菜，_____特别好吃，可有些不好吃。
  Wǒ māma zuò de cài, _____tèbié hǎochī, kě yǒuxiē bù hǎochī.

Exercise 4

Translate the following into Chinese:

a I like Chinese dumplings, but I prefer spring rolls.
b Since I started learning Chinese last month, I have become more
  and more interested in Chinese literature.

c   When I went to see my grandma last night, she was in the middle
    of practising Tai-chi.
d   There are too many characters in this film. I can't remember all of
    their names.
e   What he read were all original works of Lao She.

Dialogue 1 (CD 1; 29)

看比赛   Kàn bǐsài
Going to a match

*Daming and John are colleagues working for an accountancy firm in
Tianjin. They are having a chat during the lunch break.*

DAMING	约翰，你有什么爱好？
JOHN	体育，特别喜欢球类运动。
DAMING	真的？我也喜欢球类运动，最喜欢足球。
JOHN	我也是！我上小学的时候是校队的。你呢？
DAMING	我踢得不好，但非常喜欢看比赛。说到比赛，我有两张明天足球赛的票。你想去看吗？
JOHN	谁跟谁踢？
DAMING	北京队跟广州队。
JOHN	太好了！这两个队都很强。我当然要去看了。比赛几点开始，在什么地方？
DAMING	明天早上十一点，在北京首都体育馆。
JOHN	什么？在北京！我还以为在天津呢！
DAMING	那有什么。坐火车一个小时就到北京了。
JOHN	倒也是。好吧，我明天早点儿起床。八点半去找你，行吗？
DAMING	行。你起得来吗？用不用我八点给你打个电话？
JOHN	不用！只要是看球赛，六点起床也可以！

Dialogue 1 in pinyin ♦

DAMING	Yuēhàn, nǐ yǒu shénme àihào?
JOHN	Tǐyù, tèbié xǐhuān qiú lèi yùndòng.
DAMING	Zhēnde? Wǒ yě xǐhuān qiú lèi yùndòng, zuì xǐhuān zúqiú.

JOHN   Wǒ yě shì! Wǒ shàng xiǎoxué de shíhou shì xiào duì de.
        Nǐ ne?
DAMING Wǒ tī de bù hǎo, dàn fēicháng xǐhuān kàn bǐsài. Shuō
        dào bǐsài, wǒ yǒu liǎng zhāng míngtiān zúqiú sài de piào.
        Nǐ xiǎng qù kàn ma?
JOHN   Shuí gēn shuí tī?
DAMING Běijīng duì gēn Guǎngzhōu duì.
JOHN   Tài hǎo le! Zhè liǎng gè duì dōu hěn qiáng. Wǒ dāngrán yào
        qù kàn le. Bǐsài jǐ diǎn kāishǐ? Zài shénme dìfāng?
DAMING Míngtiān zǎoshang shíyī diǎn, zài Běijīng Shǒudū Tǐyùguǎn.
JOHN   Shénme? Zài Běijīng! Wǒ hái yǐwéi zài Tiānjīn ne!

DAMING	Nà yǒu shénme. Zuò huǒchē yī gè xiǎoshí jiù dào Běijīng le.
JOHN	Dàoyěshì. Hǎo ba, wǒ míngtiān zǎo diǎnr qǐchuáng. Bā diǎn bàn qù zhǎo nǐ, xíng ma?
DAMING	Xíng. Nǐ qǐ de lái ma? Yòng bú yòng wǒ bā diǎn gěi nǐ dǎ gè diànhuà?
JOHN	Bú yòng! Zhǐyào shì kàn qiúsài, liù diǎn qǐchuáng yě kěyǐ!

Vocabulary ◆

比赛	**bǐsài**	match (as in sports)
约翰	**Yuēhàn**	John
体育	**tǐyù**	sport
球类	**qiú lèi**	ball related
校队	**xiào duì**	school/college team
踢	**tī**	to kick
说到	**shuō dào**	talking about
球赛	**qiú sài**	(foot)ball match
跟	**gēn**	with/against
强	**qiáng**	strong; capable
首都	**shǒudū**	capital
体育馆	**tǐyù guǎn**	stadium
那有什么	**nà yǒu shénme**	that's not a problem; that is no big deal; so what?
倒也是	**dàoyěshì**	you are right; you've got a point
早点儿	**zǎo diǎnr**	a bit earlier
找	**zhǎo**	to collect; to get (a person)
起得来	**qǐ de lái**	to be able to get up
用不用...	**yòng bú yòng**	Is it necessary . . . ?
只要	**zhǐyào**	as long as . . .

Language points ◆

6.6   End of sentence 了 (le)

When 了 (**le**) occurs at the end of the sentence, it can indicate the speaker's response or feelings to a new situation. For example, the sentence in Dialogue 1 我当然要去看了 (**Wǒ dāngrán yào qù kàn le,** I certainly will go and watch it) indicates that the speaker really wants to go, now that he has found out who are playing.

Some words such as 快要 (**kuài yào**, nearly), 就 (**jiù**, then), clearly signal new situations which are often linked with end-of-sentence 了 (**le**). For example:

坐火车一个小时就到北京了。
Zuò huǒchē yī gè xiǎoshí jiù dào Běijīng le.
It takes only an hour by train to get to Beijing.

飞机　快要　　降落　了。
Fēijī　kuài yào　jiàngluò le.
lit.　plane very soon land　[le]
The plane is about to land.

6.7　Use of 倒也是 (dàoyěshì)

This phrase can be used independently as a reply to a question or a comment on an opinion. It is not a straightforward 'yes, you are right', but more of a 'now I think about it in this way, that may be right' or 'you've got a point there'. So it implies a change of mind. For example:

A　你中文说得不太好，还是我陪你去买东西吧。
　　Nǐ Zhōngwén shuō de bú tài hǎo, háishì wǒ péi nǐ qù mǎi dōngxī ba.
　　You don't speak very good Chinese. I'll go shopping with you.

B　可是如果每次你都陪我，我的中文就永远也说不好。
　　Kěshì rúguǒ měi cì nǐ dōu péi wǒ, wǒde Zhōngwén jiù yǒngyuǎn yě shuō bù hǎo.
　　But if you come with me every time (I go shopping), I'll never speak good Chinese.

A　倒也是。那，你自己去吧。
　　Dàoyěshì. Nà, nǐ zìjǐ qù ba.
　　You are right there. In that case, go by yourself.

6.8　Use of 得 (de)

In Language point 6.3 above, we discussed how 得 **de** is used to indicate possibility and ability in potential complements. Let us now compare it with the modal verb 能 **néng**. For example, the question 你起得来吗？(**Nǐ qǐ de lái ma?**) is very similar in meaning to 你能起来吗？(**Nǐ néng qǐlái ma?**), both of which translate as 'Are you able to get up/Can you get up?' However, 你起得来吗？(**Nǐ qǐ de lái**

ma?) sounds more doubtful than 你能起来吗? (**Nǐ néng qǐlái ma?**). See more examples below:

你从来没有包过饺子，包得好吗？
Nǐ cónglái méiyǒu bāo guò jiǎozi, bāo de hǎo ma?
You have never made dumplings before. Are you sure you can make them?

你好久不说上海话了，说得好吗？
Nǐ hǎojiǔ bù shuō Shànghǎi huà le, shuō de hǎo ma?
You haven't spoken the Shanghai dialect for a long time. Are you still able to speak it?

Exercises

Exercise 5

Fill in the gaps using an appropriate word from the vocabulary list for Dialogue 1:

a 你需要休息三天。_____我给你开病假条？
   Nǐ xūyào xiūxi sān tiān. _____wǒ gěi nǐ kāi bìngjià tiáo?

b 明天咱们去兵马俑。我八点来你家_____你，行不行？
   Míngtiān zánmen qù Bīngmǎyǒng. Wǒ bā diǎn lái nǐ jiā_____nǐ, xíng bù xíng?

c 北京是中国的_____，是一个非常现代化的城市。
   Běijīng shì Zhōngguó de_____, shì yī gè fēicháng xiàndàihuà de chéngshì.

d 明天你能不能_____来？我想问你一件事。
   Míngtiān nǐ néng bù néng_____lái? Wǒ xiǎng wèn nǐ yī jiàn shì.

e 在记汉字方面，他比我_____。
   Zài jì hànzì fāngmiàn, tā bǐ wǒ_____.

Exercise 6

Fill in the gaps using 的 (**de**) to signal the noun clause or 得 (**DE**) to indicate the result of the verb:

a 你想象_____太简单了。
  Nǐ xiǎngxiàng_____tài jiǎndān le.

b 我今天做_____不是西餐。
  Wǒ jīntiān zuò_____bú shì xīcān.

c 我以为看_____懂这部小说，没想到这么难。
  Wǒ yǐwéi kàn_____dǒng zhè bù xiǎo shuō, méi xiǎng dào zhème nán.

d 他喜欢看_____不是足球，是排球。
  Tā xǐhuān kàn_____bú shì zúqiú, shì páiqiú.

e 今晚我早些睡，明天早上一定起_____来。
  Jīnwǎn wǒ zǎo xiē shuì, míngtiān zǎoshàng yīdìng qǐ_____lái.

Exercise 7

Translate the following into Chinese:

a So long as you know how to look words up in a dictionary, you'll understand this article.
b Talking about celebrating Chinese New Year, I was just going to ask you for advice.
c A I know you don't like her, but she's been to China.
  B You've got a point. I should listen to what she's got to say.
d A I've finished reading the English translation of *A Dream of Red Mansions*.
  B That's nothing! Tom has almost finished reading the original Chinese version of the novel.
e The film is about to start.

Listening comprehension (CD 1; 31)

《骆驼祥子》 《Luòtuó Xiángzi》

You will hear a dialogue between two friends – John and Huaying. Try not to read the script. Bear the following questions in mind whilst listening to the dialogue and try to answer them afterwards:

1 约翰听说过《骆驼祥子》这部作品吗？
   Yuēhàn tīngshuō guò《Luòtuó Xiángzi》zhè bù zuòpǐn ma?

2 《骆驼祥子》的电影是中文的还是英文的？
   《Luòtuó Xiángzi》de diànyǐng shì Zhōngwén de háishì Yīngwén de?

3 约翰的中文怎么样？
   Yuēhàn de Zhōngwén zěnme yàng?

4 他们什么时候去看这部电影？
   Tāmen shénme shíhou qù kàn zhè bù diànyǐng?

Key words ♦

You may find the following words useful in understanding the dialogue:

| 字幕 | **zìmù** | subtitle |
| 可惜 | **kěxī** | shame; pity |

Script in characters ♦

HUAYING 约翰，你看过《骆驼祥子》的电影吗？
JOHN   没有。但是我看过这本书的英文翻译。非常喜欢。
HUAYING 你想看这部电影吗？
JOHN   有没有英文字幕？
HUAYING 可惜没有。
JOHN   那，我看得懂吗？
HUAYING 你的中文这么好，一定看得懂。
JOHN   谢谢你的夸奖。
HUAYING 你同意去看了？
JOHN   同意了。不过，我看不懂的地方，你一定要向我解释。
HUAYING 那当然了。我现在就去买票。你想看今天晚上的还是明天晚上的？
JOHN   今天晚上的。
HUAYING 没问题。一会儿我给你打电话。

Script in pinyin ◆

HUAYING	Yuēhàn, nǐ kàn guò 《Luòtuó Xiángzi》 de diànyǐng ma?
JOHN	Méi yǒu. Dànshì wǒ kàn guò zhè běn shū de Yīngwén fānyì. Fēicháng xǐhuān.
HUAYING	Nǐ xiǎng kàn zhè bù diànyǐng ma?
JOHN	Yǒu méi yǒu Yīngwén zìmù?
HUAYING	Kěxí méi yǒu.
JOHN	Nà, wǒ kàn de dǒng ma?
HUAYING	Nǐ de Zhōngwén zhème hǎo, yīdìng kàn de dǒng.
JOHN	Xièxiè nǐde kuājiǎng.
HUAYING	Nǐ tóngyì qù kàn le?
JOHN	Tóngyì le. Búguò, wǒ kàn bù dǒng de dìfang, nǐ yīdìng yào xiàng wǒ jiěshì.
HUAYING	Nà dāngrán le. Wǒ xiànzài jiù qù mǎi piào. Nǐ xiǎng kàn jīntiān wǎnshang de háishì míngtiān wǎnshang de?
JOHN	Jīntiān wǎnshang de.
HUAYING	Méi wèntí. Yīhuìr wǒ gěi nǐ dǎ diànhuà.

7   教育
Jiàoyù
Education

In this unit, you will learn about:

- sentences of comparison and contrast
- using verbal phrases to modify a noun
- shortened forms
- how to introduce a topic
- colloquial use of 厉害 (lìhai)

Text 1   🎧 (CD 2; 1)

一封信   Yī fēng xìn
A letter

Chen Qing has just started her teaching career at a primary school which is situated in a remote mountain area. She writes to a friend of hers who teaches at a school in the nearby city:

燕春：

你好！谢谢你的来信。

新的学期刚刚开始，事情特别多。加上我刚来这里，对一切都不熟悉。好在同事们和家长们都很热心，给了我很多的帮助。校长让我当一年级一个班的班主任，并且让我教一年级所有班的算术课。一年级一共有三个班，每个班有大约四十个学生。

和城里的孩子一样，这儿的孩子也是六岁上学。不过，和城里的学校比起来，这儿的条件差多了。让我高兴的是，这儿的学生十分用功，专一。农村没有什么让他们分心的事，所以他们可以集中注意力。

一会儿我要带全班去参观图书馆，不能多写了。等我有空时，再给你写封长信。

祝好！

陈青

2005, 9, 15

Chinese abacus
www.istock.com

Text 1 in pinyin ♦

Yànchūn:

Nǐ hǎo! Xièxie nǐde láixìn.

Xīn de xuéqī gānggāng kāishǐ, shìqing tèbié duō. Jiāshàng wǒ gāng lái zhèlǐ, duì yīqiē dōu bù shóuxi. Hǎozài tóngshìmen hé jiāzhǎngmen dōu hěn rèxīn, gěi le wǒ hěnduō de bāngzhù. Xiàozhǎng ràng wǒ dāng yī niánjí yī gè bān de bān zhǔrèn, bìngqiě ràng wǒ jiāo yī niánjí suǒyǒu bān de suànshù kè. Yī niánjí yīgòng yǒu sān gè bān, měi gè bān yǒu dàyuē sìshí gè xuéshēng.

Hé chénglǐ de háizi yīyàng, zhèr de háizi yě shì liù suì shàng xué. Búguò, hé chénglǐ de xuéxiào bǐ qǐlái, zhèr de tiáojiàn chà duō le. Ràng wǒ gāoxìng de shì, zhèr de xuéshēng shífēn yònggōng, zhuānyī. Nóngcūn méi yǒu shénme ràng tāmen fēn xīn de shì, suǒyǐ tāmen kěyǐ jízhōng zhùyìlì.

Yīhuìr wǒ yào dài quán bān qù cānguān túshūguǎn, bù néng duō xiě le. Děng wǒ yǒu kòng shí, zài gěi nǐ xiě fēng cháng xìn.

Zhù hǎo!

Chén Qīng

2005, 9, 15

Vocabulary ◆

教育	jiàoyù	education
学期	xuéqī	term
事情	shìqing	thing; matter
加上	jiāshàng	besides; on top of this
熟悉	shóuxi; shúxi	be familiar
好在	hǎozài	just as well; it is a good job . . .
家长	jiāzhǎng	parents
热心	rèxīn	warm; friendly
校长	xiàozhǎng	headmaster
当	dāng	to act as; become; be
一年级	yī niánjí	year one
班	bān	class (as a group)
班主任	bān zhǔrèn	class teacher
教	jiāo	to teach
算术	suànshù	arithmetic
城里	chéng lǐ	in the city
上学	shàng xué	to go to school; to start schooling
和...比起来	hé . . . bǐ qǐlái	compared with . . . ; in comparison with . . .
条件	tiáojiàn	condition
差多了	chà duō le	far worse
专一	zhuānyī	single-minded; concentrating
分心	fēn xīn	with divided attention; lack of concentration
集中	jí zhōng	to focus
注意力	zhùyìlì	attention
图书馆	túshūguǎn	library

Additional useful words

受过教育的人	shòu guò jiàoyù de rén	educated person/people
有文化的人	yǒu wénhuà de rén	educated person/people
文化程度	wénhuà chéngdù	education level; education qualification
教师	jiàoshī	teacher
老师	lǎoshī	teacher
小学	xiǎo xué	primary school
中学	zhōng xué	secondary school
大学	dàxué	university
教室	jiàoshì	classroom
暑假	shǔ jià	summer vacation (only used for school/university holidays)

寒假	hán jià	winter vacation (only used for school/university holidays)

Language points ♦

7.1 Use of 好在 (hǎozài)

This is a colloquial expression meaning 'It is just as well . . .' or 'It is a good thing that . . .'. Always place this expression at the beginning of a sentence. For example:

这几天，我得了重感冒。好在这个星期我没有课。
Zhè jǐ tiān, wǒ dé le zhòng gǎnmào. Hǎozài zhè ge xīngqī wǒ méi yǒu kè.
I've had a bad cold during the last couple of days. It's just as well that I have no classes this week.

7.2 Use of 让 (ràng)

In the above text, 让 (**ràng**) is used in two different sentences to mean different things. The first meaning is 'to ask (someone to do something)'. For example:

校长让我当一年级一个班的班主任 . . .
Xiàozhǎng ràng wǒ dāng yī niánjí yī ge bān de bān zhǔrèn . . .
The head teacher asked me to be the class teacher of one of the Year One classes . . .

我妈妈让我每天锻炼身体。
Wǒ māma ràng wǒ měitiān duànliàn shēntǐ.
My mother asks me to do exercises every day.

The second meaning is 'to make' or 'to enable'. For example:

让我高兴的是 . . .
Ràng wǒ gāoxìng de shì . . .
What makes me happy is that . . .

这件事真让我生气。
Zhè jiàn shì zhēn ràng wǒ shēngqì.
This (matter) really makes me angry.

7.3   Compare and contrast

Below are some useful expressions used in introducing sentences of comparison and contrast:

和...比起来/和...相比 (**Hé...bǐ qǐlái/Hé...xiāngbǐ**, Compared with .../In comparison with ...)

e.g.   和城里的学校比起来，这儿的条件差多了。
Hé chénglǐ de xuéxiào bǐ qǐlái, zhèr de tiáojiàn chà duō le.
Compared with schools in the city, conditions here are a lot worse.

和老张相比，我的英文差多了。
Hé Lǎo Zhāng xiāngbǐ, wǒde Yīngwén chà duō le.
Compared with Lao Zhang, my English is much worse.

和...一样 (**Hé...yī yàng**, Like ...)

e.g.   和我父母一样，我也喜欢文学。
Hé wǒ fùmǔ yīyàng, wǒ yě xǐhuān wénxué.
Like my parents, I also like literature.

和...不一样 (**hé...bù yī yàng**)

e.g.   和英国的孩子不一样，中国的孩子六岁上学。
Hé Yīngguó de háizi bù yīyàng, Zhōngguó de háizi liù suì shàng xué.
Unlike British children, Chinese children begin school when they are six.

7.4   Use of 的 (de) before a noun

A noun or noun phrase can be modified by a verbal phrase. 的 (**de**) must be placed before the noun but after the verbal phrase which modifies the noun. For example:

那个	在做健美操	的	人	是我奶奶。
Nà ge	<u>**zài zuò jiànměi cāo**</u>	<u>**de**</u>	**rén**	**shì wǒ nǎinai.**
	verbal phrase	[de]	noun	

lit.   *that   doing keep-fit exercise* [de] *person is my grandma*
The person doing the keep-fit exercise is my grandma.

Please note 那个 (**nà ge**) can be placed before 人 (**rén**), for example:

在做健美操的那个人是我奶奶
Zài zuò jiànměi cāo de nà ge rén shì wǒ nǎinai.
The person doing the keep-fit exercise is my grandma.

In fact, the above sentence consists of two parts: (1) 那个人在做健美操 (nà ge rén zài zuò jiànměi cāo), and (2) 那个人是我奶奶 (nà ge rén shì wǒ nǎinai).

Culture note

The Chinese education system

Primary and secondary education in China is composed of three stages: primary school, junior middle school and senior middle school, with a total study length of 12 years. Generally, the length of study in primary school is six years starting from age 6; junior middle school three years; and senior middle school three years. Primary and junior middle school education is compulsory. No examination is required to advance to junior middle school. Junior middle school graduates may enter senior middle school after passing examinations set by the local education authorities.

Tertiary education lasts four years. To enter university, one must take the National Entrance Examination for Higher Education.

Exercises

You may find the following words useful in doing the exercises

卡拉ok	**kǎlā ōukēi**	karaoke
网吧	**wǎng bā**	internet bar
道路	**dàolù**	road
具有	**jùyǒu**	to have
国际	**guójì**	international
标准	**biāozhǔn**	standard
开往	**kāi wǎng**	to head for

Exercise 1

Fill in the gaps using an appropriate word from the vocabulary list for Text 1:

a 这所小学校每个学期开两次_____会。这样，
 Zhè suǒ xiǎo xuéxiào měi ge xuéqī kāi liǎng cì_____huì. Zhè yang,
 学生的父母十分了解自己孩子的学习情况。
 xuéshēng de fùmǔ shífēn liǎojiě zìjǐ háizi de xuéxí qíngkuàng.

b 城里有许多_____的事情，比如卡拉OK，网吧等等。
 Chéng lǐ yǒu xǔduō_____de shìqing, bǐ rú kǎlā ōukēi, wǎngbā
 děngdeng.

c 我们的校长是一位非常_____的人，别人
 Wǒmen de xiàozhǎng shì yī wèi fēicháng_____de rén, bié rén
 有困难时，他总是帮助别人。
 yǒu kùnnán shí, tā zǒngshì bāngzhù bié rén.

d 我来这儿已经半年了，可是对这儿的路还是不_____。
 Wǒ lái zhèr yǐjīng bàn nián le, kěshì duì zhèr de lù háishì bù
 _____.

e 上个_____我们班来了个新同学。
 Shàng ge_____wǒmen bān lái le gè xīn tóngxué.

Exercise 2

Use 的 (**de**) to link the two sentences in each group together (delete unnecessary words in the original sentences) and then translate the sentence into English:

Example: 那个人在做健美操 **nà ge rén zài zuò jiànměi cāo**
 那个人是我奶奶 **nà ge rén shì wǒ nǎinai**

Linked by 的 (**de**)
 那个在做健美操的人是我奶奶。
 Nà ge zài zuò jiànměi cāo *de* rén shì wǒ nǎinai.
 The person doing the keep-fit is my grandma.

a 那个人是我的老师 nà ge rén shì wǒde lǎoshī
 他正在包饺子 tā zhèngzài bāo jiǎozi

b 我喜欢那些人 wǒ xǐhuān nàxiē rén
 他们早睡早起 tāmen zǎo shuì zǎo qǐ

c 我要去看一场比赛 wǒ yào qù kàn yī cháng bǐsài
 这场比赛具有国际标准 zhè cháng bǐsài jùyǒu guójì biāozhǔn

d 这是一辆快车   zhè shì yī liàng kuài chē
  这辆火车开往云南   zhè liàng huǒchē kāiwǎng Yúnnán

e 城里有很多事情   chéng lǐ yǒu hěnduō shìqing
  这些事情让人分心   zhèxiē shìqing ràng rén fēnxīn

Exercise 3 (CD 2; 2)

What do you say in the following situations?

a You've just met a Chinese person who is a teacher and you want to ask her what she teaches.
b You want to ask a Chinese person the age at which Chinese children begin their schooling.
c You want to find out if the library opens every day.

Exercise 4

Translate the following into Chinese:

a My bike has broken down. It's just as well that I don't have to go to work today.
b This book is too difficult. It gives me a headache.
c My father has asked me to go to my grandma's and spend Chinese New Year with her this year.
d Compared to your university library, ours is much smaller.
e Unlike Western food, cooking Chinese food is very time-consuming.

Dialogue 1 (CD 2; 3)

中英大学生活   Zhōng Yīng dàxué shēnghuó
University life at Chinese and British universities

Zhang Wei studied at a UK university for three years, and is now back in China. His friend Li Lan, a student at Peking University, is thinking about studying abroad.

Peking University
Photographer: Victoria Coleman

Lı Lan	张伟，你在英国学习了三年。能不能给我讲讲中英大学生活有什么不同？
Zhang Wei	中国大学本科一般是四年，而英国大部分学科只需要三年。英国的硕士课程一般只用一年，而中国却要学三年。
Lı Lan	这么说，和英国的学生比起来，我们在学校花的时间长得多。
Zhang Wei	没错。另外，中国的大学每年有两个学期，而英国有三个学期，所以有三次假期。放假的时候，许多学生都打工，赚些钱后，出去旅游。
Lı Lan	现在，中国的不少大学生假期也出去打工了。英国学生业余时间常常做什么？
Zhang Wei	参加各种俱乐部，比如：辩论俱乐部，戏剧俱乐部等。周末，学生们常去酒吧聚会。他们喝起酒来，比中国学生厉害得多！
Lı Lan	大学里可以谈恋爱吗？
Zhang Wei	当然可以了。这些事情校方从来不管。再说，英国学生都是一个人一间卧室，谈恋爱也比较方便！

Dialogue 1 in pinyin ♦

LI LAN   Zhāng Wěi, nǐ zài Yīngguó xuéxí le sān nián. Néng bù
                néng gěi wǒ jiǎngjiang Zhōng Yīng dàxué shēnghuó yǒu
                shénme bùtóng?

ZHANG WEI   Zhōngguó dàxué běnkē yībān shì sì nián, ér Yīngguó
                dàbùfèn xuékē zhǐ xūyào sān nián. Yīngguó de shuòshì
                kèchéng yībān zhǐ yòng yī nián, ér Zhōngguó què yào
                xué sān nián.

LI LAN   Zhème shuō, hé Yīngguó de xuéshēng bǐ qǐlái, wǒmen
                zài xuéxiào huā de shíjiān chǎng de duō.

ZHANG WEI   Méicuò. Lìngwài, Zhōngguó de dàxué měi nián yǒu liǎng
                ge xuéqī, ér Yīngguó yǒu sān ge xuéqī, suǒyǐ yǒu sān cì
                jiàqī. Fàngjià de shíhòu, xǔduō xuéshēng dōu dǎ gōng,
                zhuàn xiē qián hòu, chūqù lǚyóu.

LI LAN   Xiànzài, Zhōngguó de bùshǎo dàxué shēng jiàqī yě chūqù
                dǎ gōng le. Yīngguó xuéshēng yèyú shíjiān chángcháng
                zuò shénme?

ZHANG WEI   Cānjiā gè zhǒng jùlèbù, bǐ rú: biànlùn jùlèbù, xìjù jùlèbù
                děng. Zhōumò, xuéshēngmen cháng qù jiǔbā jùhuì.
                Tāmen hē qǐ jiǔ lái, bǐ Zhōngguó xuéshēng lìhai deduō!

LI LAN   Dàxué lǐ kěyǐ tán liàn'ài ma?

ZHANG WEI   Dāngrán kěyǐ le. Zhèxiē shìqíng xiào fāng cónglái bù
                guǎn. Zàishuō, Yīngguó xuéshēng dōu shì yī ge rén yī
                jiān wòshì, tán liàn'ài yě bǐjiào fāngbiàn!

Vocabulary ♦

生活	shēnghuó	life; living
本科	běnkē	first degree; BA
大部分	dàbùfèn	majority
而	ér	whereas; but
学科	xuékē	subject; major
硕士	shuòshì	master's; MA
课程	kèchéng	course; programme
却	què	surprisingly, but
花	huā	to spend
没错	méicuò	correct; right
假期	jiàqī	vacation; holiday

放假	**fàng jià**	to have a holiday; to be on holiday
打工	**dǎ gōng**	to do part-time work
赚些钱	**zhuàn xiē qián**	to earn some money
旅游	**lǚyóu**	to travel
业余	**yèyú**	spare (time)
俱乐部	**jūlèbù**	club
辩论	**biànlùn**	debate; debating
戏剧	**xìjù**	drama
周末	**zhōumò**	weekend
喝起酒来	**hē qǐ jiǔ lái**	when it comes to drinking
厉害	**lìhai**	aggressive; fierce; impressive
谈恋爱	**tán liàn'ài**	to court (*lit.* to talk about love)
校方	**xiào fāng**	school authority
管	**guǎn**	to be in charge; to interfere
再说	**zàishuō**	besides
卧室	**wòshì**	bedroom
方便	**fāngbiàn**	convenient

Additional useful words

留学生	**liúxué shēng**	overseas student
本科生	**běnkē shēng**	undergraduate student
研究生	**yánjiù shēng**	postgraduate student
博士	**bóshì**	doctoral; PhD; Dr
博士生	**bóshì shēng**	PhD student
考试	**kǎoshì**	examination
学位	**xué wèi**	degree
开学	**kāi xué**	to start the term
讲师	**jiǎngshī**	lecturer
教授	**jiàoshòu**	professor

Language points

7.5 Shortened form

Some country names and organization names can be shortened. For example:

中国 **Zhōngguó** + 英国 **Yīngguó** = 中英 **Zhōng Yīng**
(China, Britain; Sino-British)
中国 **Zhōngguó** + 美国 **Měiguó** = 中美 **Zhōng Měi**
(China, America; Sino-American)

北京大学 **Běijīng Dàxué** = 北大 **Běidà**
(Beijing University; Peking University)
奥林匹克运动会 **Aòlínpǐkè yùndònghuì** = 奥运会 **Aòyùnhuì**
(the Olympic Games)

Unfortunately, there aren't any rules as to which element can be deleted. It is rather arbitrary. You just have to remember them one by one.

7.6 Difference between 而 (ér) and 但是 or 可是 (dànshì, kěshì)

而 (ér) can be used either to signal a mild contrast or to link two sentences in order to make a comparison. The two sentences linked by 而 (ér) usually have different subjects. For example:

城里太杂吵，而农村太安静了。
Chénglǐ tài záchǎo, ér nóngcūn tài ānjìng le.
It is too noisy in the city, whereas in the countryside it is too quiet.

我母亲喜欢看电影，而我父亲热爱戏剧。
Wǒ mǔqīn xǐhuān kàn diànyǐng, ér wǒ fùqīn rè'ài xìjù.
My mother likes going to the cinema, whereas my father prefers the theatre.

Whilst 但是 (dànshì) and 可是 (kěshì) are normally used to introduce a sharp contrast or a change of meaning, the two parts tend to share the same subject matter or at least the same general area of discussion. For example:
(same subject matter: my daughter)

我女儿很用功，但是(她)不怎么聪明。
Wǒ nǚ'ér hěn yònggōng, dànshì (tā) bù zěnme cōngmíng.
My daughter is very hard-working, but (she is) not very bright.

(same general area of discussion: about the school)

这个学校的教室很旧，但是图书馆很现代。
Zhègè xuéxiào de jiàoshì hěn jiù, dànshì túshūguǎn hěn xiàndài.
This school's classrooms are very old, but the library is very modern.

Obviously the 'library' in discussion is the school library.

7.7 Use of 却 (què) to indicate a contrast

却 (què) can be used in conjunction with the words in 7.6 for emphasis. The basic meanings are 'surprisingly' and 'contrary to expectations'. For example:

我哥哥很会做饭，可是他的妻子却不会做。
Wǒ gēge hěn huì zuòfàn, kěshì tāde qīzi què bù huì zuò.
My brother is very good at cooking, but surprisingly his wife cannot cook.

却 (què) can also be used on its own to make a contrast. For example:

他的身体不好，脑子却很清楚。
Tāde shēntǐ bù hǎo, nǎozi què hěn qīngchǔ.
His health is poor, but his brain is very sharp.

7.8 Topic-comment

This is a very common structure in Chinese. The first part of the sentence is the topic, and the second part comments on the topic. To introduce a topic, one of the patterns used is 'verb + 起 (qǐ) + object of the verb + 来 (lái)', which can be translated as 'In terms of . . .' or 'When it comes to . . .'. For example:

喝起酒来，他比我厉害。
Hē qǐ jiǔ lái, tā bǐ wǒ lìhài.
As far as drinking is concerned, he is more capable than I.

说起她爸爸来，她眼泪汪汪。
Shuōqǐ tā bàba lái, tā yǎnlèi wāngwāng.
Talking about her father, she gets tearful.

7.9 Colloquial use of 厉害 (lìhai)

The original meaning of 厉害 (lìhai) is 'fierce'. For example:

今天的风真厉害。
Jīntiān de fēng zhēn lìhai.
Today's wind is really strong.

When describing a person, 厉害 (lìhai) can mean the following: aggressive, tough, unbelievable, great, incredible. For example:

我们班的新班主任真厉害，把我们都震住了。

Wǒmen bān de xīn bān zhǔrèn zhēn lìhai, bǎ wǒmen dōu zhèn zhù le.

Our class's new teacher is really something. She impressed all of us.

Culture note

How to address a teacher

The term 老师 (**lǎoshī**, teacher) can be used to refer to a teacher and also to speak to a teacher. Pupils and university students in China never address their teachers (including lecturers and professors) by their names. For example, if your teacher's surname is 张 (**Zhāng**), you should refer to/address him or her as 张老师 (**Zhāng lǎoshī**). If you don't know your teacher's surname, you can simply address him or her as 老师 (**lǎoshī**).

Exercises

Useful words for doing the following exercises

客厅	kètīng	sitting room
显得	xiǎnde	to appear
睡懒觉	shuìlǎnjiào	to lie in
长假	cháng jià	long holiday
短假	duǎn jià	short holiday

Exercise 5

Fill in the gaps using an appropriate word from the vocabulary list for Dialogue 1:

a 在所有的_____中，他最喜欢算术课。

  Zài suǒyǒude_____zhōng, tā zuì xǐhuān suànshù kè.

b 去你家要换三次公共汽车，太不_____了。
Qù nǐ jiā yào huàn sān cì gōnggòng qìchē, tài bù_____le.

c 我们学校有不少留学生，_____是美国人。
Wǒmen xuéxiào yǒu bùshǎo liúxué shēng, _____shì Měiguórén.

d 今年七月放假后，我打算先_____，然后去旅游。
Jīn nián Qīyuè fàng jià hòu, wǒ dǎsuàn xiān_____, ránhòu qù lǚyóu.

e 和客厅比起来，我的_____显得非常小。
Hé kètīng bǐ qǐlái, wǒde_____xiǎnde fēicháng xiǎo.

f 平常我早上七点就起床了，到了_____，我喜欢睡懒觉。
Píngcháng wǒ zǎoshàng qī diǎn jiù qǐchuáng le, dào le_____, wǒ xǐhuān shuìlǎnjiào.

Exercise 6

Ask as many questions in Chinese as you can regarding Dialogue 1:

Example: 张伟在英国学习了几年？
Zhāng Wěi zài Yīngguó xuéxí le jǐ nián?

Exercise 7

Match the sentence in the left column with an appropriate one in the right column. Then translate the complete sentences into English:

a 他在中国住了两年，
Tā zài Zhōngguó zhù
le liǎng nián,

而她的爷爷已经八十多岁了。
ér tāde yéye yǐjīng bāshí duō
suì le.

b 她的奶奶今年七十八岁，
Tāde nǎinai jīn nián
qīshí bā suì,

而英国的学校每年要放三次
长假，三次短假。
ér Yīngguó de xuéxiào měi
nián yào fàng sān cì cháng jià,
sān cì duǎn jià.

c 中国的学校每年只放两次假，
Zhōngguó de xuéxiào
měi nián zhǐ fàng liǎng cì jià,

可是他却不会说中文。
kě shì tā què bù huì shuō
Zhōngwén.

A primary school in China

Exercise 8

Translate the following into Chinese:

a How long did you spend writing this letter?
b When it comes to talking about China, he becomes very excited.
c I don't want to go to the bar tonight. Besides, the bar I like most is not open tonight.
d In Britain, children go to school at four years old; whereas in China, children begin their schooling at the age of six.
e David learnt 500 characters within three months. He is truly impressive.

Reading comprehension (CD 2; 5)

在中国教英文   Zài Zhōngguó jiāo Yīngwén
Teach English in China

Bear the following questions in mind whilst reading the letter and try to answer them afterwards. This letter is written by Susan to her Chinese teacher back in Ireland:

1   苏珊在太原做什么？
    Sūshān zài Tàiyuán zuò shénme?

2   北京和太原有什么地方不同？
    Běijīng hé Tàiyuán yǒu shénme dìfāng bù tóng?

3   学生们把苏珊叫什么？
    Xuéshēngmen bǎ Sūshān jiào shénme?

4   苏珊的学校什么时候放寒假？
    Sūshān de xuéxiào shénme shíhòu fàng hán jià?

5   苏珊准备在哪儿，和谁一起过年？
    Sūshān zhǔnbèi zài nǎr, hé shéi yīqǐ guò nián?

Key words ◆

The following key words may help you understand the letter better:

太原	**Tàiyuán**	(city name)
上课	**shàng kè**	to go to class
下课	**xià kè**	to finish class
习惯	**xíguàn**	be used to; be accustomed to
不行	**bù xíng**	not acceptable; does not work
中旬	**zhōngxún**	mid- (for month)
从前	**cóngqián**	before; a while back

Letter in characters ◆

李老师：

　　您好！

　　上次给您写信时，我还在北京学中文。今年九月，一个中国朋友介绍我来太原的一所小学教英文。我已经在这儿工作了三个月了。和北京比起来，太原的生活条件差得多，冬天也冷得多。不过，这儿的孩子特别用功。每天早上八点上课，下午五点才下课。大部分学生回家吃中午饭。孩子们把我叫 '老师'，我不太习惯。我让他们叫我名字，可是他们说不行。学生的家长们也非常热心，周末常常请我去他们家吃饭。我真的很喜欢我的工作。

　　我们一月中旬放寒假，到时候我准备去西安旅游，再去北京和我从前学中文时认识的朋友们一起过年。

　　圣诞节快到了，祝您和全家圣诞快乐！

苏珊

2005, 12, 1

Letter in pinyin ◆

Lǐ lǎoshī:

　　Nín hǎo!

　　Shàng cì gěi nín xiě xìn shí, wǒ hái zài Běijīng xué Zhōngwén. Jīnnián jiǔ yuè, yī ge Zhōngguó péngyou jièshào wǒ lái Tàiyuán de yī suǒ xiǎo xué jiāo Yīngwén. Wǒ yǐjīng zài zhèr gōngzuò le sān gè yuè le. Hé Běijīng bǐ qǐlái, Tàiyuán de shēnghuó tiáojiàn chà deduō, dōngtiān yě lěng de duō. Búguò, zhèr de háizi tèbié yònggōng. Měi tiān zǎoshàng bā diǎn shàng kè, xiàwǔ wǔ diǎn cái xià kè. Dàbùfèn xuéshēng huí jiā chī zhōngwǔ fàn. Háizimen bǎ wǒ jiào 'lǎoshī', wǒ bú tài xíguàn. Wǒ ràng tāmen jiào wǒ míngzì, kěshì tāmen shuō bù xíng. Xuéshēng de jiāzhǎngmen yě fēicháng rèxīn, zhōumò chángcháng qǐng wǒ qù tāmen jiā chī fàn. Wǒ zhēnde hěn xǐhuān wǒde gōngzuò.

　　Wǒmen Yīyuè zhōngxún fàng hán jià, dào shíhòu wǒ zhǔnbèi qù Xī'ān lǚyóu, zài qù Běijīng hé wǒ cóngqián xué Zhōngwén shí rènshi de péngyǒumen yīqǐ guò nián.

　　Shèngdàn Jié kuài dào le, zhù nín hé quán jiā Shèngdàn kuàilè

Sūshān

2005, 12, 1

8 工作
Gōngzuò
Work

In this unit, you will learn about:

▶ past and present regarding the job situation
▶ describing one's job
▶ expressions for job-hunting
▶ passive voice introduced by 由 (**yóu**)
▶ conditional sentence introduced by 如果...的话 (**rúguǒ... de huà**)

Text 1 ⟨𝅘⟩ (CD 2; 6)

找工作 Zhǎo gōngzuò
Looking for jobs

直到八十年代底，中国的大学生不用自己找工作。即便你想自己找工作，也不可能。每个毕业生的工作都是由学校分配的。当然，学校的领导也征求个人的意见，但是最后的决定是别人为你做的。所以，那个时候根本没有选择的自由，也没有什么招聘广告，工作面试。现在情况不一样了。大学毕业后要自己找工作。这样一来便出现了招聘广告，就业网站，人才市场等。同时也出现了选择带来的烦恼。

Text 1 in pinyin ♦

Zhídào bāshí niándài dǐ, Zhōngguó de dà xuéshēng bú yòng zìjǐ zhǎo gōngzuò. Jíbiàn nǐ xiǎng zìjǐ zhǎo gōngzuò, yě bù kěnéng. Měigè bìyè shēng de gōngzuò dōu shì yóu xuéxiào fēnpèi de. Dāngrán, xuéxiào de lǐngdǎo yě zhēngqiú gèrén de yìjiàn, dànshì zuìhòu de juédìng shì biérén wéi nǐ zuò de. Suǒyǐ, nàgè shíhòu

2005 Wenzhou Job Fair
Photographer: Zhang Ping

gēnběn méiyǒu xuǎnzé de zìyóu, yě méi yǒu shénme zhāopìn guǎnggào, gōngzuò miànshì. Xiànzài qíngkuàng bù yīyàng le. Dàxué bìyè hòu yào zìjǐ zhǎo gōngzuò. Zhèyàng yīlái, biàn chūxiàn le zhāopìn guǎnggào, jiùyè wǎngzhàn, réncái shìchǎng děng. Tóngshí yě chūxiàn le xuǎnzé dàilái de fánnǎo.

Vocabulary ◆

找工作	zhǎo gōngzuò	to look for jobs
直到	zhídào	until
即便	jíbiàn	even if
不可能	bù kěnéng	be impossible
毕业生	bìyè shēng	graduate students
由	yóu	by
分配	fēnpèi	to assign
领导	lǐngdǎo	leader; management
征求	zhēngqiú	to ask for; to consult
个人	gèrén	individual

意见	yìjiàn	view; opinion
决定	juédìng	decision
别人	biérén	others
根本	gēnběn	absolutely
选择	xuǎnzé	choice
自由	zìyóu	freedom
招聘	zhāopìn	to invite applications for a job
广告	guǎnggào	advertisement
面试	miànshì	interview
这样一来	zhè yàng yī lái	this way; by doing so
便	biàn	then; therefore
出现	chūxiàn	to appear; to occur
就业	jiùyè	employment
网站	wǎngzhàn	internet site
人材市场	réncái shìcháng	job market (*lit.* talents market)
带来	dàilái	to bring about
烦恼	fánnǎo	hassle; worries

Additional useful words

广告设计师	guǎnggào shèjìshī	copywriter (in advertising)
工程师	gōngchéngshī	engineer
美发师	měifàshī	hairdresser
推销员	tuīxiāoyuán	sales-person
翻译	fānyì	interpreter; translator
列车员	lièchēyuán	train attendant
老板	lǎobǎn	boss
雇员	gùyuán	employee
雇主	gùzhǔ	employer
幼儿教师	yòu'ér jiàoshī	nursery teacher
厂长	chǎngzhǎng	factory manager
工人	gōngrén	worker
失业	shīyè	unemployment; be unemployed
下岗	xiàgǎng	be laid off

Language points ♦

8.1 即便 . . . 也 (jíbiàn . . . yě . . .)

Literally, this means 'even if . . . , still/already . . .', although very often it is simply translated as 'even if . . .'. 也 (yě) must be used in the second half of the sentence, and it is placed before the verb. For example:

即便你不告诉我这件事，别人也会告诉我的。
Jíbiàn nǐ bù gàosu wǒ zhè jiàn shì, biérén yě huì gàosu wǒ de.
Even if you don't tell me about it, others (still) will.

即使你想自己找工作，也不可能。
Jíbiàn nǐ xiǎng zìjǐ zhǎo gōngzuò, yě bù kěnéng.
Even if you wanted to look for a job by yourself, it was impossible.

8.2   The passive voice

In Chinese, the passive voice is not used as extensively as in English. When it is used, there is no single unified form like the English pattern 'to be verb + ed by . . .'. Let us look at one pattern which conveys a passive voice:

subject + 由 (**yóu**) + agent of the verb + verb

For example:

我的工作	由	学校领导	分配。
Wǒde gōngzuò	**yóu**	**xuéxiào lǐngdǎo**	**fēnpèi.**
subject	passive marker	agent of verb	verb

lit.   *my job*   *by*   *university management assign*
My job is going to be assigned by the university management.

In the text above, the 是 . . . 的 (**shì . . . de**) structure was used to indicate the past tense:

每个毕业生的工作都是由学校分配的。
Měigè bìyè shēng de gōngzuò dōu shì yóu xuéxiào fēnpèi de.
The job of every graduate was assigned by the university.

When the 是 . . . 的 (**shì . . . de**) structure is used to indicate the past, the passive marker 由 (**yóu**) is often omitted. For example:

最后的决定是(由)别人为你做的。
Zuìhòu de juédìng shì yóu biérén wéi nǐ zuò de.
lit.   *final decision was by others for you made*
The final decision was made for you by others.

8.3 Use of 根本 (gēnběn, 'absolutely not')

When this phrase is used as an adverb, it is usually used in negative sentences to emphasise that something is not at all possible. For example:

他根本不可能征求我的意见。
Tā gēnběn bù kěnéng zhēngqiú wǒde yìjiàn.
It was completely out of the question that he would ask for my views.

她根本不会开车。
Tā gēnběn bú huì kāichē.
She couldn't drive at all.

8.4 Position of 便 (biàn, 'then')

This adverb can be used to indicate the consequence of an action, and hence it occurs in the second half of the sentence and it is always placed before the verb. For example:

听说北京晚报上有招聘广告，他便马上去买了一份报。
Tīngshuō Běijīng Wǎn Bào shàng yǒu zhāopìn guǎnggào, tā biàn mǎshàng qù mǎi le yī fèn bào.
Upon hearing that there were job advertisements in the *Beijing Evening News*, he immediately went out and bought a copy.

8.5 More on the use of 的 (de) before a noun or noun phrase

In Language point 7.4 of Unit 7, 的 (de) links a verbal phrase to modify a noun or noun phrase. Let us see more examples here where the noun or noun phrase functions either as a subject or an object:

我的女儿给我带来的快乐　　　　是无穷的。
<u>**Wǒde nǚ'ér gěi wǒ dàilái** *de* **kuàilè**</u> **shì wúqióng de.**
subject
lit. *my daughter to me brought happiness is endless*
My daughter has brought me endless happiness.

这是　　　我自己做的决定。
Zhè shì <u>**wǒ zìjǐ zuò** *de* **juédìng.**</u>
object
lit. *this is I myself made decision*
This is a decision made by myself (or I myself made).

Culture notes

'Iron bowl'

Before China started its economic reform programme in the late 1970s, city people either worked for state-owned factories or government organisations. The job was for life, and it was known as the 'iron bowl' (铁饭碗, **tiě fànwǎn**). There was almost no mobility in the job. To transfer from one organisation to another was an extremely lengthy and difficult task.

'Going to sea'

During the reform years, many people resigned from their 'iron bowl' posts to embark on some other ventures ranging from setting up their own food stall to launching large-scale companies. Such a daring action is described as 'going to sea' (下海, **xià hǎi**) as the sea is wild and risky.

Exercises

Exercise 1

Match the following expressions with an appropriate translation:

a	决定	**juédìng**	employment website
b	意见	**yìjiàn**	view, opinion
c	人才市场	**réncái shìcháng**	worries
d	就业网站	**jiùyè wǎngzhàn**	job interview
e	烦恼	**fánnǎo**	job market
f	工作面试	**gōngzuò miànshì**	decision

Exercise 2

Write a short account in Chinese about how you decided on what job to do or how you are going to look for a job. You may wish to use the following expressions:

. . . 的时候 . . . de shíhòu; 一开始 yī kāishǐ; 帮我出主意 bāng wǒ chū zhǔyì; 太多的选择 tài duō de xuǎnzé; 最后 zuìhòu; 决定 juédìng; 因为 yīnwéi

Exercise 3

Use either 由 (**yóu**) or 是 . . . 的 (**shì . . . de**), or both, to make up sentences in the passive voice. The key words are provided in each group.

a 昨天， 聚会，学生会，   组织
   zuótiān, jùhuì, xuéshēng huì, zǔzhī

b 今晚， 年夜饭，   奶奶， 做
   jīnwǎn, nián yè fàn, nǎinai, zuò

c 退烧药，   医生， 开
   tuìshāo yào, yīshēng, kāi

d 建议，王经理，   提出
   jiàn yì, Wáng jīnglǐ, tíchū

Exercise 4

Translate the following into Chinese:

a Having found out the real reason behind this matter, I then said to him: 'It wasn't your fault.'
b Even if I have a lot of money, I would not buy such a thing.
c Children growing up in the countryside are generally very hard-working.
d He had absolutely no idea that she could speak Chinese.

Dialogue 1   (CD 2; 8)

申请工作 Shēnqǐng gōngzuò
Applying for a job

Zhang Lan is preparing for a job interview with an American company in Beijing. She asks her American friend Jane for help.

ZHANG LAN	珍妮，今天我在《北京晚报》上看到一份工作，我想申请。
JANE	是什么工作？
ZHANG LAN	一家驻京的美国办事处需要一名经理助理兼翻译。所有的申请材料必须用英文。你能帮助我修改一下我的简历和申请信吗？
JANE	当然可以。如果你带来了的话，我现在就可以给你看看。
ZHANG LAN	太棒了。材料都在我的包里。给你。

(*a few minutes later . . .*)

JANE	简历没有问题。可以加上你的兴趣爱好，比如会弹钢琴什么的。申请信里应该说明你为什么认为自己能做好这份工作。
ZHANG LAN	那，他们会不会觉得我不谦虚，在吹牛？
JANE	要是老板是美国人，你太谦虚的话，他会认为你没有自信心。
ZHANG LAN	你的建议太宝贵了。如果我拿到面试，还要再麻烦你帮助准备。
JANE	没问题。祝你好运！

Dialogue in pinyin ♦

ZHANG LAN	Zhēnní, jīntiān wǒ zài 《Běijīng Wǎnbào》 shàng kàn dào yī fèn gōngzuò, wǒ xiǎng shēnqǐng.
JANE	Shì shénme gōngzuò?
ZHANG LAN	Yī jiā zhù Jīng de Měiguó bànshìchù xūyào yī míng jīnglǐ zhùlǐ jiān fānyì. Suǒyǒu de shēnqǐng cáiliào bìxū yòng Yīngwén. Nǐ néng bāngzhù wǒ xiūgǎi yīxià wǒde jiǎnlì hé shēnqǐng xìn ma?
JANE	Dāngrán kěyǐ. Rúguǒ nǐ dàilái le dehuà, wǒ xiànzài jiù kěyǐ gěi nǐ kànkan.
ZHANG LAN	Tàibàngle. Cáiliào dōu zài wǒde bāo lǐ. Gěi nǐ.

(*a few minutes later . . .*)

JANE	Jiǎnlì méi yǒu wèntí. Kěyǐ jiāshàng nǐde xìngqù àihào, bǐrú huì tán gāng qín shénme de. Shēnqǐng xìn lǐ yìnggāi shuōmíng nǐ wéishénme rènwéi zìjǐ néng zuòhǎo zhè fèn gōngzuò.

Zhang Lan	Nà, tāmen huì bù huì juéde wǒ bù qiānxū, zài chuīniú?
Jane	Yàoshì lǎobǎn shì Měiguórén, nǐ tài qiānxū dehuà, tā huì rènwéi nǐ méi yǒu zìxìnxīn.
Zhang Lan	Nǐde jiànyì tài bǎoguì le. Rúguǒ wǒ nádào miànshì, hái yào zài máfán nǐ bāngzhù zhǔnbèi.
Jane	Méi wèntí. Zhù nǐ hǎoyùn!

Vocabulary ◆

珍妮	Zhēnní	Jane
晚报	wǎn bào	evening news
份	fèn	(measure word for a copy of newspaper)
申请	shēnqǐng	to apply for; application
驻京	zhù Jīng	to be stationed in Beijing
办事处	bànshì chǔ	office; agency
经理助理	jīnglǐ zhùlǐ	assistant manager
兼	jiān	simultaneously (hold two or more jobs at the same time)
材料	cáiliào	materials
修改	xiūgǎi	to polish; to amend
简历	jiǎnlì	curriculum vitae
如果...的话	rúguǒ ... de huà	if
包	bāo	bag
加上	jiāshàng	to add
弹钢琴	tán gāngqín	to play the piano
说明	shuōmíng	to explain
认为	rènwéi	to think; to consider
吹牛	chuīniú	to boast; be boastful
老板	lǎobǎn	boss
要是	yàoshì	if
自信心	zìxìnxīn	confidence
宝贵	bǎoguì	precious
拿到	nádào	to have got
麻烦	máfán	to trouble
祝你好运	zhù nǐ hǎo yùn	to wish you good luck

Additional useful words

求职信	qiúzhí xìn	job application letter
申请人	shēnqǐng rén	applicant

推荐信	**tuījiàn xìn**	reference letter; reference
应聘	**yìng pìn**	to apply for a vacancy
工资	**gōngzī**	salary
年薪	**niánxīn**	annual salary

Language points ♦

8.6 Use of 什么的 (shénmede)

This is a colloquial expression meaning 'things like that' or 'etc.'. It is always placed at the end of a sentence. For example:

她喜欢画画，跳舞什么的。
Tā xǐhuān huàhuà, tiàowǔ shénmede.
She likes drawing, dancing, things like that./She likes things like drawing and dancing.

8.7 Conditional sentences (CD 2; 9)

In English, most conditional sentences are introduced by 'if'. In Chinese, they can be introduced by 如果...的话 (**rúguǒ ... dehuà**). For example:

如果你有时间的话，能不能帮助我看看我的申请信？
Rúguǒ nǐ yǒu shíjiān dehuà, néng bù néng bāngzhù wǒ kànkan wǒde shēnqǐng xìn?
If you have the time, will you please help me check my application letter?

Very often, especially in spoken Chinese, you can either omit 如果 (**rúguǒ**) or 的话 (**dehuà**). For example:

你喜欢的话，我就送给你了。
Nǐ xǐhuān dehuà, wǒ jiù sòng gěi nǐ le.
If you like it, I'll give it to you.

如果明天天气不好，我们就不去长城了。
Rúguǒ míngtiān tiānqì bù hǎo, wǒmen jiù bù qù Cháng Chéng le.
If the weather is not good tomorrow, we won't go to the Great Wall.

Please note that 就 (**jiù**) is used to mean 'then', and 了 (**le**) is used to indicate the change of state (i.e. if the condition is satisfied, there will then be a change of state).

Conditional sentences can also be introduced by 要是... 的话 (**yàoshì . . . dehuà**), which is more colloquial. Like the other phrase, either 要是 (**yàoshì**) or 的话 (**dehuà**) can be omitted. For example:

要是你大年初一不值班，一定到我家来吃饭。

Yàoshì nǐ dà nián chū yī bù zhí bān, yīdìng dào wǒ jiā lái chī fàn.

If you are not on duty on Chinese New Year's Day, you must come to our house for a meal.

Culture notes

Work unit

The term **danwei** (单位, work unit) was used before the 1980s to refer to the organisation one worked for – be it factory, shop, school, or government department. Each work unit was responsible for its employees' housing, medical care and work after retirement. Some had their own nurseries and schools. This term is still used in China amongst people over 50.

Working hours

In mainland China, working hours are mostly 8am to 6pm, with a 2-hour lunch break.

Exercises

Exercise 5

Fill in the gaps using an appropriate word from the vocabulary list for Dialogue 1:

a 我用中文写了一封信，你能不能帮我_____一下？

　　Wǒ yòng Zhōngwén xiě le yī fēng xìn, nǐ néng bù néng bāng wǒ_____yīxià?

b 小王的英文不怎么好，却_____说自己英文非常好。

　　Xiǎo Wáng de Yīngwén bù zěnme hǎo, què_____shuō zìjǐ Yīngwén fēicháng hǎo.

c 张老师也想参加咱们星期六的聚会，请在名单上_____他的
名字。

Zhāng lǎoshī yě xiǎng cānjiā zánmen Xīngqīliù de jùhuì, qǐng zài
míngdān shàng_____tāde míngzì.

d 她很有自信心，肯定能_____这份工作。

Tā hěn yǒu zìxìnxīn, kěndìng néng_____zhè fèn gōngzuò.

e 你觉得我应该_____经理助理的工作吗？

Nǐ juéde wǒ yìnggāi_____jīnglǐ zhùlǐ de gōngzuò ma?

Exercise 6

Below is a job advertisement. Read it first and then answer the questions in English:

华夏图书馆急需一名图书管理员。负责英文书籍的目录整
编。此人必须持大学文凭，精通英文。有兴趣者请将申请
信和个人简历寄给李芳。联系办法：电子信箱：
lifang@163.com；通讯地址：北京向阳东路106号华夏图书
馆，邮编：100081。

Huáxià Túshūguǎn jí xū yī míng túshū guǎnlǐyuán. Fùzé Yīngwén
shūjí de mùlù zhěngbiān. Cǐ rén bìxū chí dàxué wénpíng, jīngtōng
Yīngwén. Yǒu xìngqù zhě qǐng jiāng shēnqǐng xìn hé gèrén
jiǎnlì jì gěi Lǐ Fāng. Liánxì bànfǎ: Diànzi xìnxiāng:
lifang@163.com; Tōngxùn dìzhǐ: Běijīng Xiàngyáng Dōng Lù
106 Hào Huáxià Túshūguǎn, Yóubiān: 100081

a Who is the employer?
b What is the nature of the job?
c What are the requirements?
d To whom should the application letter be addressed?

Exercise 7

Link each pair of the sentences into one conditional sentence using either 如果...的话 (**rúguǒ...dehuà**) or 要是...的话 (**yàoshì...dehuà**):

a i 你这个周末有空。
Nǐ zhège zhōumò
yǒu kòng.

ii 我们一起去看电影。
Wǒmen yīqǐ qù kàn
diànyǐng.

b i 你能读懂这本书。
Nǐ néng dú dǒng
zhè běn shū.

ii 我就把它送给你。
Wǒ jiù bǎ tā sòng gěi nǐ.

c i 你不喜欢这个工作。
Nǐ bù xǐhuān zhège
gōngzuò.

ii 为什么不换个工作？
Wéishénme bù huàn gè
gōngzuò?

d i 你过份谦虚。
Nǐ guòfèn qiānxū.

ii 老板会认为你没有自信心。
Lǎobǎn huì rènwéi nǐ méi
yǒu zìxìnxīn.

Listening comprehension (CD 2; 10)

换工作　Huàn gōngzuò
Changing job

James works in Beijing. He's going somewhere today in a taxi, and has started a conversation with the taxi driver. You will hear a dialogue between James and the driver. Try not to read the script. Bear the following questions in mind whilst listening to the dialogue and try to answer them afterwards:

1 这个司机从前是做什么工作的？
Zhège sījī cóngqián shì zuò shénme gōngzuò de?

2 她为什么换工作？
Tā wéishénme huàn gōngzuò?

3 她每天工作几个小时？
Tā měitiān gōngzuò jǐ gè xiǎoshí?

4 她现在的工作和从前的比，有什么地方不一样？
Tā xiànzài de gōngzuò hé cóngqián de bǐ, yǒu shénme dìfāng bù
yīyàng?

Vacancy page of a local paper

Key words ♦

You may find the following words useful in understanding the dialogue:

教育部	**jiàoyù bù**	Ministry of Education
开车	**kāichē**	to drive
报纸	**bàozhǐ**	newspaper
司机	**sījī**	driver
灵活	**línghuó**	flexible

Script in characters ♦

JAMES　　你开出租车开了多久了？
DRIVER　　只有两年多。
JAMES　　从前你是做什么工作的？
DRIVER　　如果告诉你，你可能不相信。我从前在教育部为领导开车。

JAMES	真的？那，为什么换了这个工作？
DRIVER	原因很多，不过主要是太不自由。我在报纸上看到这个出租车公司在招聘司机，工作时间灵活，而且工资比我从前的高。我便申请了。
JAMES	现在的工作和从前的比，是不是忙一些？
DRIVER	是的，不过，我可以自己决定一天工作多少个小时，比较自由。
JAMES	你一般每天工作多少个小时？
DRIVER	差不多十个小时。
JAMES	这家公司有多少个雇员？
DRIVER	我也不太清楚。大概六十多个司机。
JAMES	是吗？是个不小的公司。

Script in pinyin ♦

JAMES	Nǐ kāi chūzūchē kāi le duō jiǔ le?
DRIVER	Zhǐyǒu liǎng nián duō.
JAMES	Cóngqián nǐ shì zuò shénme gōngzuò de?
DRIVER	Rúguǒ gàosù nǐ, nǐ kěnéng bù xiāngxìn. Wǒ cóngqián zài jiàoyù bù wèi lǐngdǎo kāichē.
JAMES	Zhēnde? Nà, wèishénme huàn le zhè gè gōngzuò?
DRIVER	Yuányīn hěn duō, búguò zhǔyào shì tài bù zìyóu. Wǒ zài bàozhǐ shàng kàndào zhè ge chūzūchē gōngsī zài zhāopìn sījī, gōngzuò shíjiān línghuó, érqiě gōngzī bǐ wǒ cóngqián de gāo. Wǒ biàn shēnqǐng le.
JAMES	Xiànzài de gōngzuò hé cóngqián de bǐ, shì bú shì máng yīxiē?
DRIVER	Shìde, búguò, wǒ kěyǐ zìjǐ juédìng yī tiān gōngzuò duō shǎo gè xiǎoshí. Bǐjiào zìyóu.
JAMES	Nǐ yībān měitiān gōngzuò duō shǎo ge xiǎoshí?
DRIVER	Chàbuduō shí ge xiǎoshí.
JAMES	Zhè jiā gōngsī yǒu duō shǎo gè gùyuán?
DRIVER	Wǒ yě bù tài qīngchǔ. Dàgài liùshí duō gè sījī.
JAMES	Shì ma? Shì ge bù xiǎo de gōngsī.

9 交通与环境
Jiāotōng yǔ huánjìng
Transport and environment

In this unit, you will learn about:

▶ the formal passive voice marker 被 (**bèi**)
▶ informal passive voice markers
▶ notional passive voice, i.e. passive voice with no marker
▶ use of 得 (**děi**, have to)

Text 1 〔🔊〕 (CD 2; 11)

自行车与汽车　Zìxíngchē yǔ qìchē
Bikes and cars

上个世纪六十年代，七十年代，中国被称为'自行车王国'。那个时候几乎没有私家车，自行车是大多数人的主要交通工具，自行车比汽车多得多。上班的人要骑车，许多上学的学生也得骑车。有些人家每人都有一辆自行车。现在情况不同了，私家车和出租车越来越多，路面上的汽车也就越来越多。汽车数量增加带来的两大后果是：交通堵塞和空气污染。这是中国城市目前急需解决的两个严重问题，特别是在北京和其他一些大城市。

Text 1 in pinyin ♦

Shàng ge shìjì liùshí niándài, qīshí niándài, Zhōngguó bèi chēng wéi 'zìxíngchē wángguó'. Nà ge shíhòu jīhū méi yǒu sījiā chē, zìxíngchē shì dàduōshù rén de zhǔyào jiāotōng gōngjù, zìxíngchē bǐ qìchē duō deduō. Shàng bān de rén yào qí chē, xǔduō shàng

Traffic jam in a Chinese city
Photographer: Jian Miao

xué de xuéshēng yě děi qí chē. Yǒuxiē rén jiā měi rén dōu yǒu yī
liàng zìxíngchē. Xiànzài qíngkuàng bùtóng le, sījiā chē hé chūzūchē
yuè lái yuè duō, lùmiàn shàng de qìchē yě jiù yuè lái yuè duō.
Qìchē shùliàng zēngjiā dàilái de liǎng dà hòuguǒ shì: jiāotōng dǔsè

hé kōngqì wūrǎn. Zhè shì Zhōngguó chéngshì mùqián jíxū jiějué
de liǎng gè yánzhòng wèntí, tèbié shì zài Běijīng hé qítā yīxiē dà
chéngshì.

Vocabulary ♦

汽车	qìchē	vehicle; car
世纪	shìjì	century
六十年代	liùshí niándài	60s (as in 1960s)
被	bèi	(passive marker)
王国	wángguó	kingdom
那个时候	nà ge shíhòu	at that time
几乎	jīhū	nearly
私家车	sījiā chē	private cars
大多数	dàduōshù	majority
主要	zhǔyào	main; major
交通工具	jiāotōng gōngjù	means of transport
路面上	lùmiàn shàng	on the road
也就	yějiù	therefore
数量	shùliàng	amount; quantity
增加	zēngjiā	increase; to increase
后果	hòuguǒ	consequence
交通堵塞	jiāotōng dǔsè	traffic jam
空气污染	kōngqì wūrǎn	air pollution
城市	chéngshì	city
目前	mùqián	at the moment; currently
急需	jí xū	urgently need
解决	jiějué	to resolve
严重	yánzhòng	serious

Additional useful words

存车处	cúnchē chù	bike park
停车场	tíngchē chǎng	car park
交通警	jiāotōng jǐng	traffic police
人行横道	rénxíng héngdào	pedestrian crossing
请勿吸烟	qǐng-wù-xī-yān	No smoking
闲人免进	xián-rén-miǎn-jìn	No entry
警察	jǐngchá	police; policeman
摩托车	mótuō chē	motorbike

Language points ♦

9.1 Formal passive voice marker

In Unit 8 (Language point 8.2), we saw the use of passive marker 由 (**yóu**). In Text 1 above, 被 (**bèi**) is used as a passive marker to signal that the subject of the sentence is the receiver of the action. The initiator of the action can be revealed immediately after 被 (**bèi**) or often left unstated. For example:

他的病　　　被　　　　王大夫　　治好了。
Tāde bìng bèi　　　Wáng dàifū zhì hǎo le.
lit.　*his illness* [marker] *Dr Wang　　cured*
He was cured by Dr Wang.

他的自行车　　　被　　　偷了。
Tāde zìxíngchē bèi　　　tōu le.
lit.　*his bike*　　　　[marker] *stolen*
His bike was stolen (we don't know who did it).

Please see 9.3 and 9.4 below for other types of passive voice.

9.2 Use of 得 (**děi**, 'have to')

得 (**děi**) is used in colloquial speech to mean 'have to'. It must be followed by another verb. For example:

今天那条路堵车，我得骑车去上班。
Jīntiān nà tiáo lù dǔchē, wǒ děi qí chē qù shàng bān.
That road is blocked by traffic today. I've got to cycle to work.

得 (**děi**) is never used in negative sentences. To negate 得 (**děi**), we use 不必 (**bú bì**), 不用 (**bú yòng**). For example:

我们家离这儿很近，不必坐公共汽车。
Wǒmen jiā lí zhè hěn jìn, bú bì zuò gōnggòng qìchē.
As our house is very close to here, there's no need to take a bus.

Culture notes

Noise pollution

In mainland China, drivers sound their horns simply to announce their arrival or to tell the cyclists or pedestrians to give way. So you can imagine how bad the noise level is. The government is tackling this problem, and some cities have begun to give penalties to people who abuse the use of horns.

Traffic police

At many road junctions, the traffic lights do not work properly, so instead you see traffic police standing on a raised platform in the middle of the road, directing traffic.

Exercises

Exercise 1

Fill in the gaps using an appropriate word from the vocabulary list for Text 1:

a 在我们班，＿＿＿＿＿＿每个人都有一辆自行车。
   Zài wǒmen bān, ＿＿＿＿＿＿měigèrén dōu yǒu yī liàng zìxíngchē.

b 今年的毕业生，＿＿＿＿＿＿已经找到工作了。
   Jīnnián de bìyèshēng, ＿＿＿＿＿＿yǐjīng zhǎodào gōngzuò le.

c 近几年在中国的城市，私家车的数量大大＿＿＿＿＿＿了。
   Jìn jǐ nián zài Zhōngguó de chéngshì, sījiā chē de shùliàng dàdà＿＿＿＿＿＿le.

d 在面试中太谦虚的＿＿＿＿＿＿可能是别人以为你没有自信心。
   Zài miànshì zhōng tài qiānxū de＿＿＿＿＿＿kěnéng shì biérén yǐwéi nǐ méi yǒu zìxìnxīn.

e 这个问题很严重，急需王经理来＿＿＿＿＿＿。
   Zhègè wèntí hěn yánzhòng, jí xū Wáng jīnglǐ lái＿＿＿＿＿＿.

Exercise 2

Turn the following sentences/phrases into the passive voice using 被 (**bèi**):

a 同学们称她为'热心的妈妈'。
   Tóngxuémen chēng tā wéi 'rèxīn de māma'.

b 小弟弟弄坏了电话。
   Xiǎo dìdi nòng huài le diànhuà.

c 她训了我一顿。
   Tā xùn le wǒ yī dùn.

d 很多人知道了他的秘方。
   Hěnduō rén zhīdào le tāde mìfāng.

Exercise 3

Translate the following into Chinese:

a We are going to the Great Wall early tomorrow morning. I've got to go to bed early tonight.
b You don't have to cycle to school. You decide yourself.
c There are a lot more female students than male students in my school.
d I can't believe it. All the dumplings were eaten by my elder brother!

Dialogue 1   (CD 2; 13)

骑自行车的好处   Qí zìxíngchē de hǎochù
The benefits of riding a bike

Mike works in Beijing. He has a car, but he cycles to work. His Chinese colleague Lin Mei asks him why.

LIN MEI   麦克，你为什么不开车上班？

MIKE   原因很多。主要原因是，我住得离咱们办公室不远，骑车只需十五分钟，可开车的话，这条路常常堵塞。有一次我开车来上班，结果叫车给堵了一个多小时。

LIN MEI 这倒也是。不过，下雨时骑车不太方便。

MIKE 好在北京气候比较干燥，不常常下雨。从环境保护的角度来说，自行车不消耗能源，不污染环境。

LIN MEI 我完全同意。我认为政府应该限制私家车，提倡骑自行车，并且给骑车人提供安全措施。

MIKE 太对了。比如，骑车人的专用车道。我骑车的另一个原因是为了锻炼身体。否则，工作那么忙，没有时间锻炼身体。

LIN MEI 有道理，我也应该考虑骑车上班。最近，我的体重增加了不少。

Dialogue 1 in pinyin ♦

LIN MEI Màikè, nǐ wèishénme bù kāichē shàng bān?

MIKE Yuányīn hěnduō. Zhǔyào yuányīn shì, wǒ zhù de lí zánmen bàngōngshì bù yuǎn, qíchē zhǐ xū shíwǔ fēnzhōng, kě kāichē dehuà, zhè tiáo lù chángcháng dǔsè. Yǒuyīcì, wǒ kāichē lái shàng bān, jiéguǒ jiào chē gěi dǔ le yī gè duō xiǎoshí.

LIN MEI   Zhè dào yě shì. Búguò, xiàyǔ shí qí chē bú tài fāngbiàn.

MIKE   Hǎo zài Běijīng qìhòu bǐjiào gānzào, bù chángcháng xiàyǔ. Cóng huánjìng bǎohù de jiǎodù láishuō, zìxíngchē bù xiāohào néngyuán, bù wūrǎn huánjìng.

LIN MEI   Wǒ wánquán tóngyì. Wǒ rènwéi zhèngfǔ yīnggāi xiànzhì sījiā chē, tíchāng qí zìxíngchē, bìngqiě gěi qíchērén tígòng ānquán cuòshī.

MIKE   Tài duì le. Bǐrú, qíchērén de zhuānyòng chēdào. Wǒ qí chē de lìng yī gè yuányīn shì wèile duànliàn shēntǐ. Fǒuzé gōngzuò nàme máng, méi yǒu shíjiān duànliàn shēntǐ.

LIN MEI   Yǒu dàolǐ, wǒ yě yīnggāi kǎolǜ qí chē shàng bān. Zuìjìn, wǒde tǐzhòng zēngjiā le bù shǎo.

Vocabulary ◆

麦克	**Màikè**	Mike
主要	**zhǔyào**	main
气候	**qìhòu**	climate
干燥	**gānzào**	dry
从...角度来说	**cóng ... jiǎodù láishuō**	looking from the angle of . . . ; in terms of . . .
环境	**huánjìng**	environment, environmental
保护	**bǎohù**	protection, preservation
消耗	**xiāohào**	to consume, to use up
能源	**néngyuán**	energy
政府	**zhèngfǔ**	government
限制	**xiànzhì**	to restrict
提倡	**tíchāng**	to promote; to advocate
骑车人	**qíchērén**	cyclist
提供	**tí gòng**	to provide
安全	**ānquán**	safety; safe
措施	**cuòshī**	measures
专用车道	**zhuānyòng chēdào**	specially designated/reserved lane
为了	**wèile**	for; in order to
否则	**fǒuzé**	otherwise
考虑	**kǎolǜ**	to consider
体重	**tǐzhòng**	weight

Language points ♦

9.3 Notional passive voice

In Chinese this is the most common form of passive voice where no passive marker is used. Or we can treat the sentence as having the passive marker omitted. For example:

问题　　解决　了。
Wèntí　　jiějué le.
lit.　problem solve [past marker]
The problem has been solved.

Based on our knowledge of the world, the problem cannot solve itself, so it must be a passive. Although it is grammatically correct to say 问题被解决了 (**wèntí bèi jiějué le**), it is not commonly used. Another way of looking at a notional passive is to treat it as a 'topic-comment' sentence. It is an explanatory comment on a situation.

9.4 Informal passive markers

In spoken Chinese, the more formal passive marker 被 (**bèi**) is often replaced by 让 (**ràng**), 叫 (**jiào**), 给 (**gěi**) or 让 . . . 给 (**ràng . . . gěi**), 叫 . . . 给 (**jiào . . . gěi**). When these markers are used, there must be an initiator of the action either clearly specified or vaguely specified. For example:

我的自行车　　让　　　　　我弟弟　　　　弄坏了。
Wǒde zìxíngchē ràng　　　wǒ dìdi　　　nònghuài le.
lit. my bike　　[passive marker] my younger brother broke
My bike was broken by my younger brother (the initiator is clearly specified).

Let us look at another sentence in Dialogue 1 above:

(我)　叫　车　　给　　堵了　一个多小时。
(wǒ) jiào chē　gěi　　dǔ le　yī gè duō xiǎoshí.
lit.　I　[marker]cars [marker] held up more than an hour
I was held up by the traffic for over an hour (the initiator is vaguely specified).

Please note that the initiator must always follow 让 (**ràng**) or 叫 (**jiào**), and that the verb follows 给 (**gěi**). 人 (**rén**) is often used as

Bicycle park

a vaguely specified initiator, meaning 'someone, somebody'. For example:

那个老人让人(给)撞倒了。
Nàgè lǎorén ràng rén (gěi) zhuàngdǎo le.
That old man was knocked down by someone.

Culture note

Bicycle park

In cities and towns, there are bicycle parks outside public places such as department stores and parks. These bike parks are normally attended by retired or elderly people. They charge a small flat fee for the service. If you leave your bike elsewhere, you may face a fine or find the bike taken away by the traffic police. These bike parks are actually on their way out. They are increasingly being replaced by motorbike parks.

Exercises

Exercise 4))) (CD 2; 14)

Find expressions in Dialogue 1 which mean the following:

a It is not very convenient to cycle.
b It is just as well that the climate of Beijing is rather dry.
c I agree completely.
d Lanes especially dedicated to/reserved for cyclists.
e I've put on quite a bit of weight.

Exercise 5

Re-write the following sentences (with the formal passive marker 被 (**bèi**)) using informal passive markers such as 让 (**ràng**), 叫 (**jiào**), 给 (**gěi**), 让...给 (**ràng...gěi**) or 叫...给 (**jiào...gěi**):

a 这个工人被老板解雇了。
 Zhè ge gōngrén bèi lǎobǎn jiěgù le.

b 这顿饭被我做坏了。
 Zhè dùn fàn bèi wǒ zuò huài le.

c 这条路被警察包围了。
 Zhè tiáo lù bèi jǐngchá bāowéi le.

d 我的钱包被偷了。
 Wǒde qiánbāo bèi tōu le.

Exercise 6

Circle the sentences below which are notional passive voice and then translate them into English:

a 汽车修好了   qìchē xiū hǎo le
b 老师同意了   lǎoshī tóngyì le
c 这个城市污染了   zhè ge chéngshì wūrǎn le
d 南方常下雨   nánfāng cháng xiàyǔ
e 去上班的路又堵塞了   qù shàng bān de lù yòu dǔsè le
f 学中文的人数增加了   xué Zhōngwén de rénshù zēngjiā le
g 交通堵塞的问题解决了   jiāotōng dǔsè de wèntí jiějué le

Exercise 7

Fill in the gaps using appropriate expressions given in the box below (not all words are needed):

a 很多家长_____他们的孩子每天看电视的时间。
   Hěnduō jiāzhǎng_____tāmen de háizi měitiān kàn diànshì de shíjiān.

b 他开车时注意力不集中，_____撞倒了一个骑车人。
   Tā kāichē shí zhùyìlì bù jízhōng, _____zhuàngdào le yī gè qíchērén.

c 这个小学给学生们_____了很好的学习环境。
   Zhè ge xiǎoxué gěi xuéshēngmen_____le hěn hǎo de xuéxí huánjìng.

d 他_____了很久，还是决定这个暑假去打工。
   Tā_____le hěn jiǔ, háishì juédìng zhègè shǔjià qù dǎgōng.

考虑 kǎolǜ, 限制 xiànzhì, 结果 jiéguǒ, 路面上 lùmiàn shàng, 有道理 yǒu dàolǐ, 消耗 xiāohào, 提供 tígòng

---

Reading comprehension (CD 2; 15)

水污染   Shuǐ wūrǎn
Water pollution

Below is a letter by Wang Hong to the editor of a newspaper which is having a discussion on how to tackle the pollution problem. Read the letter first and then try to write a summary about the problem in Wang Hong's hometown.

Key words ♦

The following words may help you to understand the letter better:

| 尊敬 | zūnjìng | respected; respectful |
| 编辑 | biānjí | editor |

老家	**lǎojiā**	hometown
浙江	**Zhèjiāng**	(a province in China)
村子	**cūnzi**	village
小河	**xiǎo hé**	small river
记得	**jìde**	(still) remember
小时候	**xiǎo shíhòu**	when I was small
后来	**hòulái**	later
离开	**líkāi**	to leave
家乡	**jiā xiāng**	hometown
变化	**biànhuà**	change
脏	**zāng**	dirty
臭	**chòu**	smelly
建起	**jiànqǐ**	to build
化肥厂	**huàféi chǎng**	chemical fertiliser factory
废水	**fèi shuǐ**	waste water
往 . . . 倒	**wǎng . . . dào**	to pour into
提意见	**tí yìjiàn**	to voice one's view (always negative)
要求	**yāoqiú**	to demand
清理	**qīnglǐ**	to clear up
希望	**xīwàng**	to hope; to wish
说到做到	**shuō-dào-zuò-dào**	to do as promised

Letter in characters

尊敬的编辑：

　　我的老家在浙江的一个农村。村子边上有一条小河，我记得河水清清的。小时候，夏天的时候，我和朋友们常在这条小河里游泳。后来我上大学，离开了家乡。上个月我回老家看奶奶，高兴地看到家乡的许多变化。但是其中有一个变化真让我难过：这条河被污染了！河水比从前脏得多，而且也臭。我问奶奶这是为什么。她告诉我：村里建起了几个小化工厂，这些工厂把废水往河里倒。村里的人们都提意见，要求这些工厂清理这条河，否则就关门。这几个厂的厂长们都同意了。我希望这些厂长们说到做到。

祝好！

王红

2005, 7, 12

Letter in pinyin

Zūnjìng de biānjí:

Wǒde lǎojiā zài Zhèjiāng de yī gè nóngcūn. Cūnzi biānshàng yǒu yī tiáo xiǎo hé, wǒ jìde hé shuǐ qīngqīng de. Xiǎo shíhòu, xiàtiān de shíhòu, wǒ hé péngyǒumen cháng zài zhè tiáo xiǎo hé lǐ yóuyǒng. Hòulái wǒ shàng dàxué, líkāi le jiāxiāng. Shàng ge yuè wǒ huí lǎojiā kàn nǎinai, gāoxìng de kàn dào jiāxiāng de xǔduō biànhuà. Dànshì qí zhōng yǒu yī gè biànhuà zhēn ràng wǒ nánguò: zhè tiáo hé bèi wūrǎn le! Hé shuǐ bǐ cóngqián zāng deduō, érqiě yě chòu. Wǒ wèn nǎinai zhè shì wèishénme. Tā gàosù wǒ: cūn lǐ jiànqǐ le jǐ gè xiǎo huàgōng chǎng, zhèxiē gōngchǎng bǎ fèishuǐ wǎng hé lǐ dào. Cūn lǐ de rénmen dōu tí yìjiàn, yàoqiú zhèxiē gōngchǎng qīnglǐ zhè tiáo hé, fǒuzé jiù guānmén. Zhè jǐ ge chǎng de chǎngzhǎngmen dōu tóngyì le. Wǒ xīwàng zhèxiē chǎngzhǎngmen shuō-dào-zuò-dào.

Zhù hǎo!

Wáng Hóng

2005, 7, 12

10 电脑和互联网
Diànnǎo hé hùliánwǎng
Computers and the internet

In this unit, you will learn about:

▶ computer and internet jargon
▶ end-of-sentence 了 (**le**)
▶ complex structures such as 不但...而且 (**bú dàn ... ér qiě**); 不仅...还 (**bù jǐn ... hái**)
▶ 了 (**liǎo**) as potential compliment of a verb
▶ how to negate 学会 (**xué huì**, to have learnt)
▶ 得 (**de**) before a verbal phrase or clause

Text 1 (CD 2; 16)

信息革命 Xìnxī gémìng
Information revolution

二十年前，大部分中国老百姓家庭连电话都没有，更别说电脑了。那时候，人们根本没想到二十年后的今天，在城里几乎每家都有电话，手机也十分普及。很多人家不但有电脑，而且还安装了宽带。人们不仅可以随时上网查询需要的信息，发电子邮件，还可以在网上用信用卡购物，甚至在网上同国外的亲戚朋友免费聊天。即便家里不能上网，去网吧也很方便。这真是一场名副其实的信息革命。

Text 1 in pinyin ♦

Èrshí nián qián, dàbùfen Zhōngguó lǎobǎixìng jiātíng lián diànhuà dōu méi yǒu, gèng biéshuō diànnǎo le. Nà shíhòu, rénmen gēnběn méi xiǎngdào èrshí nián hòu de jīntiān, zài chénglǐ jīhū měijiā dōu yǒu diànhuà, shǒu jī yě shífēn pǔjí. Hěnduō rén jiā bú dàn yǒu diànnǎo, ér qiě hái ānzhuāng le kuāndài. Rénmen bú jǐn kěyǐ suí shí shàng wǎng cháxún xūyào de xìnxī, fā diànzǐ yóujiàn, hái kěyǐ zài wǎng shàng yòng xìnyòng kǎ gòu wù, shènzhì zài wǎng shàng tóng guówài de qīnqi péngyǒu miǎnfèi liáotiān. Jíbiàn jiā lǐ bù néng shàng wǎng, qù wǎngbā yě hěn fāngbiàn. Zhè zhēn shì yī chǎng míng-fù-qí-shí de xìnxī gémìng.

Vocabulary ◆

信息	xìnxī	information
革命	gémìng	revolution
老百姓	lǎo bǎixìng	ordinary people (*lit.* old hundred surnames)
家庭	jiātíng	family
更别说	gèng bié shuō	let alone; not to mention
电脑	diànnǎo	computer
人们	rénmen	people
想到	xiǎng dào	to think of; think about
手机	shǒu jī	mobile phone
普及	pǔjí	popular
不但...而且	bú dàn ... ér qiě	not only ... but also
不仅...还	bù jǐn ... hái	not only ... also
安装	ānzhuāng	to install; to connect
宽带	kuāndài	broadband
随时	suí shí	at any time
上网	shàng wǎng	to go on the net; to connect to the net
查询	cháxún	to check
发	fā	to send
电子邮件	diànzǐ yóujiàn	email
网上	wǎng shàng	on the net
信用卡	xìnyòng kǎ	credit card
购物	gòu wù	to purchase goods; to make a purchase
甚至	shènzhì	even
国外	guówài	abroad
免费	miǎn fèi	free of charge
网吧	wǎng bā	internet bar
场	chǎng	(measure word for campaigns, matches, etc.)
名副其实	míng-fù-qí-shí	the name matches the reality; worthy of the name

Additional useful words

软件	**ruǎnjiàn**	software
硬件	**yìngjiàn**	hardware
下载	**xiàzǎi**	to download
主页	**zhǔ yè**	home page

Language points ♦

10.1 Use of 连 . . . 都 (lián . . . dōu, 'even')

In Unit 1, there is a similar structure 连 . . . 也 (lián . . . yě). It means exactly the same as 连 . . . 都 (lián . . . dōu). Normally a noun or noun phrase follows 连 (lián) and what is after 都 (dōu) can be either positive or negative. For example:

我爷爷精通电脑，连电脑游戏都会玩！
Wǒ yéye jīng tōng diànnǎo, lián diànnǎo yóuxì dōu huì wán!
My grandfather is extremely familiar with computers. He can even play computer games!

他连这么简单的问题都不会回答。我真失望！
Tā lián zhème jiǎndān de wèntí dōu bú huì huídá. Wǒ zhēn shīwàng!
He can't even answer such a simple question. I'm so disappointed.

10.2 More on end-of-sentence 了 (le)

When a speaker expresses his/her feelings, positive or negative, about the impact of a new situation on him/her, 了 (le) is added to the end of the sentence to help convey such meanings. For example:

我连电脑都不会用，更别说发电子邮件了。
Wǒ lián diànnǎo dōu bú huì yòng, gèng bié shuō fā diànzǐ yóujiàn le.
I don't even know how to use a computer, not to mention sending an email!

我以为手机被偷了。急死我了！
Wǒ yǐwéi shǒu jī bèi tōu le. Jí sǐ wǒ le!
I thought my mobile had been stolen. I've been worried to death!

太谢谢你了！
Tài xièxie nǐ le!
Thank you so much!

10.3 Not only . . . but also

In Text 1 above, there are two constructions (both meaning 'not only . . . but also'): 不但 . . . 而且 **bú dàn . . . ér qiě** and 不仅 . . . 还 **bù jǐn . . . hái**. Let us see how they are used:

很多人家不但有电脑，而且还安装了宽带。
Hěnduō rén jiā bú dàn yǒu diànnǎo, ér qiě hái ānzhuāng le kuāndài.
Not only do many families have computers, but they also have broadband connections.

人们不仅可以随时上网查询需要的信息，发
Rénmen bù jǐn kěyǐ suí shí shàng wǎng cháxún xūyào de xìnxī, fā
电子邮件，还可以在网上用信用卡购物 . . .
diànzǐ yóujiàn, hái kěyǐ zài wǎng shàng yòng xìnyòng kǎ gòuwù . . .
Not only can one go on the net at any time to check for information needed or send emails, but one can also make purchases by credit card on the net . . .

We can also use 不仅 . . . 而且 **bù jǐn . . . ér qiě**. Also, 还 **hái** is often used after 而且 **ér qiě** for the purpose of emphasis. For example:

他不仅会说中文，而且还会说日文。
Tā bù jǐn huì shuō Zhōngwén, ér qiě hái huì shuō Rìwén.
Not only can he speak Chinese, but he also speaks Japanese.

Please note that unlike in English where a noun can follow 'but also', a verbal phrase must follow 而且 **ér qiě**.

10.4 Use of 在 . . . 上 (**zài . . . shàng**, 'at/on/in')

The pattern '在 **zài** + noun + 上 **shàng**' can be used to refer to a physical location such as 在桌子上 (**zài zhuōzi shàng**, on the table/desk), 在床上 (**zài chuáng shàng**, in bed/on the bed), 在火车上 (**zài huǒchē shàng**, on the train) or an abstract location such as 在网上 (**zài wǎng shàng**, on the net), 在会上 (**zài huì shàng**, at the meeting), 在电话上 (**zài diànhuà shàng**, on the phone).

Culture note

Internet users

The first email was sent from China as early as 1987, but the internet in China did not really begin to develop until the mid-1990s. According to the official statistics published by the China Internet Information Centre, the number of internet users in China was fewer than 40,000 in 1995, but that figure had leapt to more than 80 million by July 2004.

Exercises

Exercise 1

Fill in the gaps using an appropriate word from the vocabulary list for Text 1:

a 她连北京都没去过，_____英国了。
   Tā lián Běijīng dū méi qù guò, _____Yīngguó le.

b 在中国，有信用卡的人不少，可是，用
   Zài Zhōngguó, yǒu xìnyòng kǎ de rén bù shǎo, kěshì, yòng
   信用卡购物还不怎么_____。
   xìnyòng kǎ gòuwù hái bù zěnme_____.

c 这个商店24小时都开门，你可以_____去买东西。
   Zhègè shāngdiàn 24 xiǎoshí dōu kāimén, nǐ kěyǐ_____qù mǎi
   dōngxi.

d 如果你是这个大学的学生，就可以_____上网。
   Rúguǒ nǐ shì zhègè dàxué de xuéshēng, jiù kěyǐ_____shàng wǎng.
   其他的人得付钱。
   qítā de rén děi fùqián.

e 在英国，不管多大年龄都可以上大学，
   Zài Yīngguó, bùguǎn duō dà niánlíng dōu kěyǐ shàng dàxué,
   _____退休的人也可以上大学。
   _____tuìxiū de rén yě kěyǐ shàng dàxué.

Exercise 2

Match the following phrases with their English translations:

a	信息革命	xìnxī gémìng	i	email
b	老百姓	lǎo bǎixìng	ii	information revolution
c	电子邮件	diànzi yóujiàn	iii	on the net
d	名副其实	míng-fù-qí-shí	iv	ordinary people
e	在网上	zài wǎng shàng	v	the name matches the reality; worthy of the name

Exercise 3

Translate the following into Chinese:

a This question is too difficult. Even our teacher does not know the answer.
b Not only can he cook Western-style food, he can also cook Chinese food.
c I never thought you would come. I'm so happy!
d I seldom ring my mother, but I send her an email everyday.

Dialogue 1 (CD 2; 17)

去网吧 Qù wǎng bā
Going to the internet bar

Jane studies Chinese at Beijing Foreign Studies University. She is on her way to the internet bar and bumps into her classmate Yusuki from Japan.

YUSUKI 嗨，珍妮！去哪儿？
JANE 别提了。不知是我的电脑出毛病了，还是今天学院的互联网有问题。反正我怎么也上不了网。我去校外的网吧试试。
YUSUKI 别急！你的电脑没问题，是学院的服务器今天在维修。不瞒你说，我的电脑也上不了网。我也刚从网吧回来。
JANE 这下我放心了。校外的哪个网吧网速快？

An internet bar
Photographer: Zhan Lan

| YUSUKI | 都差不多，不过，咱们学院大门对面的那家叫 '蓝天' 的环境比较好。 |
| JANE | 谢谢！我这就去。 |

Dialogue 1 in pinyin ♦

YUSUKI	Hāi! Zhēnní, qù nǎr?
JANE	Bié tí le! Bù zhī shì wǒde diànnǎo chū máobìng le, háishì jīntiān xuéyuàn de hùliánwǎng yǒu wèntí, fǎnzhèng wǒ zěnme yě shàng bù liǎo wǎng. Wǒ qù xiào wài de wǎngbā shìshi.
YUSUKI	Bié jí! nǐde diànnǎo méi wèntí, shì xuéyuàn de fúwùqì jīntiān zài wéixiū. Bù mán nǐ shuō, wǒde diànnǎo yě shàng bù liǎo wǎng. Wǒ yě gāng cóng wǎngbā huílái.
JANE	Zhèxià wǒ fàngxīn le. Xiào wài de nǎ gè wǎngbā wǎng sù kuài?
YUSUKI	Dōu chàbuduō, búguò, zánmen xuéyuàn dàmén duìmiàn de nà jiā jiào 'Lán Tiān' de huánjìng bǐjiào hǎo.
JANE	Xièxie! Wǒ zhè jiù qù.

Vocabulary ♦

嗨	hāi	hey
不知	bù zhī	do not know; be unsure; not sure
是... 还是	shì ... háishì	is it ... or ... ?; whether ... or ...
出毛病	chū máobìng	to break down
学院	xuéyuàn	college
互联网	hùliánwǎng	internet
怎么也	zěnme yě	no matter how
校外	xiào wài	outside the college
别急	bié jí	don't worry
服务器	fúwùqì	server
维修	wéixiū	to be serviced; to service
不瞒你说	bù mán nǐ shuō	to tell you the truth (*lit.* not hiding from you)
放心	fàng xīn	to feel at ease; to have no worries
网速	wǎng sù	internet speed
差不多	chàbuduō	more or less the same
大门	dàmén	entrance
对面	duìmiàn	opposite
蓝天	Lán Tiān	Blue Sky
这就	zhè jiù	this minute

Language point ♦

10.5 了 (liǎo) used after 得 (de) or 不 (bù)

When 了 is used after a verb and with 得 (de) or 不 (bù), it is pronounced 'liǎo' and it indicates the possibility or impossibility of the verb (see Language point 6.3 in Unit 6). Please note that 不 carries a neutral tone here. For example, 上不了网 (**shàng bu liǎo wǎng**) in Dialogue 1 above means 'cannot connect to the net/go on the net'. Here are some other examples:

上得了网
shàng de liǎo wǎng
can connect to the net/go on the net

吃得了
chī de liǎo
can eat up

来得了
lái de liǎo
can come

去得了
qù de liǎo
can go

来不了
lái bu liǎo
cannot come

去不了
qù bu liǎo
cannot go

Exercises

Exercise 4

Listen to Dialogue 1 and answer the following questions in English:

a   Why can't Jane get connected to the internet?
b   Where is Jane going now?
c   Why is the name 'Lan Tian' mentioned?

Exercise 5

Can you find expressions in Dialogue 1 which mean the following:

a   Please don't worry yourself.
b   More or less the same
c   Tell me about it.
d   To tell you the truth

Exercise 6

Translate the following sentences into Chinese:

a   I tried various methods, but simply couldn't fall asleep.
b   My car has broken down. I have to go to work by bike.
c   Really, I can't finish off (i.e. drink up) this much beer.
d   I don't know whether he is going to cycle or drive.

Dialogue 2 (CD 2; 18)

电子邮件   Diànzǐ yóujiàn
Email

Below is a conversation between two mothers, both of whom are retired. Ren Yuan is older than Huang Wei.

HUANG WEI   听说你买了个笔记本电脑，好用吗？
REN YUAN   挺好用的。我正在学怎么用。昨天刚学会了怎么发电子邮件。
HUANG WEI   我早就听说过电子邮件，可就是不知道是什么。大姐，你真不简单。怎么发电子邮件？

Inside an internet bar
Photographer: Wu Han

REN YUAN   一时半会儿说不清。下次你到我家来，我给你演示一下。
            可神啦！昨晚，我收到了我儿子从法国发回来的邮件，激
            动得半天睡不着觉。
HUANG WEI   好，我过几天去你家见识见识。

Dialogue 2 in pinyin ♦

HUANG WEI   Tīng shuō nǐ mǎi le ge bǐjìběn diànnǎo, hǎo yòng ma?
REN YUAN   Tǐng hǎo yòng de. Wǒ zhèngzài xué zěnme yòng. Zuótiān
            gāng xué huì le zěnme fā diànzǐ yóujiàn.
HUANG WEI   Wǒ zǎo jiù tīng shuō guo diànzǐ yóujiàn, kě jiù shì bù
            zhīdào shì shénme. Dà jiě, nǐ zhēn bù jiǎndān. Zěnme fā
            diànzǐ yóujiàn?
REN YUAN   Yī-shí-bàn-huìr shuō bù qīng. Xià cì nǐ dào wǒ jiā lái, wǒ
            gěi nǐ yǎnshì yīxià. Kě shén la! Zuówǎn, wǒ shōudào le
            wǒ érzi cóng Fǎguó fā huílái de yóujiàn, jīdòng de bàn
            tiān shuì bù zháo jiào.
HUANG WEI   Hǎo, wǒ guò jǐ tiān qù nǐ jiā jiànshi jiànshi.

Vocabulary ♦

笔记本	bǐjìběn	notebook; laptop
好用	hǎo yòng	easy to use
学会	xué huì	have learnt to
早就	zǎo jiù	for a long time
一时半会儿	yī-shí-bàn-huìr	within a short time; a little while
演示	yǎnshì	to demonstrate
可神啦！	kě shén la	it's amazing
收到	shōudào	to have received
法国	Fǎguó	France
半天	bàn tiān	for a long time (*lit.* half a day)
睡不着觉	shuì bù zháo jiào	cannot go to sleep
过几天	guò jǐ tiān	in a couple of days
见识	jiànshi	to widen one's knowledge; to broaden one's experience

Language points

10.6 Use of 好 (hǎo) before the verb

When 好 (hǎo) is placed before some verbs, it means 'easy to' such as 好用 (hǎoyòng, easy to use) in Dialogue 2. Other examples are: 好找 (hǎo zhǎo, easy to find), 好骑 (hǎo qí, easy to ride), 好开 (hǎo kāi, easy to drive/easy to open). However, 好看 (hǎokàn), 好吃 (hǎochī) and 好喝 (hǎohē) are adjectives and they mean 'good-looking', 'tasty (to eat)' and 'nice (to drink)' respectively.

10.7 How to negate 学会 (xué huì, 'to have learnt')

Here, 会 (huì) is the result of 学 (xué, learn) indicating potential ability. To negate it, both 没 (méi) and 不 (bù) can be used in different places and with different implications. Let us compare the following sentences:

我已经学会了开车。
Wǒ yǐjīng xué huì le kāichē.
I have learnt how to drive (have succeeded; have managed).

我已经开始学开车了，但还没学会。
Wǒ yǐjīng kāishǐ xué kāichē le, dàn hái méi xué huì.

I have started learning to drive, but haven't succeeded yet (simply to report the fact, i.e. have started learning but can't drive yet).

A 我学开车已经学了半年了，怎么也学不会。
  Wǒ xué kāichē yǐjīng xué le bàn nián le, zěnme yě xué bú huì.
  I have been learning to drive for six months but am unable to learn no matter how (hard I try) (potentially unable to).

B 别急！你肯定学得会。
  Bié jí! Nǐ kěndìng xué de huì.
  Don't worry, you'll definitely learn to do so (potentially able to).

10.8 Affectionate terms

Terms such as 大姐 (**dà jiě**, big sister) can either be used to address or refer to one's eldest sister, or a female who is older than you and who you feel very close to. The same applies to the term 大哥 (**dà gē**, big brother).

10.9 得 (de) before a verbal phrase or clause

得 (**de**) can be used after a predicate (verbal or adjectival), but before a verbal phrase or a clause to indicate the consequential state of the predicate. Grammatically, it is known as a 'complement of sequential state'. Let us analyse one sentence in Dialogue 2 above:

	(我)	激动	得	半天睡不着觉。
	<u>Wǒ</u>	<u>jīdòng</u>	<u>*de*</u>	<u>**bàn tiān shuì bù zháo jiào.**</u>
	subject	predicate	[**de**]	clause
lit.	I	be excited	[de]	*a long time could not fall asleep*

I was so excited that I couldn't fall asleep for a long time.

Let us see two other examples:

	她	伤心	得	哭 了。
	<u>Tā</u>	<u>shāngxīn</u>	*de*	<u>kū</u> le
	subject	predicate	[de]	verbal phrase
lit.	She	be sad	[de]	*cry* [past particle]

She was so sad that she cried.

我高兴得连话都说不出来了。
Wǒ gāoxìng de lián huà dōu shuō bù chūlái le.
I was so happy that I couldn't even get my words out.

Culture note

Chinese newspaper

The *People's Daily* is the number one official newspaper in China, known as *Renmin Ribao* (人民日报). The paper is now online and there is both a Chinese version and an English version. For the Chinese version the website address is: http://www.people.com.cn/; and for the Engish version it is: http://english.peopledaily.com.cn/. The number one English newspaper in China is *China Daily*, aiming at English speakers living and working in China. Each province and city has its own local paper.

Exercises

Exercise 7

Match the questions with the answers:

Questions:

a 你最近在学什么？
Nǐ zuìjìn zài xué shénme?

b 你的笔记本好用吗？
Nǐde bǐjìběn hǎo yòng ma?

c 怎么发电子邮件？
Zěnme fā diànzǐ yóujiàn?

d 昨晚你为什么睡不着觉？
Zuówǎn nǐ wèishénme shuì bù zháo jiào?

Answers:

i 挺好用的。
Tǐng hǎo yòng de.

ii 学怎么用电脑。
Xué zěnme yòng diànnǎo.

iii 收到了儿子的电子邮件，太激动了！
Shōudào le érzi de diànzi yóujiàn, tài jīdòng le!

iv 一时半会儿说不清。你到我家来，我给你演示
一下，你就明白了。
Yī-shí-bàn-huìr shuō bù qīng. Nǐ dào wǒ jiā lái, wǒ gěi nǐ yǎnshì
yīxià, nǐ jiù míngbái le.

Exercise 8

Link the following two parts into one sentence using 得 (de) and then
translate the sentence into English:

Examples: 她最近很累；她常常不吃饭就睡觉了。
            Tā zuìjìn hěn lèi; tā chángcháng bù chīfàn jiù shuìjiào le.

她最近累得常常不吃饭就睡觉了。
Tā zuìjìn lèi de chángcháng bù chīfàn jiù shuìjiào le.
She is so tired recently that she often goes to bed without
eating anything.

a 见到了多年不见的好朋友，我太激动了：
Jiàndào le duō nián bù jiàn de hǎo péngyou, wǒ tài jīdòng le;
我说不出话来。
wǒ shuō bùchū huà lái.

b 拿到了这份工作，我很高兴：
Ná dào le zhè fèn gōngzuò, wǒ hěn gāoxìng;
我好几晚没睡好觉
wǒ hǎo jǐ wǎn méi shuì hǎo jiào.

c 她这几天很忙：
Tā zhè jǐ tiān hěn máng;
她没有时间吃饭。
tā méi yǒu shíjiān chīfàn.

Listening comprehension (CD 2; 20)

查电子邮件　Chá diànzǐ yóujiàn
Checking emails

The following conversation is between John and Mingfu who are
friends. They are on a postgraduate programme at a university in
China. Listen to the dialogue first. Try not to read the script. Afterwards, do the following multiple choice exercises:

1 明富今天为什么上不了网？
Míngfù jīntiān wèishénme shàng bù liǎo wǎng?

    a 因为他的电脑坏了。
      Yīnwèi tāde diànnǎo huài le.

    b 因为他学院的服务器坏了。
      Yīnwèi tā xuéyuàn de fúwùqì huài le.

    c 因为他学院的服务器在维修。
      Yīnwèi tā xuéyuàn de fúwùqì zài wéixiū.

2　明富今天为什么必须查电子邮件？
　　Míngfù jīntiān wèishénme bìxū chá diànzi yóujiàn?

　　a　因为他想知道是否拿到一份工作。
　　　　Yīnwèi tā xiǎng zhīdào shìfǒu nádào yī fèn gōngzuò.

　　b　因为他想知道是否有工作面试。
　　　　Yīnwèi tā xiǎng zhīdào shìfǒu yǒu gōngzuò miànshì.

　　c　因为有一家公司要他去修电脑。
　　　　Yīnwèi yǒu yī jiā gōngsī yào tā qù xiū diànnǎo.

Key words ♦

You may find the following words useful in understanding the dialogue:

修一修	xiūyixiū	to fix it
原来如此	yuán-lái-rú-cǐ	So that's how it is!
通知	tōngzhī	to notify
价钱	jiàqián	price
收到	shōudào	to receive; to get
消息	xiāoxi	news (as in 'good news')

Script in characters ♦

MINGFU　约翰，我的电脑坏了。你能不能帮我修一修？
JOHN　　我试试吧。我刚好现在有空。
MINGFU　太谢谢你了！

(*after checking the computer . . .*)

JOHN　　明富，我看你的电脑没有什么问题。为什么你说坏了？
MINGFU　因为刚才我想上网，可是上不了。
JOHN　　别急！那是因为学校的服务器今天在维修。
MINGFU　原来如此！那我就放心了。可是我今天必须查我的电子邮件，
　　　　　那天给我工作面试的公司说今天通知我们。
JOHN　　你可以去校外的网吧查。
MINGFU　我从来没有去过。哪家好？
JOHN　　都差不多，价钱也差不多。
MINGFU　好吧，我这就去。

John 希望你收到好消息！

Mingfu 谢谢！

Script in pinyin ♦

Mingfu Yuōhàn, wǒde diànnǎo huài le. Nǐ néng bù néng bāng wǒ xiūyixiū?

John Wǒ shìshi ba. Wǒ gānghǎo xiànzài yǒu kòng.

Mingfu Tài xièxie nǐ le!

(after checking the computer . . .)

John Míngfù, wǒ kàn nǐde diànnǎo méi yǒu shénme wèntí. Wèishénme nǐ shuō huài le?

Mingfu Yīnwèi gāngcái wǒ xiǎng shàng wǎng, kěshì shàng bù liǎo.

John Bié jí! Nà shì yīnwèi xuéxiào de fúwùqì jīntiān zài wéixiū.

Mingfu Yuán-lái-rú-cǐ! Nà wǒ jiù fàngxīn le. Kěshì wǒ jīntiān bìxū chá wǒde diànzǐ yóujiàn, nà tiān gěi wǒ gōngzuò miànshì de gōngsī shuō jīntiān tōngzhī wǒmen.

John Nǐ kěyǐ qù xiào wài de wǎngbā chá.

Mingfu Wǒ cónglái méi yǒu qù guò. Nǎ jiā hǎo?

John Dōu chàbuduō, jiàqián yě chàbuduō

Mingfu Hǎo ba, Wǒ zhè jiù qù.

John Xīwàng nǐ shōudào hǎo xiāoxi!

Mingfu Xièxie!

Authentic text (CD 2; 21)

上网聊天是坏事吗?
Is it a bad thing to chat online?

The following article is an extract from a column of a popular Chinese youth magazine, *China Youth*. A reader who signed her name as 'a troubled girl' wrote in to seek advice about the following question: 'Is it a bad thing to chat online?' An 'agony aunt' kind of person replied to her question. As this is the original text, some sentences are rather complex both in terms of grammar and structure. For the English translation of the text, please see Appendix B on page 262.

上网聊天是坏事吗？

上网聊天是不是件很坏的事？我这人自制力差，一上网就想聊天，你能帮助我吗？

心烦女孩

心烦女孩：

你好！上网聊天是网络时代的一种人际沟通和交往的方式，就像打电话一样，本身没好坏之分。但是，如果你上网聊天没有节制，以至于影响了学习，甚至影响身体健康或像报纸上报道的一样上了坏人的当，那网上聊天对你来说就是有害的事情了。我想，你写这封信就说明上网聊天已经给你的生活带来了麻烦，你希望能对此有一定的控制，这要求你对上网聊天给自己带来的害处有深深的反省和认识，并下定决心改变现状。你的决心越大，见效越快。

戒除或者控制上网聊天有两类办法：渐进法和厌恶法。如果实行渐进法，你应该逐步减少每天的上网聊天时间。例如，如果你现在每天都要花1小时聊天，那你可以规定下周每天聊天时间不能超过50分钟，下下周每天聊天不能超过40分钟等等。逐步减少聊天时间，达到你认为合适的量。...

选自《中国青年》2002/3, 64页 (*China Youth*, Beijing, 2002, Issue 3: 64)

Vocabulary ♦

坏事	huài shì	bad thing
自制力	zìzhì lì	power of self-discipline
差	chà	not good
一...就	yī...jiù...	as soon as ... then
心烦	xīn fán	troubled
网络时代	wǎngluò shídài	internet era
人际	rénjì	human
沟通	gōutōng	to communicate
交往	jiāowǎng	to interact
方式	fāng shì	way; method

本身	**běnshēn**	itself
之分	**zhī fēn**	difference
节制	**jiézhì**	control; be moderate in
以至于	**yǐzhìyú**	even; go as far as
报道	**bàodào**	to report
上 . . . 当	**shàng . . . dàng**	to be tricked by . . .
坏人	**huài rén**	bad people
有害	**yǒuhài**	harmful; detrimental
说明	**shuōmíng**	to demonstrate; illustrate
此	**cǐ**	this (formal)
一定	**yīdìng**	definitely
控制	**kòngzhì**	to control
要求	**yāoqiú**	to require
深深的	**shēnshēn de**	deep; in depth
反省	**fǎnxǐng**	to reflect
认识	**rènshí**	to come to understand
下定决心	**xiàdìng juéxīn**	to have firm determination
现状	**xiànzhuàng**	current situation
见效	**jiàn xiào**	to take effect; be effective
戒除	**jiè chú**	to give up
渐进法	**jiànjìn fǎ**	the gradual approach
厌恶法	**yànwù fǎ**	aversion approach
实行	**shíxíng**	to carry out
逐步	**zhúbù**	gradual
减少	**jiǎnshǎo**	to reduce
例如	**lì rú**	for example .
规定	**guīdìng**	to set; to formulate
超过	**chāoguò**	exceed
等等	**děngděng**	etc.
达到	**dádào**	to reach
合适	**héshì**	appropriate
量	**liàng**	amount; quantity

11　婚姻与子女
Hūnyīn yǔ zǐnǚ
Marriage and children

In this unit, you will learn about:

▶ Chinese marriages
▶ China's one-child policy
▶ wedding expressions
▶ complex patterns such as 宁愿...也 (**níng yuàn ... yě ...**)
▶ differences between 问 (**wèn**), 让 (**ràng**), 叫 (**jiào**), and 请 (**qǐng**)
▶ 把 (**bǎ**) sentence

Text 1　⑼🕪　(CD 2; 22)

昨天和今天的婚姻　Zuótiān hé jīntiān de hūnyīn
Yesterday and today's marriage

中国曾是世界上离婚率最低的国家之一。这也许和传统的婚姻观念有关系。从前，很多的婚姻是包办婚姻，也就是说：父母决定你和谁结婚。不管你爱不爱对方，一旦结了婚，就必须白头到老。许多夫妇说他们是先结婚再恋爱。还有许多夫妇在没有爱的婚姻中生活了一辈子。如今，年青人重视爱情，追求幸福，比他们的长辈浪漫得多。他们不愿意别人给自己介绍对象，因为那样太不浪漫。他们宁愿不结婚，也不愿和自己不爱的人结婚。即使结了婚，如果爱情消逝，他们也不愿意凑合着过。所以，离婚率开始逐渐上升。

Text 1 in pinyin ♦

Zhōngguó céng shì shìjiè shàng líhūn lǜ zuì dī de guójiā zhī yī. Zhè yěxǔ hé chuántǒng de hūnyīn guānniàn yǒu guānxì. Cóngqián,

hěnduō de hūnyīn shì bāobàn hūnyīn, yě jiù shì shuō: fùmǔ juédìng
nǐ hé shéi jiéhūn. Bùguǎn nǐ ài bú ài duìfāng, yīdàn jié le hūn, jiù
bìxū bái-tóu-dào-lǎo. Xǔduō fūfù shuō tāmen shì xiān jiéhūn zài
liàn'ài. Hái yǒu xǔduō fūfù zài méi yǒu ài de hūnyīn zhōng
shēnghuó le yī bèizi. Rújīn, niánqīng rén zhòngshì àiqíng, zhuīqiú
xìngfú, bǐ tāmen de zhǎng bèi làngmàn deduō. Tāmen bú yuànyì
biérén gěi zìjǐ jièshào duìxiàng, yīnwéi nà yàng tài bú làngmàn.
Tāmen níng yuàn bù jiéhūn, yě bú yuàn hé zìjǐ bú ài de rén jiéhūn.
Jíshǐ jié le hūn, rúguǒ àiqíng xiāoshì, tāmen yě bú yuànyì còuhe
zhe guò. Suǒyǐ, líhūn lù kāishǐ zhújiàn shàngshēng.

Vocabulary ♦

婚姻	hūnyīn	marriage
世界	shìjiè	world
离婚率	líhūn lǜ	divorce rate
低	dī	low
国家	guójiā	country
观念	guānniàn	view; concept
和...有关系	hé ... yǒu guānxì	to have something to do with; to be related to
包办婚姻	bāobàn hūnyīn	arranged marriage
不管	bùguǎn	regardless of
爱	ài	to love
对方	duì fāng	the other person
一旦...就...	yīdàn ... jiù ...	once ... then ...
白头到老	bái-tóu-dào-lǎo	grow old together (*lit.* white hair till old)
夫妇	fūfù	married couple
恋爱	liàn'ài	to fall in love; courtship
一辈子	yī bèizi	the whole life
如今	rújīn	nowadays
年青人	niánqīng rén	young people
重视	zhòngshì	to pay attention to; to attach importance to
爱情	àiqíng	love (noun)
追求	zhuīqiú	to seek after
幸福	xìngfú	happiness
长辈	zhǎng bèi	older generations
浪漫	làngmàn	romantic
对象	duìxiàng	boyfriend or girlfriend

宁愿 . . . 也	níngyuàn . . . yě	would rather . . . than
消逝	xiāoshì	to disappear; to disintegrate
凑合	còuhe	to make do
所以	suǒyǐ	therefore; so
逐渐	zhújiàn	gradually
上升	shàngshēng	to go up; to increase

Language points ♦

11.1 Use of 宁愿 . . . 也 (níng yuàn . . . yě . . .)

In English, when the sentence pattern 'would rather . . . than . . .' is used, whatever one does not want to do is put after 'than'. In Chinese, whatever one does not want to do is also put in the second half after 也 yě but the negation word must be used. For example:

我宁愿下岗，也不愿去做这样没有意思的工作。
Wǒ níng yuàn xià gǎng, yě bú yuàn qù zuò zhèyàng méi yǒu yìsī de gōngzuò.
I would rather be laid off work than do a boring job like this.

The first half of the sentence can also be negated. For example:

我宁愿不结婚，也不和他结婚。
Wǒ níng yuàn bù jiéhūn, yě bù hé tā jiéhūn.
I would rather not marry at all than marry him.

If a positive clause follows 也 (yě), the whole meaning changes:

我宁愿今晚不睡觉，也要学会用这个软件。
Wǒ níngyuàn jīnwǎn bù shuìjiào, yě yào xué huì yòng zhè ge ruǎnjiàn.
I must learn to use this software even if it means no sleep tonight.

11.2 你 (nǐ, 'you') as general reference

Like in English, 你 (nǐ, you) can be used as general reference (as opposed to specific reference). For example, the sentence in Text 1 above:

父母决定你和谁结婚。
Fùmǔ juédìng nǐ hé shéi jiéhūn.
Parents decide whom you will be married to.

11.3 Verb formation

There is one type of Chinese verb which is formed by a verb and its object. For example: 游泳 (**yóuyǒng**, *lit.* swim a swim → to swim), 做饭 (**zuòfàn**, *lit.* make food → to cook), 开车 (**kāichē**, *lit.* operate a car → to drive), 结婚 (**jié hūn**, *lit.* tie the marriage → to marry). When modifying this type of verb, the modifying word or phrase is inserted in between the verb and its object. For example:

游了一个小时的泳（or 游泳游了一个小时）
yóu le yī ge xiǎoshí de yǒng (or **yóuyǒng yóu le yī ge xiǎoshí**)
swam for an hour

开了一上午的车（or 开车开了一上午）
kāi le yī shàngwǔ de chē (or **kāichē kāi le yī shàngwǔ**)
drove for the whole morning

11.4 Use of 凑合 (còuhe, 'make do')

It is very much a colloquial expression. When 凑合 (**còuhe**) is used as a verb, it means 'to make do'; and it is often used together with 着 (**zhe**) plus a specific verb. Let us take the sentence from Text 1 as an example:

他们不愿意凑合着过。
Tāmen bú yuànyì còuhe zhe guò.
lit. they not willing make do [particle] live together
They don't want to just settle for it.

Please note that 日子 (**rìzi**, life, day) is omitted after 过 (**guò**, to lead, to spend) in the above sentence. 过日子 (**guò rìzi**) is a fixed expression which means 'to lead a family life' or 'to live a life' depending on the context.

凑合 (**còuhé**) is often used when one tries to be modest and polite:

我做饭做得不好，你凑合着吃吧。
Wǒ zuòfàn zuò de bù hǎo, nǐ còuhé zhe chī ba.
I'm not a good cook. You'll just have to put up with that and have some.

When it is used as adjective, it means 'passable' or 'just so so'. For example:

他做的饭还凑合。
Tā zuò de fàn hái còuhe.
His cooking is passable.

Exercises

Exercise 1

Fill in the gaps using an appropriate word from the vocabulary list for Text 1:

a 中国是_____上人口最多的国家。
Zhōngguó shì_____shàng rénkǒu zuì duō de guójiā.

b 我的自行车不太好,你_____着骑吧。骑坏了也没关系。
Wǒde zìxíngchē bú tài hǎo, nǐ_____zhe qí ba. Qíhuài le yě méiguānxi.

c _____你同意不同意,我都要和他结婚。
_____nǐ tóngyì bù tóngyì, wǒ dōu yào hé tā jiéhūn.

d 中国的父母特别_____孩子的教育。
Zhōngguó de fùmǔ tèbié_____háizi de jiàoyù.

e 离婚率低也许_____传统的婚姻观念_____。
Líhūn lǜ dī yěxǔ_____chuán tǒng de hūnyīn guānniàn_____.

Exercise 2

Translate the following phrases into Chinese using the phrase given in brackets (see Language point 11.3):

a have married twice (结婚, jiéhūn)
b cooked an Italian meal (做饭, zuòfàn)
c had a good sleep (睡觉, shuìjiào)
d met once (见面, jiànmiàn)

Text 2))))🎧 (CD 2; 24)

关于子女 Guānyú zǐnǚ
About children

传统的观念是：多子多福，意思是：孩子越多，福气越多。生孩
子首先是为了传宗接代，所以就出现了重男轻女的现象；其次是
为了老年时有人照顾自己，所以老人总是同子女住在一起。现在
的观念变了：由于独生子女政策，许多家庭只有一个孩子，所以
无论男孩还是女孩，他们都是父母的宝贝。再说，现在的生活条
件好了，老人不像从前那么依靠子女，所以越来越多的老人愿意
独立生活。

Text 2 in pinyin ♦

Chuántǒng de guānniàn shì: duō-zǐ-duō-fú, yìsī shì: háizi yuè duō,
fúqì yuè duō. Shēng háizi shǒuxiān shì wéi le chuán-zōng-jiē-dài,
suǒyǐ jiù chūxiàn le zhòng-nán-qīn-nǚ de xiànxiàng; qícì shì wéi le
lǎo nián shí yǒu rén zhàogù zìjǐ, suǒyǐ lǎo rén zǒngshì tóng zǐnǚ
zhù zài yīqǐ. Xiànzài de guānniàn biàn le: yóuyú dúshēng-zǐnǚ
zhèngcè, xǔduō jiātíng zhǐ yǒu yī gè háizi, suǒyǐ wúlùn nánhái
háishì nǚhái, tāmen dōu shì fùmǔ de bǎobèi. Zài shuō, xiànzài de
shēnghuó tiáojiàn hǎo le, lǎo rén bú xiàng cóngqián nàme yīkào
zǐnǚ, suǒyǐ yuè lái yuè duō de lǎo rén yuànyì dúlì shēnghuó.

Vocabulary ♦

关于	guānyú	about; on
子女	zǐnǚ	children (*lit.* son daughter)
多子多福	duō-zǐ-duō-fú	the more children, the more blessings
福气	fúqì	blessing
生	shēng	to give birth to
首先	shǒuxiān	firstly; first of all
传宗接代	chuán-zōng-jiē-dài	to continue the family line
重男轻女	zhòng-nán-qīn-nǚ	favour the boy and discriminate against the girl; regard men as superior to women
现象	xiànxiàng	phenomenon

其次	**qícì**	secondly
老年时	**lǎonián shí**	in one's old age; when getting old
照顾	**zhàogù**	to look after
变	**biàn**	to change
由于	**yóuyú**	due to; because of
独生子女	**dúshēng zǐnǚ**	only child
政策	**zhèngcè**	policy
无论...还是	**wúlùn...háishì**	regardless whether...or...
宝贝	**bǎobèi**	treasure; sweetheart
生活条件	**shēnghuó tiáojiàn**	living condition
不像	**bú xiàng**	be not like
依靠	**yīkào**	to rely on
独立	**dúlì**	independently; independent

Language points ♦

11.5 ...时 (shí) is the abbreviated form of ... 的时候 (de shíhòu, 'when ...')

Both of them are only used in statements (as opposed to questions) to introduce a time-related clause. For example:

上大学时/上大学的时候，我喜欢打网球。
Shàng dàxué shí/Shàng dàxué de shíhòu, wǒ xǐhuān dǎ wǎngqiú.
When (I was) at the university, I liked to play tennis.

11.6 Use of 无论...还是... (wúlùn...háishì...) and 不管...还是... (bùguǎn...háishì...)

In terms of the meaning, both of them mean 'regardless of whether...or...'. For example:

无论晴天还是雨天，我都要去看网球赛。
Wúlùn qíng tiān háishì yǔ tiān, wǒ dōu yào qù kàn wǎngqiú sài.
Regardless whether it is a sunny or rainy day, I'll go to watch the tennis match.

We can replace 无论 (**wúlùn**) with 不管 (**bùguǎn**):

不管晴天还是雨天，我都要去看网球赛。
Bùguǎn qíng tiān háishì yǔ tiān, wǒ dōu yào qù kàn wǎngqiú sài.

还是 (háishì) can be omitted from both patterns if we have 'verb + 不 bù' or '没 méi + the same verb'. For example, in Text 1, we have seen the phrase 不管你爱不爱对方 (bùguǎn nǐ ài bú ài duìfāng, regardless of whether or not you love the other person). Let us see two other examples:

无论你喜欢不喜欢，我都要说。
Wúlùn ni xihuǎn bù xǐhuǎn, wǒ dōu yào shuō.
Regardless of whether you like it or not, I'm going to say it.

不管你结婚没结婚，我都要说。
Bùguǎn nǐ jiéhūn méi jiéhūn, wǒ dōu yào shuō.
Regardless of whether or not you are married, I'm going to say it.

Culture notes

One-child policy

The one-child policy was adopted in 1979 by the Chinese government as an attempt to control the population. Prior to that, the government had already adopted a series of policies to encourage later marriage, later pregnancies and fewer births, all of which paved the way for the one-child policy. However, it was still strongly resisted by the people, especially people in the rural areas. People in cities gradually get used to it, or have to get used to it as there are heavy financial penalties for having a second child. Recently, the policy has been relaxed and some provinces allow people in the countryside to have a second child if the first one is a girl.

Kinship terms

Kinship terms are very complex in Chinese. Age and sex always play an important role. For example: 哥哥 (**gēge**, elder brother), 姐姐 (**jiějie**, elder sister), 弟弟 (**dìdi**, younger brother), 妹妹 (**mèimei**, younger sister). In families with only one child, the child has no brothers and sisters any more. But one still can hear a Chinese child talking about his/her elder sister or brother. They actually use those terms to refer to their cousins now. One of the reasons might be that they want to be close to their cousins as they are the only child. Also, it may have something to do with the fact that the Chinese terms for cousins are too complex. The English term 'cousin' can be translated into eight different terms in Chinese depending on the age, sex and the side of the family the cousin belongs to. Please see the table below:

táng gē 堂哥	elder, male, child of father's brothers	biǎo gē 表哥	elder, male, child of mother's brothers or sisters or of father's sisters
táng dì 堂弟	younger, male, child of father's brothers	biǎo dì 表弟	younger, male, child of mother's brothers or sisters or of father's sisters
táng jiě 堂姐	elder, female, child of father's brothers	biǎo jiě 表姐	elder, female, child of mother's brothers or sisters or of father's sisters
táng mèi 堂妹	younger, female, child of father's brothers	biǎo mèi 表妹	younger, female, child of mother's brothers or sisters or of father's sisters

Imagine in a few years' time when these only children become parents, as they don't have brothers and sisters themselves, their children will have no cousins! What will happen to the kinship terms?

Exercise 3

Translate into Chinese:

a   Regardless of whether you are an elderly person or child, everybody must take this medicine.
b   When driving, one should not use a mobile phone.

c   When I was in China, my Chinese was much better than it is now.
d   Because it is a present from you, I'll treasure it regardless of
    whether it is expensive or inexpensive.

Dialogue 1   (CD 2; 26)

婚礼 Hūnlǐ
Wedding

*Lao Wang and Lao Liu are neighbours. Lao Wang and his wife have
only one daughter who is getting married. Lao Liu is asking about
the wedding arrangements:*

LAO LIU   你们什么时候给宝贝女儿办喜事？
LAO WANG   本来准备大年初一办的，可不巧她从初一到初三在医院
           值班。只好把婚礼推迟到十五。
LAO LIU   这样也好，先过年再办喜事。

Double happiness
www.istock.com

Lao Wang	到时候你们两口子一定要来喝喜酒。
Lao Liu	谢谢，一定来。如果需要我们帮忙，尽管说。
Lao Wang	好的。

Dialogue 1 in pinyin ♦

Lao Liu   Nǐmen shénme shíhòu gěi bǎobèi nǚ'ér bàn xǐshì?

Lao Wang   Běnlái zhǔnbèi dà nián chū yī bàn de, kě bù qiǎo tā cóng chū yī dào chū sān zài yīyuàn zhí bān. Zhǐ hǎo bǎ hūnlǐ tuīchí dào shíwǔ.

Lao Liu   Zhèyàng yě hǎo, xiān guò nián zài bàn xǐ shì.

Lao Wang   Dào shíhòu nǐmen liǎng kǒuzi yīdìng yào lái hē xǐ jiǔ.

Lao Liu   Xièxie, yīdìng lái. Rúguǒ xūyào wǒmen bāngmáng, jǐnguǎn shuō.

Lao Wang   Hǎode.

Vocabulary ♦

办喜事	bàn xǐshì	to get married (*lit.* sort out a happy event)
本来	běnlái	originally
不巧	bùqiǎo	unfortunately
只好	zhǐ hǎo	to have to
推迟到	tuīchí dào	to postpone
到时候	dào shíhòu	when the time comes
两口子	liǎng kǒuzi	married couple
喝喜酒	hē xǐjiǔ	to attend the wedding reception (*lit.* drink happy wine)
尽管说	jǐnguǎn shuō	to feel free to let us know

Additional useful words

嫁	jià	to marry (a man)
娶	qǔ	to marry (a woman)
新郎	xīnláng	bridegroom (*lit.* new man)
新娘	xīnniáng	bride (*lit.* new woman)
丈人	zhàng rén	father-in-law (wife's father)
丈母娘	zhàngmǔ niáng	mother-in-law (wife's mother)

婆婆	pópo	mother-in-law (husband's mother)
公公	gōnggong	father-in-law (husband's father)
儿媳妇	ér xífù	daughter-in-law
女婿	nǚ xù	son-in-law

Language points ♦

11.7　办喜事 (bàn xǐ shì)

Literally, it means 'to sort out/organise a happy event'. Actually, it can mean 'to get married' or 'to organise one's wedding'. The emphasis is on the organisation of the event. For example:

我妹妹上个月办了喜事。
Wǒ mèimei shàng ge yuè bàn le xǐ shì.
My younger sister got married last month.

你什么时候给你的女儿办喜事？
Nǐ shénme shíhòu gěi nǐde nǚ'ér bàn xǐ shì?
lit. *you when for your daughter organise happy event*
When is your daughter's wedding?

Chinese weddings inevitably consist of an elaborate sit-down banquet. 喝喜酒 (hē xǐ jiǔ, *lit.* drink happy wine) is a colloquial way of saying 'to attend a wedding reception'. For example:

小王明天结婚。他请我去喝喜酒。
Xiǎo Wáng míngtiān jiéhūn, tā qǐng wǒ qù hē xǐ jiǔ.
Xiao Wang is getting married tomorrow. He's invited me to attend his wedding reception.

11.8　把 (bǎ) sentence

In Language point 4.9 of Unit 4, we introduced 把 (bǎ) when it is used in sentences where the object of the main verb is either something tangible or a person. 把 (bǎ) can also be used in sentences where the object of the main verb is a definite event or something intangible. For example:

我决定把婚礼推迟到八月份。
Wǒ juédìng bǎ hūnlǐ tuīchí dào bāyuè fèn.
I've decided to postpone the wedding until August.

他把去中国工作的打算告诉了我。

Tā bǎ qù Zhōngguó gōngzuò de dǎsuàn gàosù le wǒ.

He told me his plan of going to work in China.

11.9 Use of 到时候 (dào . . . shíhòu)

This phrase can be used at the beginning of a sentence to mean 'when the time comes . . .' if the context makes it clear what this time refers to. For example:

A: 你什么时候结婚？

Nǐ shénme shíhòu jiéhūn?

When are you getting married?

B: 还没决定。

Hái méi juédìng.

Not decided yet.

A: 到时候，你一定要通知我。

Dào shíhòu, nǐ yīdìng yào tōngzhī wǒ.

When the time comes, you must let me know.

If this time needs to be specified, simply insert a verbal phrase plus 的 (**de**) in between 到 (**dào**) and 时候 (**shíhòu**). For example:

到　　大学毕业　　　的　时候，我就二十二岁了。

Dào　dàxué bìyè　　de　shíhòu, wǒ jiù èrshí'èr suì le.

lit.　*arrive university graduate [de] time,　I will be 22*

When I graduate/By the time I graduate, I'll be 22.

Dialogue 2 (CD 2; 28)

布置新房　**Bùzhì xīn fáng**

Decorating the bridal chamber

Lao Wang and his wife, Ying, are decorating their daughter's new flat for her. This is the house the newly-weds will live in after they get married:

YING　　　　老头子，昨天我让你买一束玫瑰花，你买了吗？

LAO WANG　　糟糕！我把这件事忘了！我现在马上去买。

YING　　　　快去快回。

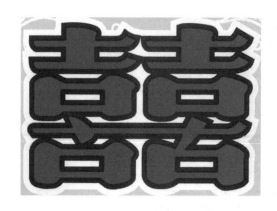

(*a little later . . .*)

Lao Wang	花来了！放在哪儿？
Ying	你顺手把那个水晶花瓶给我拿过来，我来放。
Lao Wang	行。对了，你妹妹送来的那个双喜剪纸大字到哪儿去了？
Ying	你转过身往上看。
Lao Wang	嘿，真棒！这个新房让你这么一布置，更漂亮了！
Ying	还是我的老头子会说话！

Dialogue 2 in pinyin ♦

Ying	Lǎo tóuzi, zuótiān wǒ ràng nǐ mǎi yī shù méiguīhuā, nǐ mǎi le ma?
Lao Wang	Zāogāo! Wǒ bǎ zhè jiàn shì wàng le! Wǒ xiànzài mǎshàng qù mǎi.
Ying	Kuài qù kuài huí.

(*a little later . . .*)

Lao Wang	Huā lái le! Fàng zài nǎr?
Ying	Nǐ shùnshǒu bǎ nà ge shuǐjīng huāpíng gěi wǒ ná guòlái, wǒ lái fàng.
Lao Wang	Xíng. Duì le, nǐ mèimei sònglai de nà ge shuāng xǐ jiǎnzhǐ dào nǎr qù le?
Ying	Nǐ zhuǎn guò shēn wǎng shàng kàn.
Lao Wang	Hēi, zhēn bàng! Zhè ge xīn fáng ràng nǐ zhème yī bùzhì, gèng piàoliàng le!
Ying	Háishì wǒde lǎo tóuzi huì shuōhuà!

Vocabulary ♦

布置	bùzhì	to decorate
新房	xīn fáng	bridal chamber (*lit.* new room)
老头子	lǎo tóuzi	old man (affectionate term used by one's wife)
束	shù	bunch
玫瑰花	méiguīhuā	rose
放	fàng	to put
顺手	shùnshǒu	on passing
水晶	shuǐjīng	crystal
花瓶	huāpíng	vase
拿过来	ná guòlái	to bring over
送	sòng	to give something as present
双喜	shuāng xǐ	double happiness
剪纸	jiǎnzhǐ	paper-cut
到哪儿去了	dào nǎr qù le	where has it gone to
转过身	zhuǎn guò shēn	to turn (the body) over
往上看	wǎng shàng kàn	to look upward
嘿	hēi	gosh!
真棒	zhēn bàng	wonderful
会说话	huì shuōhuà	to know how to 'sweet talk' people

Language points ♦

11.10 Differences between 问 (wèn), 让 (ràng), 叫 (jiào), and 请 (qǐng)

In English, the verb 'ask' can be used in 'to ask (someone) a question' and 'to ask someone to do something', but in Chinese, different verbs are used. 问 (wèn) is only used to ask a question or ask about something. For example:

我能不能问你一个问题？
Wǒ néng bù néng wèn nǐ yī gè wèntí?
Can I ask you a question?

If you ask someone to do something, you must use 让/叫 (ràng/jiào). For example:

我没有让/叫你做这件事。
Wǒ méi yǒu ràng/jiào nǐ zuò zhè jiàn shì.
I didn't ask you to do this.

请 (**qǐng**) is normally used either when the person you ask to do the task is your senior, or you want to make it obvious that the other person is doing you a big favour. It is a politeness expression. For example:

我请我的舅舅教我开车。
Wǒ qǐng wǒde jiùjiu jiāo wǒ kāichē.
I asked my uncle to teach me to drive.

11.11 More on the 把 (bǎ) sentence

One of the requirements of the 把 (**bǎ**) sentence is that the main verb must be followed by another word indicating the result of the main verb (see 4.9 of Unit 4). The particle 了 (**le**) can be placed after certain verbs to indicate the change of state (i.e. the result of the main verb). Take the verbs 卖 (**mài**, to sell), 忘 (**wàng**, to forget) for example. 卖了 (**mài le**) becomes 'have sold' and 忘了 (**wàng le**) becomes 'have forgotten'. For example:

我把咱们家的那辆红车卖了。
Wǒ bǎ zánmen jiā de nà liàng hóng chē mài le.
I've sold that red car of ours.

我把这件事忘了。
Wǒ bǎ zhè jiàn shì wàng le.
I've forgotten about this matter.

We can re-write the above two sentences and leave 把 (**bǎ**) out of them without changing the meaning:

我卖了咱们家的那辆红车。
Wǒ mài le zánmen jiā de nà liàng hóng chē.

我忘了这件事。
Wǒ wàng le zhè jiàn shì.

However, 把 (**bǎ**) must be used with some verbs such as 放 (**fàng**, put), 摆 (**bǎi**, put, arrange), 挂 (**guà**, hang) when indicating the location of an object. For example:

我把花瓶放在窗台上了。
Wǒ bǎ huāpíng fàng zài chuāngtái shàng le.
I've put the vase on the window-sill.

老师把世界地图挂在了教室的墙上。
Lǎoshī bǎ shìjiè dìtú guà zài le jiàoshì de qiáng shàng.
The teacher has hung the map of the world on the wall of the classroom.

11.12 让 (ràng) as informal passive marker

In Language point 9.4 of Unit 9, 让 (ràng) was introduced as an informal passive marker. There is one sentence in Dialogue 2 above where 让 (ràng) functions as an informal passive marker:

这个新房让你这么一布置，更漂亮了！
Zhè gè xīn fáng ràng nǐ zhème yī bùzhì, gèng piàoliàng le!
This bridal chamber, having been arranged in this way by you, is even more beautiful!

11.13 来 (lái) in '我来放' (Wǒ lái fàng)

来 (lái) here is not a verb. It functions as a tone softener. By putting it in front of a verb it makes the sentence sound less like an order and as a result more friendly. For example:

我来开，你休息一下。
Wǒ lái kāi, nǐ xiūxi yīxià.
Let me drive. You have a rest.

What follows 来 (lái) tends to be a single-syllable verb. If it is a double-syllable verb, or if the verb takes an object, the object is usually omitted as the context makes it redundant. For example:

A wife is doing the cooking in the kitchen, the husband comes in and says:

我来做(饭)，你去看电视吧。
Wǒ lái zuò (fàn), nǐ qù kàn diànshì ba.
Let me do the cooking. You go and watch some TV.

Culture notes

Double-happiness character

By putting two characters of 'happiness' (喜, **xǐ**) together, a symbol of 'double-happiness' is formed: 喜喜. This symbol is only used for weddings.

Wedding colours

The wedding colour is red. The traditional Chinese wedding dress for a bride is bright red, and the bridegroom wears a red flower. Nowadays, there are more and more Western-style white satin wedding dresses.

Married women

Nowadays, Chinese women keep their own surnames after the marriage. So it is really not appropriate to put the title 'Mrs' in front of a married Chinese woman's surname. In the old days, women used to change to their husbands' surnames after getting married. This practice gradually died out after 1949 when the Communist Party came to power.

Exercises

Exercise 4

Listen to or read Dialogue 1 and answer the following questions in Chinese:

a 谁要结婚？
Shéi yào jiéhūn?

b 她本来准备什么时候结婚？
Tā běnlái zhǔnbèi shénme shíhòu jiéhūn?

c 为什么推迟到十五？
Wéishénme tuīchí dào shíwǔ?

Exercise 5

Find expressions in Dialogues 1 and 2 which mean the following:

a Wonderful!
b You turn around and look up.
c If you need our help, please feel free to let us know.
d Celebrate the Chinese New Year first and then have the wedding.
e You two must come to the wedding reception.

Exercise 6

Fill in the gaps using 问 (wèn), 让 (ràng), 叫 (jiào), or 请 (qǐng):

a 你能不能_____你妈妈接电话。
   Nǐ néng bù néng_____nǐ māma jiē diànhuà.

b 昨天我_____王平来帮我修了一下电脑。
   Zuótiān wǒ_____Wáng Píng lái bāng wǒ xiū le yīxià diànnǎo.

c 我_____他叫什么名字，他就是不告诉我。
   Wǒ_____tā jiào shénme míngzì, tā jiù shì bú gàosù wǒ.

d 妈妈_____我把电视关掉。
   Māma_____wǒ bǎ diànshì guān diào.

e 我_____张老师给我修改一下我的简历。
   Wǒ_____Zhāng lǎoshī gěi wǒ xiūgǎi yīxià wǒde jiǎnlì.

Exercise 7

Use 把 (bǎ) to re-write the following sentences:

a 我忘了他的名字。
   Wǒ wàng le tāde míngzì.

b 她布置好了女儿的房间。
   Tā bùzhì hǎo le nǚ'ér de fángjiān.

c 请你拿过来那个双喜剪纸。
   Qǐng nǐ ná guò lái nà ge shuāng xǐ jiǎnzhǐ.

d 小王推迟了他的婚礼，推迟到九月份。
Xiǎo Wáng tuīchí le tāde hūnlǐ, tuīchí dào jiǔyuè fèn.

e 奶奶让我打开礼物。
Nǎinai ràng wǒ dǎkāi lǐwù.

Reading comprehension (CD 2; 29)

我父母的婚姻 Wǒ fùmǔ de hūnyīn
My parents' marriage

Read the following passage and then decide if each of the following statements is true or false:

a 村里的人不喜欢我的爷爷和奶奶。
Cūnlǐ de rén bù xǐhuān wǒde yéye hé nǎinai.

b 父亲和母亲结婚前见过面。
Fùqīn hé mǔqīn jiéhūn qián jiàn guò miàn.

c 父亲结婚的那天很难过，因为他知道母亲不爱他。
Fùqīn jiéhūn de nà tiān hěn nánguò, yīnwéi tā zhīdào mǔqīn bú ài tā.

d 结婚后，父亲和母亲才恋爱，慢慢地有了爱情。
Jiéhūn hòu, fùqīn hé mǔqīn cái liàn'ài, mànmàn de yǒu le àiqíng.

e 父亲和母亲凑合着过了一辈子，生活得不幸福。
Fùqīn hé mǔqīn còuhe zhe guò le yī bèizi, shēnghuó de bú xìngfú.

Key words ♦

You may find the following words helpful in understanding the passage:

开明	kāimíng	open; liberal
难过	nánguò	sad
姑娘	gūniang	girl
紧张	jǐnzhāng	tense
幸运的是	xìngyùn de shì	fortunately
相处	xiāng chǔ	to get along; to get on
感情	gǎnqíng	affection; emotion; feeling

Passage in characters ♦

我的爷爷奶奶被大家认为是村里最开明的人，可是，他们就是不同意父亲自己找的对象，一定要让他娶我的母亲。父亲和母亲结婚前只见过一面，根本不了解对方，更别说爱情了。父亲说，结婚的那天，他很难过，因为他不能和他爱的姑娘结婚。而母亲呢，她的心里也很紧张，因为她不知道父亲会不会喜欢她。幸运的是，他们结婚后相处得很好，慢慢地有了感情。而有很多和我父母情况一样的人结婚后却相处得不好，在没有爱的婚姻中凑合了一辈子，一辈子不幸福。

Passage in pinyin ♦

Wǒde yéye nǎinai bèi dàjiā rènwéi shì cūnlǐ zuì kāimíng de rén, kěshì tāmen jiù shì bù tóngyì fùqīn zìjǐ zhǎo de duìxiàng, yídìng yào ràng tā qǔ wǒde mǔqīn. Fùqīn hé mǔqīn jiéhūn qián zhǐ jiàn guò yī miàn, gēnběn bù liǎojiě duìfāng, gèng bié shuō àiqíng le. Fùqīn shuō, jiéhūn de nà tiān, tā hěn nánguò, yīnwéi tā bù néng hé tā ài de gūniang jiéhūn. Ér mǔqīn ne, tāde xīn lǐ yě hěn jǐnzhāng, yīnwéi tā bù zhīdào fùqīn huì bú huì xǐhuān tā. Xìngyùn de shì, tāmen jiéhūn hòu xiāngchǔ de hěn hǎo, mànmàn de yǒu le gǎnqíng. Ér yǒu hěnduō hé wǒ fùmǔ qíngkuàng yīyàng de rén jiéhūn hòu què xiāngchǔ de bù hǎo, zài méi yǒu ài de hūnyīn zhōng còuhe le yī bèizi, yī bèizi bú xìngfú.

Authentic text (CD 2; 30)

日子 '各过各' **Rìzi 'gè guò gè'**
Leading one's own life

This text is an extract from an article entitled 'Leading one's own life' published in a Chinese popular youth magazine, *Young Generation*. The article is about the changes in traditional ways of life. As this is the original text, some sentences are rather complex both in terms of grammar and structure. For the English translation of the text, please see Appendix B on page 262.

日子 '各过各'

传统观念认为，老人应该与儿女晚辈生活在一起，共享天伦之乐。然而，如今的老人则不然，他们一个个要与儿女分开过，想享享晚年清闲。'宁愿出钱不愿心烦'已经在一些老年人中形成共识。据近期对一些大、中城市的调查结果表明，有70%以上的老人与儿女'各过各'。

现今城市的老人们，经济上大都独立支撑，也有自己安身的住房。退休后，他们要参加各种社会活动，有的还根据自己的特长，受聘于各企业、社团去发挥余热。如果他们与晚辈住在一起，势必要受一辈子买菜、煮饭、带孩子等家务杂活的牵累。

一位与儿子分开过的老人直率地说，'我们老了，应把保健身体放在第一位。如果与儿孙住在一起，表面上看热闹得很，其实这对我们和儿孙都不利。我们奋斗大半辈子了，为子女付出了很多，该休息休息了。同时，我们与年轻人在思想认识、生活习惯等诸多方面都存有分歧，如果长期生活在一起，容易产生矛盾。因此，还是分开过好。'

选自《青年一代》，2004/7, 4页 (*Young Generation*, Beijing, 2004, Issue 7: 4)

Vocabulary ♦

日子	rìzi	life
各过各	gè guò gè	to live separately
儿女	érnǚ	children (*lit.* son daughter)
晚辈	wǎn bèi	a generation below (i.e. children)
共享	gòng xiǎng	to enjoy . . . together
天伦之乐	tiānlún zhī lè	the pleasure of family life
然而	rán'ér	however
则	zé	on the other hand
不然	bùrán	be not so; be not like this
分开过	fēn kāi guò	to lead separate lives
享享清闲	xiǎngxiǎng qīngxián	to enjoy the happiness of leisurely and relaxed life
晚年	wǎn nián	old age
宁愿	níngyuàn	would rather
出钱	chū qián	to contribute financially
不愿	búyuàn	not willing to
形成	xíngchéng	to form; to take shape

共识	gòngshí	common belief; common understanding
据	jù	according to
近期	jìnqī	recently
调查	diàochá	investigation; to investigate
结果	jiéguǒ	result
表明	biǎomíng	to show; to demonstrate
经济上	jīngjì shàng	financially
大都	dàdōu	majority
支撑	zhīchēng	to support
安身	ānshēn	sheltering; take shelter
住房	zhùfáng	house; accommodation
参加	cānjiā	to take part in
社会活动	shèhuì huódòng	social activity
根据	gēnjù	according to
特长	tècháng	strength; strong point
受聘于	shòupìn yǔ	to be employed with
社团	shètuán	community
势必	shìbì	must; be bound to
受...牵累	shòu . . . qiānlèi	be tied down with . . .
煮饭	zhǔfàn	cooking
带孩子	dài háizi	to look after children
家务杂活	jiāwù záhuó	household chore
直率	zhíshuài	frankly; directly
保健	bǎo jiàn	to protect and care for one's health
表面上	biǎomiàn shàng	on surface
其实	qíshí	in fact
不利	búlì	harmful; detrimental
奋斗	fèn dòu	to work hard
付出	fùchū	to put in a lot of hard work; to pay
同时	tóng shí	at the same time; besides
思想认识	sīxiǎng rènshi	thinking and understanding
诸	zhū	various; all
存有	cúnyǒu	to have; to exist
分歧	fēnqí	difference
长期	cháng qī	long term
产生	chǎnshēng	to produce; to emerge
矛盾	máodùn	conflict
因此	yīncǐ	therefore

12 改革和变化
Gǎigé hé biànhuà
Reform and change

In this unit, you will learn about:

- Chinese economic reform
- township and village enterprises
- four-character expressions
- expressing changes and one's wishes
- using 虽然 . . . 但是 (**suīrán . . . dànshì**, although . . . but)
- distinguishing between 新闻 (**xīnwén**, news) and 消息 (**xiāoxi**, news)

Text 1 ⸙🎧 (CD 2; 31)

成功的乡镇企业 chénggōng de xiāngzhèn qǐyè
Successful township and village enterprise

中国的经济改革带来的成果之一是乡镇企业。昨天，我参观了一家乡镇企业，给我留下了很深的印象。这是一家生产皮鞋的厂家。十年前才成立，当时只有十个人，现在已经有两百个雇员了。他们生产的鞋子款式新颖，质量好，很受消费者的欢迎。百分之五十的产品出口到世界各地。这个厂成功的经验是：保证质量，注重款式，重视消费者提的意见，并且定期做市场调研。他们成功的另一条经验是：无论是经理还是普通工人，大家平等相待，互相尊重。

Text 1 in pinyin ◆

Zhōngguó de jīngjì gǎigé dàilái de chéngguǒ zhī yī shì xiāng zhèn qǐyè. Zuótiān, wǒ cānguān le yī jiā xiāng zhèn qǐyè, gěi wǒ liúxià le hěn shēn de yìnxiàng. Zhè shì yī jiā shēngchǎn pí xié de chǎngjiā. Shí nián qián cái chénglì, dāng shí zhǐ yǒu shí ge rén, xiànzài yǐjīng yǒu liǎng bǎi ge gùyuán le. Tāmen shēngchǎn de xiézi kuǎnshì xīnyǐng, zhíliàng hǎo, hěn shòu xiāofèizhě de huānyíng. Bǎi fēn zhī wǔshí de chǎnpǐn chūkǒu dào shìjiè gè dì. Zhè ge chǎng chénggōng de jīngyàn shì: bǎozhèng zhíliàng, zhùzhòng kuǎnshì, zhòngshì xiāofèizhě tí de yìjiàn, bìngqiě dìngqī zuò shìcháng diàoyán. Tāmen chénggōng de lìng yī tiáo jīngyàn shì: wúlùn shì jīnglǐ háishì pǔtōng gōngrén, dàjiā píngděng xiāngdài, hù xiāng zūnzhòng.

Vocabulary ◆

经济改革	jīngjì gǎigé	economic reform
成果	chéngguǒ	achievement
乡镇	xiāng zhèn	village and town
企业	qǐ yè	enterprise; firm; company
留下	liúxià	to leave (behind)
深	shēn	deep
生产	shēngchǎn	to produce; production
皮鞋	pí xié	leather shoes
厂家	chǎngjiā	factory; firm
成立	chénglì	to set up; to establish
款式新颖	kuǎnshì xīnyǐng	original in style
受欢迎	shòu huānyíng	be popular (*lit.* receive welcome)
消费者	xiāofèizhě	consumer
百分之	bǎifēnzhī	per cent
产品	chǎnpǐn	product
出口	chūkǒu	to export; export
各地	gè dì	various places
成功	chénggōng	successful; success
经验	jīngyàn	experience; good practice; tip
保证	bǎozhèng	to guarantee
注重	zhùzhòng	to pay attention to
定期	dìngqī	regularly
普通	pǔtōng	ordinary
大家	dàjiā	everybody
平等相待	píngděng xiāngdài	to treat everyone equally
尊重	zūnzhòng	to respect

Language points ◆

12.1 Four-character expressions

One of the features of the Chinese language is the use of four-character expressions, especially in written Chinese. Many proverbs and famous sayings consist of four characters. Besides, phonologically, four-character expressions sound more rhythmical and hence are easy to remember. Some of the four-character expressions are fixed such as 名副其实 (**míng-fù-qí-shí**, worthy of the name), 款式新颖 (**kuǎnshì xīnyǐng**, original in style) and others are more of a loose nature: 平等相待 (**píngděng xiāngdài**, to treat each other equally), 互相尊重 (**hùxiāng zūnzhòng**, to respect each other).

12.2 给 . . . 留下印象 (gěi . . . liúxià yìnxiàng, 'leave an impression on . . .')

Please note that the sentence order here is different from the equivalent English phrase. In Chinese, one must say 'on (somebody) leave impression'. For example:

> 这部电影给我奶奶留下了很深的印象。
> **Zhè bù diànyǐng gěi wǒ nǎinai liúxià le hěn shēn de yìnxiàng.**

lit. *this film on my grandmother left very deep impression*
This film left a very deep impression on my grandmother.

Exercises

Exercise 1

Fill in the gaps using an appropriate word from the vocabulary list for Text 1:

a 这所英文学校是五年前才_____的。
　Zhè suǒ Yīngwén xuéxiào shì wǔ nián qián cái_____de.

b 那个小镇的出租车司机给我_____了很好的印象。
　Nà ge xiǎo zhèn de chūzūchē sījī gěi wǒ_____le hěn hǎo de yìnxiàng.

c 他是一个_____的工人，不过，他们工厂的
　Tā shì yī gè_____de gōngrén, búguò, tāmen gōngchǎng de

领导却很重视他提的意见。
lǐngdǎo què hěn zhòngshì tā tí de yìjiàn.

d 这个厂家生产的皮鞋特别_____。
Zhè gè chǎngjiā shēngchǎn de pí xié tèbié_____.

e 他学习中文的_____是：多和中国人交流。
Tā xuéxí Zhōngwén de_____shì: duō hé Zhōngguórén jiāoliú.

Exercise 2

List as many four-character expressions used in this book as you can, and make a sentence using each of them.

Text 2 〃⑨ (CD 2; 33)

一封来自中国农村的信
Yī fēng láizì Zhōngguó nóngcūn de xìn
A letter from China's countryside

David is doing a postgraduate degree in Chinese Studies. During one of his fieldwork trips, David visited some villages in the countryside and made friends with Xiaofang's family. Below is a letter from Xiaofang to David:

大卫：

你好！近来学习忙吗？

好久没有联系。我们家里变化很大，我们村的变化更大。先说说我们家，我上个月结了婚，丈夫在一家乡镇企业当会计。我从农业银行贷款办了个流动图书馆，每天在附近几个村来回跑，很受大家的欢迎。在你的影响下，我开始学习英文了！下次，我会用英文给你写信的。我哥哥和我爸妈还是忙着种菜，今年又增加了两个新品种 – 西蓝花和樱桃西红柿。村子里好多人家都盖起了二层小楼房，装上了电话，还有几家买了电脑呢！

你最近有什么新闻？有空请来信。大家都很想你。

祝好！

小芳

2005, 7, 20

A vegetable farm
Photographer: Kan Yigang

Text 2 in pinyin ♦

Dàwèi:

Nǐ hǎo! Jìnlái xuéxí máng ma?

Hǎo jiǔ méi yǒu liánxì. Wǒmen jiā lǐ biànhuà hěn dà, wǒmen cūn de biànhuà gèng dà. Xiān shuōshuo wǒmen jiā, wǒ shàng ge yuè jié le hūn, zhàngfū zài yī jiā xiāng zhèn qǐyè dāng kuàijì. Wǒ cóng nóngyè yínháng dài kuǎn bàn le gè liúdòng túshūguǎn. Měitiān zài fùjìn jǐ ge cūn láihuí pǎo, hěn shòu dàjiā de huānyíng. Zài nǐde yǐngxiǎng xià, wǒ kāishǐ xuéxí Yīngwén le! Xià cì, wǒ huì yòng Yīngwén gěi nǐ xiěxìn de. Wǒ gēge hé wǒ bà mā háishì máng zhe zhòng cài, jīn nián yòu zēngjiā le liǎng ge xīn pǐnzhǒng – xīlánhuā hé yīngtáo xīhóngshì. Cūnzi lǐ hǎo duō rén jiā dōu gàiqǐ le èr céng xiǎo lóufáng, zhuāng shàng le diànhuà, hái yǒu jǐ jiā mǎi le diànnǎo ne!

Nǐ zuìjìn yǒu shénme xīnwén? Yǒu kòng qǐng lái xìn. Dàjiā dōu hěn xiǎng nǐ.

Zhù hǎo!

Xiǎofāng

2005, 7, 20

Vocabulary ◆

大卫	**Dàwèi**	David
联系	**liánxì**	be in touch; to contact
家里	**jiā lǐ**	in the family; at home
会计	**kuàijì**	accountant
农业	**nóngyè**	agriculture
贷款	**dài kuǎn**	to get a loan
办	**bàn**	to run; to manage
流动	**liúdòng**	mobile
附近	**fùjìn**	nearby
来回跑	**láihuí pǎo**	to go around
在 . . . 下	**zài . . . xià**	under . . .
影响	**yǐngxiǎng**	influence
种菜	**zhòng cài**	to grow vegetables
新品种	**xīn pǐnzhǒng**	new produce
西蓝花	**xīlánhuā**	broccoli
樱桃	**yīngtáo**	cherry
西红柿	**xīhóngshì**	tomato
盖起	**gàiqǐ**	to build; to erect
二层	**èr céng**	two-storey
楼房	**lóufáng**	building
新闻	**xīnwén**	news

Language points ◆

12.3   Omission of '一 (yī, "one")' before the measure word

When a measure word is not preceded by a number, the omitted number must be '一 (yī)'. If it is any other number, it cannot be omitted. For example:

今天早上，我去北京饭店看了个朋友。
Jīntiān zǎoshàng, wǒ qù Běijīng fàndiàn kàn le ge péngyou.
This morning, I went to the Beijing Hotel to visit a friend.

我打了三个电话，才花了一块钱。
Wǒ dǎ le sān ge diànhuà, cái huā le yī kuài qián.
I made three telephone calls, and it only cost me one kuai.

However, when '一 (yī)' appears at the beginning of a sentence or functions as part of a subject, it cannot be omitted. For example:

刚才，一个年轻姑娘来找你。
Gāngcái, yī gè niánqīng gūniang lái zhǎo nǐ.
Just now, a young lady came to look for you.

12.4 印象 (yìnxiàng, 'impression') and 影响 (yǐngxiǎng, 'influence/to influence')

Please note that the pronunciation of these two terms is very similar. But they carry different tones and very different meanings.

Culture note

Township and village enterprises

Before 1978, the Chinese economy was a planned economy, and there was virtually no private ownership. In 1978, Deng Xiaoping came to power and introduced the market economy. He was the mastermind behind China's economic reform. Under the economic reform plan, farmers were given enormous freedom and hence became energetic and productive. They were allowed to put their money together and set up township and village enterprises. As these enterprises were not under the control of any government departments, their decision-making process was not lengthy. As a result, they quickly flourished and became the most dynamic element for growth in the 1980s and early 1990s. Nowadays, there are over 20 million township and village enterprises that are involved in a variety of economic activities such as processing agricultural products, industry, transport, building and commerce.

Exercises

Exercise 3

Translate the following into Chinese:

a Under the influence of my parents, I became more and more interested in Chinese literature.
b Can you write a letter for me in Chinese?
c Our village has changed greatly and our village primary school has changed even more.

Exercise 4

Read Text 2 again. Suppose you are David in Text 2. Write a reply to Xiaofang in Chinese.

Dialogue 1   (CD 2; 34)

小镇的变化 Xiǎo zhèn de biànhuà
Change in a small town

The following dialogue is between a mother and her son who has just returned from Germany where he had been doing a postgraduate degree for the last three years:

ZHIYUAN 妈妈，咱们镇的变化太大了。我都认不出来了。
MAMA 别说你认不出来，就连你哥哥上次回家还差点儿迷了路。你快三年没回来了吧？
ZHIYUAN 是啊！哥哥多久回来一次？
MAMA 他几乎每半年回来一次。
ZHIYUAN 我做梦也没想到人们的生活水平提高得这么快。
MAMA 谁能想到！要是你父亲还活着该多好！
ZHIYUAN 是啊！不过，他会为我们高兴的。对了，我和父亲最喜欢的那条小河还在吗？

China's Venice: Zhou Zhuang

MAMA	在，前几年河水被污染了，最近才清理干净。
ZHIYUAN	太好了！明天我就去游个泳。
MAMA	虽然清理干净了，但是河水不像从前那么清了。你自己去看看吧。

Dialogue 1 in pinyin ♦

ZHIYUAN	Māma, zánmen zhèn de biànhuà tài dà le, wǒ dōu rèn bu chūlái le.
MAMA	Bié shuō nǐ rèn bu chūlái, jiù lián nǐ gēge shàng cì huí jiā hái chà diǎnr mí le lù. Nǐ kuài sān nián méi huí lái le ba?
ZHIYUAN	Shì a! Gēge duō jiǔ huí lái yī cì?
MAMA	Tā jīhū měi bàn nián huílái yī cì.
ZHIYUAN	Wǒ zuòmèng yě méi xiǎng dào rénmen de shēnghuó shuǐpíng tígāo de zhème kuài.
MAMA	Shéi néng xiǎngdào! Yàoshì nǐ fùqīn hái huózhe gāi duō hǎo!

ZHIYUAN   Shì a! Bú guò, tā huì wéi wǒmen gāoxìng de. Duì le, wǒ hé fùqīn zuì xǐhuān de nà tiáo xiǎo hé hái zài ma?

MAMA   Zài, qián jǐ nián héshuǐ bèi wūrǎn le, zuìjìn cái qīnglǐ gānjìng.

ZHIYUAN   Tài hǎo le! Míngtiān wǒ jiù qù yóu ge yǒng.

MAMA   Suīrán qīnglǐ gānjìng le, dànshì hé shuǐ bú xiàng cóngqián nàme qīng le. Nǐ zìjǐ qù kànkan ba.

Vocabulary ♦

镇	zhèn	small town
认不出来	rèn bu chūlái	cannot recognise
差点儿	chàdiǎnr	nearly
迷了路	mí le lù	got lost
做梦	zuòmèng	to dream
提高	tígāo	to raise
谁能想到	shéi néng xiǎngdào	who would have thought
活着	huózhe	be alive
该多好	gāi duō hǎo	would be nice
干净	gānjìng	clean
虽然 . . . 但是	suīrán . . . dànshì	although . . . but
清	qīng	clear

Language points ♦

12.5 出来 (chūlái) to indicate the result of a verb

In Unit 6 (Language point 6.3), we saw that some words are used to indicate the result of a verb. In Dialogue 1, 出来 (chūlái) in 认不出来 (rèn bù chū lái) indicates the result of the verb 认 (rèn, to recognise). By placing 不 (pronounced with a neutral tone 'bu') in front of 出来 (chūlái), the speaker conveys the meaning that the result is potentially impossible. 出来 (chūlái) often follows verbs that have to do with the recognition or production of things such as 认 (rèn, to recognise), 看(kàn, to look), 写 (xiě, to write), 唱 (chàng, to sing). For example:

你的变化太大了，我都认不出来你了。
Nǐde biànhuà tài dà le, wǒ dōu rèn bu chūlái nǐ le.
You have changed so much that I do not recognise you.

看不出来你的体重增加了。
Kàn bu chūlái nǐde tǐzhòng zēngjiā le.
(I) cannot tell that you've put on some weight.

12.6 要是 . . . 该多好/就好了 (yàoshì . . . gāi duō hǎo/jiù hǎo le)

This pattern is used to express one's wish. It is equivalent to the English expression 'If only . . .' or 'It would be . . . if . . .'. For example:

要是你会说中文该多好！
Yàoshì nǐ huì shuō Zhōngwén gāi duō hǎo!
If only you could speak Chinese!

12.7 会 . . . 的 (huì . . . de, 'would')

We have seen 会 . . . 的 (huì . . . de) used to express one's determination to do something. 会 . . . 的 (huì . . . de) can also be used in an imaginary situation to mean 'would'. It is often used with a conditional sentence. For example:

如果父亲还活着的话，他会为我们高兴的。
Rúguǒ fùqīn hái huó zhe dehuà, tā huì wéi wǒmen gāoxìng de.
If father was alive, he would be pleased for us.

12.8 虽然 . . . 但是 (suīrán . . . dànshì, 'although . . . but')

In English, if 'although' is used, 'but' cannot be used in the second half of the sentence. In Chinese, they can appear in the same sentence. For example:

虽然我只见过他一面，但是他给我留下了很深的印象。
Suīrán wǒ zhǐ jiàn guò tā yī miàn, dànshì tā gěi wǒ liúxià le hěn shēn de yìnxiàng.
Although I only met him once, he left a deep impression on me.

虽然 (suīrán) can also be used in conjunction with 还是 (háishì, still) or 仍 (réng, still). For example:

虽然我知道他不喜欢别人给他提意见，我还是要说。
Suīrán wǒ zhīdào tā bù xǐhuān biérén gěi tā tí yìjiàn, wǒ háishì yào shuō.
Although I know that he doesn't like others being critical of him, I'm still going to say it.

Dialogue 2 (CD 2; 36)

合资企业 Hézī qǐyè
Joint venture companies

Wu Yu has just been offered a job and is phoning her father to tell him the good news ...

WU YU	爸爸，告诉你一个好消息！远森药品有限公司给了我一份工作。
FATHER	是吗？这是一家什么样的企业？
WU YU	是中美合资企业。
FATHER	真的！那，你具体做什么工作？
WU YU	销售部经理。
FATHER	赫！一个很重要的职务。我的女儿真不简单！
WU YU	别夸我了。说真的，我昨晚高兴得一晚上睡不着觉。
FATHER	那，你今天在家好好休息休息。

Zhejiang Haisen Pharmaceutical Co.
Photographer: Wang Shiyue

Dialogue 2 in pinyin ◆

WU YU Bàba, gàosù nǐ yī gè hǎo xiāoxi! Yuǎn Sēn Yàopǐn Yǒuxiàn Gōngsī gěi le wǒ yī fèn gōngzuò.
FATHER Shì ma? Zhè shì yī jiā shéme yàng de qǐyè?
WU YU Shì Zhōng Měi hé zī qǐyè.
FATHER Zhēn de! Nà, nǐ jùtǐ zuò shénme gōngzuò?
WU YU Xiāoshòu Bù jīnglǐ.
FATHER Hè! Yī gè hěn zhòngyào de zhíwù. Wǒde nǚ'ér zhēn bù jiǎndān!
WU YU Bié kuā wǒ le. Shuō zhēn de, wǒ zuó wǎn gāoxìng de yī wǎnshang shuì bù zháo jiào.
FATHER Nà, nǐ jīntiān zài jiā hǎohāo xiūxi xiūxi.

Vocabulary ◆

远森	**Yuǎn Sēn**	Far Forest (proper name)
药品	**yàopǐn**	medicine; pharmaceutical
有限公司	**yǒuxiàn gōngsī**	limited company
中美合资	**Zhōng Měi hé zī**	Sino-American joint venture
具体	**jùtǐ**	exactly; in detail
销售部	**xiāoshòu bù**	sales department
赫	**hè**	hey
职务	**zhíwù**	position
说真的	**shuō zhēn de**	to be honest; honestly

Extra useful vocabulary

国有企业	**guó yǒu qǐyè**	state-owned enterprise
私有企业	**sī yǒu qǐyè**	private enterprise
企业家	**qǐyèjiā**	entrepreneur
市场经济	**shìcháng jīngjì**	market economy

Language point ◆

12.9 The difference between 新闻 (**xīnwén**) and 消息 (**xiāoxi**)

Although both mean 'news' in English, 新闻 (**xīnwén**) refers to those items of news that are reported in the media, or things that have never been heard before. For example:

你看今天的新闻了吗？
Nǐ kàn jīntiān de xīnwén le ma?
Have you watched today's news?

我早就知道这件事了，这不是新闻。
Wǒ zǎo jiù zhīdào zhè jiàn shì le, zhè bú shì xīnwén.
I knew about it a long time ago. This is not news.

消息 (**xiāoxi**) refers to a specific piece of information:

这是个坏消息。
Zhè shì ge huài xiāoxi.
This is bad news.

好长时间没有他的消息了。
Hǎo cháng shíjiān méi yǒu tāde xiāoxi le.
Haven't heard from him for a long time (*lit.* a long time no his news).

Exercises

Exercise 5

Match the questions with the answers in Dialogues 1 and 2:
Questions:

a   这是一家什么样的企业？
　　Zhè shì yī jiā shénme yàng de qǐyè?

b   你具体做什么工作？
　　Nǐ jùtǐ zuò shénme gōngzuò?

c   哥哥多久回来一次？
　　Gēge duō jiǔ huílái yīcì?

d   我和父亲最喜欢的那条小河还在吗？
　　Wǒ hé fùqīn zuì xǐhuān de nà tiáo xiǎo hé hái zài ma?

Answers:

i   他几乎每半年回来一次。
　　Tā jīhū měi bàn nián huílái yīcì.

ii 在，前几年河水被污染了。
   Zài, qián jǐ nián héshuǐ bèi wūrǎn le.

iii 销售部经理。
    Xiāoshòu Bù jīnglǐ.

iv 是中美合资企业。
   Shì Zhōng Měi hézī qǐyè.

Exercise 6

Fill in the gaps using an appropriate measure word provided in the box:

a 我把这_____事忘了！真对不起。
  Wǒ bǎ zhè_____shì wàng le! Zhēn duìbuqǐ.

b 我想请你吃一_____中国饭。
  Wǒ xiǎng qǐng nǐ chī yī_____Zhōngguó fàn.

c 他连一_____自行车都没有。
  Tā lián yī_____zìxíngchē dōu méi yǒu.

d 这_____公司不仅注重质量，而且还重视环境保护。
  Zhè_____gōngsī bù jǐn zhùzhòng zhíliàng, ér qiě hái zhòngshì huánjìng bǎohù.

e 你顺着这_____街一直往前走。
  Nǐ shùnzhe zhè_____jiē yīzhí wǎng qián zǒu.

f 这是一_____古典长篇小说。
  Zhè shì yī_____gǔdiǎn chángpiān xiǎoshuō.

g 我对这_____工作特别感兴趣。
  Wǒ duì zhè_____gōngzuò tèbié gǎn xìngqù.

条， 家， 份， 件， 部， 顿， 辆
tiáo, jiā, fèn, jiàn, bù, dùn, liàng

Exercise 7

Decide if 新闻 (xīnwén) or 消息 (xiāoxi) should be used in the following two sentences:

a　他每天看报，主要是读_____和天气预报。
　　Tā měi tiān kàn bào, zhǔyào shì dú_____hé tiānqì yùbào.

b　昨天，我弟弟告诉了我一个好_____：他拿到了一份奖学金！
　　Zuótiān, wǒ dìdi gàosù le wǒ yī gè hǎo_____: tā nádào le yī fèn
　　jiǎngxuéjīn!

Exercise 8

Translate into Chinese:

a　I was so excited that I could not get my words out.
b　If only he could come to spend Chinese New Year with us!
c　Although he has problems with the four tones, he always speaks
　　Chinese with the locals.
d　If you didn't come to the get-together, Xiao Lin would be very
　　disappointed.
e　Honestly, I would never have dreamt that our village had its own
　　primary school.

Listening comprehension

开网吧　Kāi wǎng bā
Opening an internet bar   (CD 2; 38)

The following dialogue is between Daping and Huifeng, who used to
work for the same company. Daping now works for a small computer firm. Listen to the dialogue first. Try not to read the script.
Afterwards, do the following multiple choice exercises:

1　What business does Huifeng plan to get into?
　　a　an internet bar
　　b　market research
　　c　software design

2　How is Huifeng going to fund her business?
　　a　with her own savings
　　b　with a loan from the bank
　　c　with her savings and some money borrowed from the bank

3 What preparation has Huifeng made to set up her business?
   a attended a computer training programme
   b installed broadband at home
   c did market research

4 What does Daping think of Huifeng's business idea?
   a He thinks it's a bad idea.
   b He didn't make any comment.
   c He thinks it's a good idea and it will be profitable.

5 What is Daping doing next Wednesday?
   a showing and explaining some software to Huifeng
   b going to Shanghai on a business trip
   c going to the bank to borrow some money

Key words ♦

You may find the following words useful in understanding the dialogue:

区	qū	district
听上去	tīngshàngqu	it sounds . . .
赚钱	zhuànqián	profitable (*lit.* earn money)
生意	shēngyì	business
资金	zījīn	capital; money
存款	cúnkuǎn	savings; deposit
常用	cháng yòng	in everyday use
哎呀	āi'yā	Ah; my God
约	yuē	to arrange

Script in characters ♦

DAPING   听说你上个月下岗了？
HUIFENG 是的，不过也许不是一件坏事。我想开一个网吧。
DAPING   你做市场调研了吗？
HUIFENG 做了，咱们这个区一个网吧都没有。想上网的人不少，可自
         己家有宽带的人很少。

DAPING	听上去是一个能赚钱的生意。你有足够的资金吗？
HUIFENG	我自己有一些存款，还可以从银行贷一些款。
DAPING	你真不简单！
HUIFENG	我还没开始呢，你就夸我了。说真的，我想请你帮个忙。
DAPING	尽管说。
HUIFENG	我对电脑不太熟悉。你能不能抽空给我介绍一些常用的软件？
DAPING	当然可以。
HUIFENG	你哪天有空？
DAPING	下周三吧。哎呀，不行。下周三我去上海出差。下周末吧。
HUIFENG	可以，过几天我给你打电话约具体的时间。

Script in pinyin ♦

DAPING	Tīngshuō nǐ shàng ge yuè xià gǎng le?
HUIFENG	Shì de. Búguò, yěxǔ bú shì yī jiàn huài shì. Wǒ xiǎng kāi yī gè wǎng bā.
DAPING	Nǐ zuò shìcháng diàoyán le ma?
HUIFENG	Zuò le, zánmen zhè ge qū yī gè wǎng bā dōu méi yǒu. Xiǎng shàng wǎng de rén bù shǎo, kě zìjǐ jiā yǒu kuāndài de rén hěn shǎo.
DAPING	Tīngshàngqu shì yī gè néng zhuànqián de shēngyì. Nǐ yǒu zúgòude zījīn ma?
HUIFENG	Wǒ zìjǐ yǒu yīxiē cúnkuǎn, hái kěyǐ cóng yínháng dài yī xiē kuǎn.
DAPING	Nǐ zhēn bù jiǎndān.
HUIFENG	Wǒ hái méi kāishǐ ne, nǐ jiù kuā wǒ le. Shuō zhēn de, wǒ xiǎng qǐng nǐ bāng gè máng.
DAPING	Jìnguǎn shuō.
HUIFENG	Wǒ duì diànnǎo bú tài shóuxi. Nǐ néng bù néng chōu kòng gěi wǒ jièshào yīxiē cháng yòng de ruǎnjiàn?
DAPING	Dāngrán kěyǐ.
HUIFENG	Nǐ nǎ tiān yǒu kòng?
DAPING	Xià zhōu sān ba. Aiyā, bù xíng. Xià zhōu sān wǒ qù Shànghǎi chū chāi. Xià zhōu mò ba.
HUIFENG	Kěyǐ, guò jǐ tiān wǒ gěi nǐ dǎ diànhuà yuē jùtǐ de shíjiān.

Authentic text (CD 2; 39)

江西实现全省村村通电话
All the villages in Jiangxi Province have had a telephone connection

The following article is part of a news bulletin from China's major newspaper, the *People's Daily*. It reports on a major modernisation programme in Jiangxi Province in which every village in the province had a telephone line installed. As this is the original text, some sentences are rather complex both in terms of grammar and structure. For the English translation of the text, please see Appendix B on page 262.

江西实现全省村村通电话

　　江西省宜黄县仙坪村村民管常福给在广东南海打工的爱人拨通了电话：'喂！家里装电话了，以后有事记得就打这个电话。'随着仙坪村通上电话，江西省17955个行政村实现了村村通电话，成为我国中西部地区第一个实现村村通电话的省份。

　　到去年底，江西省还有933个行政村未通电话。这些村多半属于'老、山、边、穷'地区，自然、交通状况差，施工难度也大。为帮助电信企业克服资金困难，确保工程按时完成，江西省政府出台了一系列优惠奖励措施，......对村村通电话工程大开绿灯。

　　村村通电话工程不仅给农民生活带来便利，也为农民创造了实实在在的经济财富。...村民胡典发激动地说：'以前，我们都是挑着茶油走20公里的小路到山外去卖，因为没有事先联系好，老卖不出去，还白跑冤枉路。现在有了电话，我们就可以随时和外面联系，做买卖方便多了！'

选自《人民日报》2005年9月25日头版 (*People's Daily*, 25 September 2005: front page)

Vocabulary ♦

江西	**Jiāngxī**	(a province in the southwest China)
实现	**shíxiàn**	to realise
全省	**quán shěng**	entire province
村村	**cūn cūn**	every village
通电话	**tōng diànhuà**	to have a telephone installed
宜黄县	**Yíhuáng Xiàn**	Yihuang county

仙坪村	**xiānpíng cūn**	Xianping village
村民	**cūnmín**	villager
管常福	**Guǎn Chángfú**	(personal name)
广东	**Guǎngdōng**	(a province in southeast China)
南海	**Nánhǎi**	(a city in Guangdong province)
拨通	**bō tōng**	to have (the call) connected
随着	**suí zháo**	as . . .
行政村	**xíngzhèng cūn**	administrative village
成为	**chéngwéi**	to become; turn into
省份	**shěng fèn**	province
到去年底	**dào qù nián dǐ**	up till the end of last year
未	**wèi**	have not yet
多半	**duō bàn**	majority
属于	**shǔyú**	to belong to
山、边、穷	**shān, biān, qióng**	mountainous, remote, poor
地区	**dìqū**	area
状况	**zhuàngkuàng**	condition
差	**chà**	not good
施工	**shīgōng**	construction
电信	**diànxìn**	telecommunications
克服	**kèfú**	to overcome
确保	**quèbǎo**	to guarantee
工程	**gōngchéng**	project
完成	**wánchéng**	to complete
出台	**chūtái**	to announce (e.g. policy, measures)
一系列	**yī xìliè**	a series
优惠奖励	**yōuhuì jiǎnglì**	preferential and with rewards
对 . . . 大开绿灯	**duì . . . dà kāi lǜdēng**	to provide help to . . . (*lit.* to switch on the green light to . . .)
便利	**biànlì**	convenience
创造	**chuàngzào**	to create
实实在在	**shí-shí-zài-zài**	concrete; real
财富	**cáifù**	wealth
胡典发	**Hú Diǎnfā**	(personal name)
挑	**tiāo**	to carry with a pole
茶油	**chá yóu**	tea tree oil
公里	**gōnglǐ**	kilometre
事先	**shìxiān**	in advance
联系好	**liánxì hǎo**	to get things arranged
老	**lǎo**	always
白跑冤枉路	**bái pǎo yuānwang lù**	to make a fruitless trip
做买卖	**zuò mǎimài**	to do business

Key to exercises and reading/listening comprehension questions

Unit 1

Exercise 1

a 外语 wài yǔ,   **b** 不过 búguò,   **c** 认识 rènshí,
d 有问题 yǒu wèntí,   **e** 整整/差不多 zhěngzhěng/chàbuduō,
f 差不多 chàbuduō

Exercise 2

a 你的四声不错。
Nǐde sì shēng bú cuò.

b 他说普通话时有上海口音。
Tā shuō pǔtōnghuà shí, yǒu Shànghǎi kǒuyīn.

c 我在英国住了一年，可是连一句英语也不会说。
Wǒ zài Yīngguó zhù le yī nián, kěshì lián yī jù Yīngyǔ yě bú huì shuō.

d 她很不简单，连广东话也会说。
Tā hěn bù jiǎndān, lián Guǎngdōng huà yě huì shuō.

Exercise 3

a 你家有几个人？
Nǐ jiā yǒu jǐ gè rén?

b 你们班有多少人？
Nǐmen bān yǒu duō shǎo rén?

c 他会说几种外语？
Tā huì shuō jǐ zhǒng wài yǔ?

Exercise 4 (for reference)

a 你会说英文吗？
  Nǐ huì shuō Yīngwén ma?

b 你学了几年中文了？
  Nǐ xué le jǐ nián Zhōngwén le?

c 过奖，过奖/哪里，哪里/谢谢
  Guò jiǎng, guò jiǎng/nǎlǐ, nǎlǐ/xièxie.

Exercise 5

a 同意 tóngyì,   b 味道 wèidào,   c 品种 pǐnzhǒng,
d 特别 tèbié,   e 方面 fāngmiàn   f 到处 dàochù

Exercise 6

a 个 ge (I went to five or six cities, and also the countryside in the north.)
b no measure word required (She is planning to go to China this September.)
c 个 ge (I'm graduating next month.)
d 个 ge (Last year, I lived in Beijing for six months.)

Exercise 7

a 总的来说，我对中国的印象很好。
  Zǒngde láishuō, wǒ duì Zhōngguó de yìnxiàng hěn hǎo.

b 这个城市比我想象的挤得多。
  Zhè ge chéngshì bǐ wǒ xiǎngxiàng de jǐ de duō.

c 我十分喜欢这个小城，又漂亮又安静。还有就是当地人很友好。
  Wǒ shífēn xǐhuān zhè ge xiǎo chéng, yòu piāoliàng yòu ānjìng. Hái yǒu jiù shì dāngdìrén hěn yǒuhǎo.

d 你能不能具体点？
  Nǐ néng bù néng jùtǐ diǎn?

e 你(是)什么时候来的北京？/你(是)什么时候来北京的？
   Nǐ shì shénme shíhòu lái de Běijīng?/Nǐ shì shénme shíhòu lái
   Běijīng de?

Listening comprehension questions

1 小燕的男朋友。　　Xiǎoyàn de nán péngyou.
2 快三个月了。　　　Kuài sān gè yuè le.
3 因为他要去北京见小燕的父母。
   Yīnwéi tā yào qù Běijīng jiàn Xiǎoyàn de fùmǔ.

Unit 2

Exercise 1

a 出出 chūchu,　　b 一边，一边 yībiān, yībiān,
c 帮 bāng,　　　　d 美丽的 měilìde,　　e 沿途 yán tú

Exercise 2 (for reference)

a 快到出发的时间了，小王怎么还没来？
   Kuài dào chūfā de shíjiān le, Xiǎo Wáng zěnme hái méi lái?
   (It's nearly time to set off. How come Xiao Wang is not here yet?)

b 我不太喜欢这个电影，一是因为结尾太奇怪，
   Wǒ bú tài xǐhuān zhè ge diànyǐng, yī shì yīnwéi jiéwěi tài qíguài,
   二是因为主题音乐不好听。
   èr shì yīnwéi zhǔtí yīnyuè bù hǎotīng.
   (I'm not keen on this film. First because the ending is very strange,
   and second because the theme music is not nice.)

c 上海人喜欢饭后喝汤，而广东人却恰恰
   Shànghǎirén xǐhuān fàn hòu hē tāng, ér Guǎngdōngrén què qiàqià
   相反，他们喜欢先喝汤再吃饭。
   xiāngfǎn, tāmen xǐhuān xiān hē tāng zài chī fàn.
   (The Shanghainese like to have soup after the main meal, whilst
   the Cantonese are just the opposite – they like to have soup first
   and then eat the main course.)

Exercise 3 (for reference)

a 老王，这个星期天我想请你吃晚饭。
Lǎo Wáng, zhè ge Xīngqītiān wǒ xiǎng qǐng nǐ chī wǎnfàn.

b 去云南的路上，沿途的风景特别美。
Qù Yúnnán de lù shàng, yán tú de fēngjǐng tèbié měi.
我真高兴我是坐火车去的。
Wǒ zhēn gāoxìng wǒ shì zuò huǒchē qù de.

c 他刚才说的有道理。
Tā gāng cái shuō de yǒu dàolǐ.

d 好好玩！/度假快乐！
Hǎohào wán!/Dù jiǎ kuàilè!

e 快到吃晚饭的时间了。我们必须快一点。
Kuài dào chī wǎnfàn de shíjiān le. Wǒmen bìxū kuài yīdiǎn.

Exercise 4

a 参观 cānguān,   b 多亏了 duōkuīle,
c 外地人 wàidìrén,   d 而且 érqiě,   e 了解 liǎojiě

Exercise 5

a 的 de (One can cycle on Xi'an's city wall.)
b 得 DE (He speaks very good Chinese.)
c 得 DE (This train goes very slowly.)
d 的 de (Yunnan has a lot of beautiful natural scenery.)
e 得 DE (She went to the Three Gorges during the summer holidays.
She had a really good time.)

Exercise 6 (for reference)

a 真让人佩服。   Zhēn ràng rén pèifú.
b 离这儿很远。   Lí zhèr hěn yuǎn.
c 对学习外语有兴趣。   Duì xuéxí wài yǔ yǒu xìngqu.

Exercise 7 (for reference)

a 多谢夸奖/哪里，哪里。
Duō xiè kuājiǎng/Nǎlǐ, nǎlǐ.

b 真不好意思，我没带钱。
Zhēn bù hǎo yìsi, wǒ méi dài qián.

c 你想和我一起参观城墙吗？
Nǐ xiǎng hé wǒ yīqǐ cānguān chéng qiáng ma?

Reading comprehension questions

1 西安火车站 Xī'ān huǒchē zhàn
2 坐火车 zuò huǒchē
3 长安 Cháng'ān
4 兵马俑，钟楼，古城墙 Bīngmǎyǒng, Zhōnglóu, gǔ Chéng Qiáng
5 四个 sì ge

Unit 3

Exercise 1

a 不舒服 bù shūfu,   b 当然 dāngrán,   c 得 dé,
d 好象 hǎoxiàng,   e 按时 àn shí,   f 反正 fǎnzhèng,
g 多 duō

Exercise 2 (for reference)

1 我肚子特别疼。   Wǒ dùzi tèbié téng.
2 今天早上。   Jīntiān zǎoshàng.
3 大夫，我得了什么病？   Dàifu, wǒ dé le shénme bìng?

Exercise 3

a de (He coughs so badly that he can't sleep at night.)
b dé (My father has gone down with appendicitis.)

c dé (I heard that Xiao Wang is poorly recently. What exactly is he suffering from?)

d de (Our teacher speaks too fast. Often I can't understand him/her.)

Exercise 4

a 发烧 fā shāo, b 量体温 liáng tǐwēn,
c 开退烧药 kāi tuì shāo yào, d 病假条 bìng jià tiáo,
e 全身没劲 quán shēn méi jìn

Exercise 5

a 规律 guīlǜ, b 秘方 mìfāng, c 气色 qìsè,
d 学习 xuéxí, e 锻炼 duànliàn

Exercise 6

A 病假条 bìng jià tiáo, B 大夫 dàifu, C 头晕 tóuyūn

Exercise 7

a 你应该多吃蔬菜，并且开始锻炼身体（OR 做些运动）。
Nǐ yīnggāi duō chī shūcài, bìngqiě kāishǐ duànliàn shēntǐ (OR zuò xiē yùndòng).

b 他生活很有规律，而且每天早上锻炼身体。
Tā shēnghuó hěn yǒu guīlǜ, érqiě měi tiān zǎoshàng duànliàn shēntǐ.

c 他告诉你的不是真的。
Tā gàosù nǐ de bú shì zhēnde.

d 从明天开始，我要早些起床。
Cóng míngtiān kāishǐ, wǒ yào zǎo xiē qǐchuáng.

Listening comprehension questions (for reference)

1 六十八岁 liùshí bā suì

2 很好 hěn hǎo

3 每天早上锻炼身体，晚饭后散步。
Měi tiān zǎoshàng duànliàn shēntǐ, wǎnfàn hòu sàn bù.

4 打太极拳，做健美操。
Dǎ tàijíquán, zuò jiànměi cāo.

5 打太极拳，做健美操，跳舞。
Dǎ tàijíquán, zuò jiànměi cāo, tiàowǔ.

Unit 4

Exercise 1

a 聚会 jùhuì,   b 费时间 fèishíjiān,
c 说不清 shuō bu qīng,   d 周日 zhōurì

Exercise 2

a verb,   b direction indicator,
c direction indicator,   d verb

Exercise 3

a 件 jiàn,   b 棵 kē,   c 个 gè,   d 根 gēn

Exercise 4

a 我弟弟爱足球。他什么足球比赛都看。
Wǒ dìdi ài zúqiú. Tā shénme zúqiú bǐsài dōu kàn.

b 你是我最好的朋友，一定要来我的婚礼。

Nǐ shì wǒ zuìhǎode péngyou, yīdìng yào lái wǒde hūnlǐ.

c 你下个星期六来的时候，能不能带些中国音乐来？

Nǐ xià ge xīngqīliù lái de shíhou, néng bù néng dài xiē Zhōngguó yīnyuè lái?

d 别着急。等我到了你家后咱们再开始包饺子。

Bié zháojí. Děng wǒ dào le nǐ jiā hòu, zánmen zài kāishǐ bāo jiǎozi.

Exercise 5

a 意思 yìsi,　　**b** 简单 jiǎndān,　　**c** 不同 bùtóng,
d 方法 fāngfǎ,　　**e** 主要 zhǔyào

Exercise 6

a 先，然后，最后 xiān, ránhòu, zuìhòu
b 先，再 xiān, zài

Exercise 7

a 还是 háishì,　　**b** 或者 huòzhě,
c 或者 huòzhě,　　**d** 还是 háishì

Exercise 8 (for reference only)

a 南方人喜欢吃春卷，而北方人喜欢吃饺子。

Nánfāngrén xǐhuān chī chūnjuǎn, ér běifāngrén xǐhuān chī jiǎozi.

b 昨天晚上的音乐会以中国音乐为主。

Zuótiān wǎnshang de yīnyuèhuì yǐ Zhōngguó yīnyuè wéizhǔ.

c 筷子，我用得不好。

Kuàizi, wǒ yòng de bù hǎo.

d 请把这些刀叉洗干净。
Qǐng bǎ zhèxiē dāo chā xǐ gānjìng.

e 请你七点把我叫醒。
Qǐng nǐ qī diǎn bǎ wǒ jiào xǐng.

Exercise 9 (Please ask your tutor or a native speaker to check your presentation.)

Listening comprehension

1 剩米饭，鸡蛋和葱。 Shèng mǐfàn, jīdàn hé cōng.

2 菜油，盐和五香粉。 Cài yóu, yán hé wǔ xiāngfěn.

3 第一：把鸡蛋打碎，加点盐一起打。第二：把葱切碎。
Dìyī, bǎ jīdàn dǎ suì, jiā diǎn yán yīqǐ dǎ. Dìèr, bǎ cōng qiē suì.

4 先把葱倒进去炒几下，再把打碎的鸡蛋倒
Xiān bǎ cōng dào jìnqu, chǎo jǐ xià, zài bǎ dǎsuì de jīdàn dào
进去，炒一分钟左右，最后把剩饭倒进去。
jìnqu, chǎo yī fēnzhōng zuǒyòu, zuìhòu bǎ shèng fàn dào jìnqu.

Unit 5

Exercise 1

a 西方人 xīfāngrén, **b** 团圆饭/年夜饭 tuányuán fàn/niányè fàn,
c 传统 chuántǒng, **d** 按照 àn zhào, **e** 同事 tóngshì

Exercise 2

a 吃团圆饭，看电视，包饺子
chī tuányuán fàn, kàn diànshì, bāo jiǎozi

b 整个晚上不睡觉
zhěnggè wǎnshàng bú shuìjiào

c 互相拜年
hù xiāng bài nián

d 从初二开始
cóng chū èr kāishǐ

e 十五天/两个星期
shíwǔ tiān/liǎng gè xīngqī

Exercise 3 (for reference)

a 这是我第一次在中国过年/过春节。
Zhè shì wǒ dì yī cì zài Zhōngguó guò nián/guò Chūn Jié.

b 大年初一，我们去我们的老师家给他拜年。
Dà nián chū yī, wǒmen qù wǒmen de lǎoshī jiā gěi tā bài nián.

c 我们说好了八点吃全家团圆饭，可是我哥哥九点才到！
Wǒmen shuō hǎo le bā diǎn chī quán jiā tuányuán fàn, kěshì wǒ gēge jiǔ diǎn cái dào!

d 我知道小明是你家的亲戚。你把他叫什么？
Wǒ zhīdào Xiǎo Míng shì nǐ jiā de qīnqī. Nǐ bǎ tā jiào shénme?

Exercise 4

a 老大 lǎo dà, **b** 留 liú, **c** 值班 zhí bān,
d 春卷 chūn juǎn, **e** 以为 yǐwéi

Exercise 5

a 就 jiù, **b** 就 jiù, **c** 才 cái,
d 就 jiù, **e** 才 cái

Exercise 6

a matches D, **b** matches E, **c** matches A,
d matches B, **e** matches C

Exercise 7

a 今年你打算在哪儿过年？
Jīn nián nǐ dǎsuàn zài nǎr guò nián?

b 我还以为你不会包饺子。
Wǒ hái yǐwéi nǐ bú huì bāo jiǎozi.

c 别提了！看孩子了可累了。
Bié tí le! Kān háizi kě lèi le.

d 你不用带什么礼物来。
Nǐ bú yòng dài shénme lǐwù lai.

e 我正要给你打电话。
Wǒ zhèng yào gěi nǐ dǎ diànhuà.

Reading comprehension questions

1 医生
Yīshēng

2 在天津
Zài Tiānjīn

3 去看王强的父母
Qù kàn Wáng Qiáng de fùmǔ

Unit 6

Exercise 1

a 人物 rénwù, **b** 电影迷 diànyǐng mí, **c** 作品 zuòpǐn,
d 不得不 bù de bù, **e** 好几遍 hǎo jǐ biàn, **f** 困难 kùnnán

Exercise 2 (for reference)

a 他的父母喜欢音乐，哥哥爱好足球，奶奶喜欢养
Tāde fùmǔ xǐhuān yīnyuè, gēge àihào zúqiú, nǎinai xǐhuān yǎng
花，爷爷爱看电影。
huā, yéye ài kàn diànyǐng.

b 他喜欢电影，但更喜欢文学。
Tā xǐhuān diànyǐng, dàn gèng xǐhuān wénxué.

c 他读过《红楼梦》,《家》,正在读《骆驼祥子》。
Tā dú guò 《Hóng Lóu Mèng》,《Jiā》, zhèngzài dú
《Luòtuó Xiángzi》.

d 古典长篇小说。
Gǔdiǎn chángpiān xiǎoshuō.

Exercise 3

a 有些，有些 yǒuxiē, yǒuxiē,   **b** 一些 yīxiē,
c 一些 yīxiē,   **d** 有些 yǒuxiē

Exercise 4 (for reference)

a 我喜欢中国饺子，但我更喜欢春卷。
Wǒ xǐhuān Zhōngguó jiǎozi, dàn wǒ gèng xǐhuān chūnjuǎn.

b 自从上个月开始学中文以来，我对中国文学越来越感兴趣。
Zìcóng shàngge yuè kāishǐ xué Zhōngwén yǐlái, wǒ duì Zhōngguó
wénxué yuè lái yuè gǎn xìngqu.

c 昨天晚上我去看我奶奶时，她正在打太极拳。
Zuótiān wǎnshàng wǒ qù kàn wǒ nǎinai shí, tā zhèngzài dǎ
tàijíquán.

d 这部电影里面的人物太多，我记不住他们所有人的名字。
Zhè bù diànyǐng lǐmiàn de rénwù tài duō, wǒ jì bu zhù tāmen
suǒyǒu rén de míngzì.

e 他读的全是老舍的原著。
Tā dú de quán shì Lǎo Shě de yuán zhù.

Exercise 5

a 用不用 yòng bú yòng,   **b** 找 zhǎo,   **c** 首都 shǒudū,
d 早点儿 zǎo diǎnr,   **e** 强 qiáng

Exercise 6

a 的 de,   b 的 de,   c 得 DE,   d 的 de,   e 得 DE

Exercise 7

a 只要你知道怎么查字典，你一定能看懂这篇文章。
  Zhǐyào nǐ zhīdào zěnme chá zìdiǎn, nǐ yīdìng néng kàn dǒng zhè piān wénzhāng.

b 说到过年，我正要请你帮我出出主意。
  Shuō dào guò nián, wǒ zhèng yào qǐng nǐ bāng wǒ chūchu zhǔyi.

c A 我知道你不喜欢她，但她去过中国。
    Wǒ zhīdào nǐ bù xǐhuān tā, dàn tā qù guò Zhōngguó.
  B 到也是。我应该听听她怎么说。
    Dàoyěshì. Wǒ yìnggāi tīngting tā zěnme shuō.

d A 我已经看完了《红楼梦》的英文翻译。
    Wǒ yǐjīng kàn wán le《Hóng Lóu Mèng》de yīngwén fānyì.
  B 那有什么！汤姆几乎马上就看完了这部小说的中文原著。
    Nà yǒu shénme! Tāngmǔ jīhū mǎshàng jiù kàn wán le zhè bù xiǎoshuō de Zhōngwén yuán zhù.

e 电影马上就要开始了。
  Diànyǐng mǎshàng jiùyào kāishǐ le.

Listening comprehension questions

1 听说过 tīng shuō guò,   2 中文的 Zhōngwén de,
3 很好 hěn hǎo,   4 今天晚上 jīntiān wǎnshang

Unit 7

Exercise 1

a 家长 jiāzhǎng,   b 分心 fēnxīn,   c 热心 rèxīn,
d 熟悉 shóuxi, shúxi,   e 学期 xuéqī

Exercise 2

a 那个正在包饺子的人是我的老师。/正在包
Nà gè zhèngzài bāo jiǎozi de rén shì wǒde lǎoshī./Zhèngzài bāo
饺子的那个人是我的老师。
jiǎozi de nà ge rén shì wǒde lǎoshī.

b 我喜欢那些早睡早起的人。
Wǒ xǐhuān nàxiē zǎo shuì zǎo qǐ de rén.

c 我要去看一场具有国际标准的比赛。
Wǒ yào qù kàn yī cháng jùyǒu guójì biāozhǔn de bǐsài.

d 这是一辆开往云南的火车。
Zhè shì yī liàng kāiwǎng Yúnnán de huǒchē.

e 城里有很多让人分心的事情。
Chéng lǐ yǒu hěnduō ràng rén fēnxīn de shìqing.

Exercise 3

a 你教什么？
Nǐ jiāo shénme?

b 中国孩子几岁上学？
Zhōngguó háizi jǐ suì shàngxué?

c 图书馆是不是每天开门？
Túshūguǎn shì bú shì měitiān kāimén?

Exercise 4

a 我的自行车坏了。好在我今天不用上班。
Wǒde zìxíngchē huài le. Hǎozài wǒ jīntiān bú yòng shàngbān.

b 这本书太难了，真让我头疼。
Zhè běn shū tài nán le, zhēn ràng wǒ tóuténg.

c 我爸爸让我今年去我奶奶家和她一起过春节。
Wǒ bàba ràng wǒ jīnnián qù wǒ nǎinai jiā hé tā yīqǐ guò chūnjié.

d 和你们大学的图书馆比起来，我们的小多了 or 小得多。

Hé nǐmen dàxué de túshūguǎn bǐqǐlái, wǒmende xiǎo duō le or xiǎo de duō.

e 和西餐不同，做中国饭特别费时间。

Hé xī cān bùtóng, zuò Zhōngguó fàn tèbié fèishíjiān.

Exercise 5

a 课程 kèchéng,   **b** 方便 fāngbiàn,   **c** 大部份 dàbùfèn,
d 打工 dǎ gōng (or 赚些钱 zhuàn xiē qián),
e 卧室 wòshì,   **f** 周末 zhōumò

Exercise 6 (for reference)

a 英国的大学本科需要学几年？

Yīngguó de dàxué běnkē xūyào xué jǐ nián?

b 英国的大学每年放几次假？

Yīngguó de dàxué měi nián fàng jǐ cì jià?

c 英国大学生业余时间常常做什么？

Yīngguó dàxué shēng yèyú shíjiān chángcháng zuò shénme?

d 在英国，硕士课程要学多久？

Zài Yīngguó, shuòshì kèchéng yào xué duō jiǔ?

Exercise 7

a 他在中国住了两年，可是他却不会说中文。

Tā zài Zhōngguó zhù le liǎng nián, kěshì tā què bú huì shuō Zhōngwén.

He has lived in China for two years, but he can't speak Chinese.

b 她的奶奶今年七十八岁，而她的爷爷已经八十多岁了。

Tāde nǎinai jīn nián qīshíbā suì, ér tāde yéye yǐjīng bāshí duō suì le.

Her grandma is seventy-eight this year, whilst her grandpa is over eighty.

c 中国的学校每年只放两次假，而英国的
Zhōngguó de xuéxiào měi nián zhǐ fàng liǎng cì jià, ér Yīngguó de
学校每年要放三次长假，三次短假。
xuéxiào měi nián yào fàng sān cì cháng jià, sān cì duǎn jià.
Chinese schools have only two vacations each year, whilst schools
in Britain have three long holidays and three short holidays each
year.

Exercise 8

a 你花了多长时间写这封信？
Nǐ huā le duō cháng shíjiān xiě zhè fēng xìn?

b 说起中国来，他变得十分激动。
Shuōqǐ Zhōngguó lái tā biàn de shífēn jīdòng.

c 我今晚不想去酒吧。再说，我最喜欢的酒吧今晚不开门。
Wǒ jīnwǎn bù xiǎng qù jiǔbā. Zàishuō, wǒ zuì xǐhuān de jiǔbā
jīnwǎn bù kāimén.

d 在英国，小孩四岁上学，而在中国，小孩六岁才上学。
Zài Yīngguó, xiǎohái sì suì shàng xué, ér zài Zhōngguó, xiǎohái
liù suì cái shàng xué.

e 大卫三个月之内学会了500个汉字。他真厉害。
Dàwèi sān gè yuè zhīnèi xué huì le 500 gè hànzì. Tā zhēn lìhai.

Reading comprehension questions

1 在一所小学教英文。
Zài yī suǒ xiǎoxué jiāo Yīngwén.

2 太原的生活条件没有北京的好，冬天也比北京冷。
Tàiyuán de shēnghuó tiáojiàn méi yǒu Běijīng de hǎo, dōngtiān
yě bǐ Běijīng lěng.

3 老师 lǎoshī

4 一月中旬 Yīyuè zhōngxún

5 在北京和她从前学中文时认识的朋友们一起过年。
Zài Běijīng hé tā cóng qián xué Zhōngwén shí rènshí de
péngyǒumen yīqǐ guò nián.

Unit 8

Exercise 1

a	决定	juédìng	decision
b	意见	yìjiàn	view, opinion
c	人才市场	réncái shìcháng	job market
d	就业网站	jiùyè wǎngzhàn	employment website
e	烦恼	fánnǎo	worries
f	工作面试	gōngzuò miànshì	job interview

Exercise 2 (Please ask your tutor or a Chinese friend to check it for you.)

Exercise 3

a 昨天的聚会是(由)学生会组织的。
Zuótiān de jùhuì shì yóu xuéshēng huì zǔzhī de.

b 今晚的年夜饭由奶奶做。
Jīnwǎn de niányè fàn yóu nǎinai zuò.

c 退烧药由医生开。/退烧药是医生开的。
Tuìshāo yào yóu yīshēng kāi./Tuìshāo yào shì yīshēng kāi de.

d 这个建议是王经理提出的。
Zhè ge jiànyì shì Wáng jīnglǐ tíchū de.

Exercise 4

a 找出了这件事情的真正原因后，我便对他说：'这不是你的错'。
Zhǎochū le zhè jiàn shìqíng de zhēnzhèng yuányīn hòu, wǒ biàn duì tā shuō: 'Zhè bú shì nǐde cuò'.

b 即便我有很多钱，我也不会买这样的东西。
Jíbiàn wǒ yǒu hěnduō qián, wǒ yě bú huì mǎi zhè yàng de dōngxi.

c 在农村长大的孩子通常很勤奋。
Zài nóngcūn zhǎngdà de háizi tōngcháng hěn qínfèn.

d 他根本不知道她会说中文。
Tā gēnběn bù zhīdào tā huì shuō Zhōngwén.

Exercise 5

a 修改 xiūgǎi, b 吹牛 chuīniú, c 加上 jiāshang,
d 拿到 nádào, e 申请 shēnqǐng

Exercise 6

a Huaxia Library, b librarian,
c university graduate who is good at English,
d Li Fang

Exercise 7

a 如果你这个周末有空，我们一起去看电影。
Rúguǒ nǐ zhè ge zhōumò yǒu kōng, wǒmen yīqǐ qù kàn diànyǐng.

b 如果你能读懂这本书，我就把它送给你。
Rúguǒ nǐ néng dú dǒng zhè běn shū, wǒ jiù bǎ tā sòng gěi nǐ.

c 如果你不喜欢这个工作，为什么不换个工作？
Rúguǒ nǐ bù xǐhuān zhège gōngzuò, wèishénme bù huàn gè gōngzuò?

d 如果你过份谦虚，老板会认为你没有自信心。
Rúguǒ nǐ guòfèn qiānxū, lǎobǎn huì rènwéi nǐ méi yǒu zìxìnxīn.

Listening comprehension questions

1 在教育部给领导开车。
Zài jiàoyù bù gěi lǐngdǎo kāichē.

2 从前的工作不太自由，现在的工作比较灵活。
Cóngqián de gōngzuò bú tài zìyóu, xiànzài de gōngzuò bǐjiào línghuó.

3 十个小时左右。
Shí gè xiǎoshí zuǒyòu.

4 从前的工作不太自由，现在的工作比较灵活。

Cóngqián de gōngzuò bù tài zìyóu, xiànzài de gōngzuò bǐjiào línghuó.

从前的工资低，现在的高。

Cóngqián de gōngzī dī, xiànzài de gāo.

Unit 9

Exercise 1

a 几乎 jīhū,　**b** 大多数 dàduōshù,　**c** 增加 zēngjiā,
d 后果 hòuguǒ,　**e** 解决 jiějué

Exercise 2

a 她被同学们称为'热心的妈妈'。

Tā bèi tóngxuémen chēng wéi 'rèxīn de māma'.

b 电话被小弟弟弄坏了。

Diànhuà bèi xiǎo dìdi nònghuài le.

c 我被她训了一顿。

Wǒ bèi tā xùn le yī dùn.

d 他的秘方被许多人知道了。

Tāde mìfāng bèi xǔduō rén zhīdào le.

Exercise 3

a 我们明天一大早要去长城。今天晚上我得早睡。

Wǒmen míngtiān yī dà zǎo yào qù Cháng Chéng. Jīntiān wǎnshang wǒ děi zǎo shuì.

b 你不用骑车上学。你自己决定。

Nǐ bú yòng qíchē shàng xué. Nǐ zìjǐ juédìng.

c 在我们学校，女学生比男学生多得多。
  Zài wǒmen xuéxiào, nǚ xuéshēng bǐ nán xuéshēng duō deduō.

d 我真不敢相信！饺子全被我哥哥吃完了！
  Wǒ zhēn bù gǎn xiāngxìn! Jiǎozi quán bèi wǒ gēge chī wán le!

Exercise 4

a 骑车不太方便。
  Qíchē bú tài fāngbiàn.

b 好在北京气候比较干燥。
  Hǎozài Běijīng qìhòu bǐjiào gānzào.

c 我完全同意。
  Wǒ wánquán tóngyì.

d 骑车人的专用车道。
  Qíchērén de zhuānyòng chēdào.

e 我的体重增加了不少。
  Wǒde tǐzhòng zēngjiā le bù shǎo.

Exercise 5

a 这个工人让（OR 叫）老板解雇了。/这个工人
  Zhè gè gōngrén **ràng (OR jiào)** lǎobǎn jiěgù le./Zhè gè gōngrén
  让（OR 叫）老板给解雇了。
  ràng (OR jiào) lǎobǎn **gěi** jiěgù le.

b 这顿饭让（OR 叫）我做坏了。/这顿饭让（OR 叫）我给做坏了。
  Zhè dùn fàn **ràng (OR jiào)** wǒ zuòhuài le./Zhè dùn fàn **ràng
  (OR jiào)** wǒ **gěi** zuòhuài le.

c 这条路让（OR 叫 OR 给）警察包围了。/这条路
  Zhè tiáo lù **ràng (OR jiào OR gěi)** jǐngchá bāowéi le./Zhè tiáo lù
  让（OR 叫）警察给包围了。
  ràng (OR jiào) jǐngchá **gěi** bāowéi le.

d 我的钱包让（OR 叫）人偷了。/我的钱包让（OR 叫）人给偷了。
  Wǒde qiánbāo **ràng (OR jiào)** rén tōu le./Wǒde qiánbāo **ràng
  (OR jiào)** rén **gěi** tōu le.

Exercise 6

a   The car is fixed.
c   This city is polluted.
e   The road to work is jammed again.
g   The traffic jam problem has been solved.

Exercise 7

a   限制 xiànzhì,   b   结果 jiéguǒ,
c   提供 tígòng,   d   考虑 kǎolǜ

Reading comprehension question

Check your summary with your tutor or a Chinese person.

Unit 10

Exercise 1

a   更别说 gèng bié shuō,   b   普及 pǔjí,
c   随时 suí shí,   d   免费 miǎn fèi,
e   甚至 shènzhì

Exercise 2

a	信息革命	xìnxī gémìng	ii	information revolution
b	老百姓	lǎo bǎixìng	iv	ordinary people
c	电子邮件	diànzǐ yóujiàn	i	email
d	名副其实	míng-fù-qí-shí	v	the name matches the reality; worthy of the name
e	在网上	zài wǎng shàng	iii	on the net

Exercise 3

a 这个问题太难了。连我们老师都不知道答案。

Zhè ge wèntí tài nán le. Lián wǒmen lǎoshī dōu bù zhīdào dá'àn.

b 他不但/不仅会做西餐，而且还会做中餐。

Tā bù dàn/bù jǐn huì zuò xī cān, ér qiě hái huì zuò zhōng cān.

c 我根本没想到你会来，我太高兴了！

Wǒ gēnběn méi xiǎng dào nǐ huì lái, wǒ tài gāoxìng le!

d 我很少给我妈妈打电话，但我每天给她发一封电子邮件。

Wǒ hěnshǎo gěi wǒ māma dǎ diànhuà, dàn wǒ měitiān gěi tā fā yī fēng diànzǐ yóujiàn.

Exercise 4

a Because the college server is being serviced.
b To the internet bar outside the college.
c It's an internet bar, and her friend Yusuki thinks it has got a nice environment.

Exercise 5

a 你放心吧 nǐ fàngxīn ba,
b 差不多 chàbuduō,
c 别提了 bié tí le,
d 不瞒你说 bù mán nǐ shuō

Exercise 6

a 我试了好几种办法，但怎么也睡不着。

Wǒ shì le hǎo jǐ zhǒng bànfǎ, dàn zěnme yě shuì bù zháo.

b 我的车出毛病了。我得骑车去上班。

Wǒde chē chū máo bìng le. Wǒ děi qíchē qù shàng bān.

c 真的，我喝不了这么多啤酒。

Zhēnde, wǒ hē bù liǎo zhème duō píjiǔ.

d 我不知道他是骑车还是开车。

Wǒ bù zhīdào tā shì qíchē háishì kāichē.

Exercise 7

a 你最近在学什么？
  Nǐ zuìjìn zài xué shénme?

> ii 学怎么用电脑。
>   Xué zěnme yòng diànnǎo.

b 你的笔记本好用吗？
  Nǐde bǐjìběn hǎo yòng ma?

> i 挺好用的。
>   Tǐng hǎo yòng de.

c 怎么发电子邮件？
  Zěnme fā diànzǐ yóujiàn?

> iv 一时半会儿说不清。你到我家来，我给你
>   Yī-shí-bàn-huìr shuō bu qīng. Nǐ dào wǒ jiā lái, wǒ gěi nǐ
>   演示一下，你就明白了。
>   yǎnshì yīxià, nǐ jiù míngbái le.

d 昨晚你为什么睡不着觉？
  Zuówǎn nǐ wéishénme shuì bù zháo jiào?

> iii 收到了儿子的电子邮件，太激动了！
>   Shōudào le érzi de diànzi yóujiàn, tài jīdòng le!

Exercise 8

a 见到了多年不见的好朋友，我激动得说不出话来。
  Jiàndào le duō nián bù jiàn de hǎo péngyǒu, wǒ jīdòng de shuō
  bùchū huà lái.
  Having met good friends I hadn't seen for so many years, I was
  so excited that I couldn't find the right words.

b 拿到了这份工作，我高兴得好几晚没睡好觉。
  Ná dào le zhè fèn gōngzuò, wǒ gāoxìn de hǎo jǐ wǎn méi shuì
  hǎo jiào.
  I was so pleased about getting this job that I couldn't sleep well
  for a couple of nights.

c 她这几天忙得都没有时间吃饭。/她这几天
Tā zhè jǐ tiān máng de dōu méi yǒu shíjiān chīfàn./Tā zhè jǐ tiān
忙得连吃饭的时间都没有。
máng de lián chīfàn de shíjiān dōu méi yǒu.
In the last couple of days, she was so busy that she had no time to
eat./In the last couple of days, she was so busy that she didn't
even have time to eat.

Listening comprehension questions

1 c, 2 a

Unit 11

Exercise 1

a 世界   shìjiè,
b 凑合   còuhe,
c 不管   bùguǎn,
d 重视   zhòng shì,
e 和... 有关系   hé ... yǒu guānxì

Exercise 2

a 结了两次婚/结婚结了两次
jié le liǎng cì hūn/jiéhūn jié le liǎng cì

b 做一顿意大利饭
zuò yī dùn Yìdàlì fàn

c 睡了一个好觉
shuì le yī gè hǎo jué

d 见过一面/见了一次面
jiàn guò yī miàn/jiàn le yī cì miàn

Exercise 3   (for reference)

a   无论/不管你是老人还是小孩，每个人都必须吃这种药。
Wúlùn/bùguǎn nǐ shì lǎo rén háishì xiǎo hái, měi gè rén dōu bìxū
chī zhè zhǒng yào.

b   开车的时候/开车时，(你)不应该用手机。
Kāichē de shíhòu/Kāichē shí, (nǐ) bù yìnggāi yòng shǒujī.

c   我在中国的时候，我的中文比现在好得多。
Wǒ zài Zhōngguó de shíhòu, wǒde Zhōngwén bì xiànzài hǎo
deduō.

d   因为这是你给我的礼物，无论贵还是便宜，我都会珍惜的。
Yīnwéi zhè shì nǐ gěi wǒde lǐwù, wúlùn guì háishì piányí, wǒ dōu
huì zhēnxí de.

Exercise 4

a   老王的女儿。
Lǎo Wáng de nǚ'ér.

b   大年初一。
Dà nián chū yī.

c   因为老王的女儿从初一到初三在医院值班。
Yīnwéi Lǎo Wáng de nǚ'ér cóng chū yī dào chū sān zài yīyuàn
zhí bān.

Exercise 5

a   真棒！
Zhēnbàng!

b   你转过身往上看。
Nǐ zhuǎn guò shēn wǎng shàng kàn.

c   如果(你)需要我们帮忙，尽管说。
Rúguǒ (nǐ) xūyào wǒmen bāng máng, jìnguǎn shuō.

d   先过年再办喜事。
Xiān guò nián zài bàn xǐ shì.

e　你们俩一定要来喝喜酒。
　　Nǐmen liǎng yīdìng yào lái hē xǐ jiǔ.

Exercise 6

a　让/叫 ràng/jiào,
b　请 qǐng ('让/叫 ràng/jiào' can be used, but is not very polite),
c　问 wèn,　　d　让/叫 ràng/jiào,　　e　请 qǐng

Exercise 7

a　我把他的名字忘了。
　　Wǒ bǎ tā de míngzì wàng le.

b　她把女儿的房间布置好了。
　　Tā bǎ nǚ'ér de fángjiān bùzhì hǎo le.

c　请你把那个双喜剪纸拿过来。
　　Qǐng nǐ bǎ nà ge shuāng xǐ jiǎnzhǐ ná guò lái.

d　小王把他的婚礼推迟到九月份。
　　Xiǎo Wáng bǎ tāde hūnlǐ tuīchí dào jiǔyuèfen.

e　奶奶让我把礼物打开。
　　Nǎinai ràng wǒ bǎ lǐwù dǎkāi.

Reading comprehension questions

a　false,　　b　true,　　c　false,　　d　true,　　e　false

Unit 12

Exercise 1

a　成立 chénglì,　　　　b　留下 liú xià,　　c　普通 pǔtōng,
d　受欢迎 shòu huānyíng,　　e　经验 jīngyàn

Exercise 2 (for reference)

名副其实 míng-fù-qí-shí,　款式新颖 kuǎnshì xīnyǐng,　白头到老 bái-tóu-dào-lǎo,　包办婚姻 bāobàn hūnyīn,　传宗接代 chuán-zōng-jiē-dài, 名胜古迹 míng-shèng-gǔ-jī,　重男轻女 zhòng-nán-qīng-nǚ

Exercise 3

a　在我父母的影响下，我对中国文学越来越感兴趣。
　　Zài wǒ fùmǔ de yǐngxiǎng xià, wǒ duì Zhōngguó wénxué yuè lái yuè gǎn xìngqù.

b　你能用中文给我写信吗？
　　Nǐ néng yòng Zhōngwén gěi wǒ xiě xìn ma?

c　我们村的变化很大，我们村的小学的变化更大。
　　Wǒmen cūn de biànhuà hěn dà, wǒmen cūn de xiǎo xué de biànhuà gèng dà.

Exercise 4 (for reference)

小芳：

　　你好！

　　很高兴收到你的来信。祝贺你结了婚，并祝你们白头到老！你的丈夫叫什么名字？请你给我寄一张你们的结婚照。真高兴你开始学英文了。今后，我们可以互相帮助：你用英文给我写信，我用中文给你写信！

　　我也要告诉你一个好消息：我有女朋友了！她是中国人，也叫小芳！明年春天我们可能要去中国。到时候，我一定和小芳一起去你们家玩。

　　我也很想你们全家。请代我向大家问好。

祝好！

大卫

2005, 8, 10

Letter in pinyin

Xiǎofāng:

Nǐ hǎo!

Hěn gāoxìng shōudào nǐde láixìn. Zhùhè nǐ jié le hūn, bìng zhù nǐmen bái-tóu-dào-lǎo! Nǐde zhàngfū jiào shénme míngzì? Qǐng nǐ gěi wǒ jì yī zhāng nǐmende jiéhūn zhào. Zhēn gāoxìng nǐ kāishǐ xué Yīngwén le. Jīnhòu, wǒmen kěyǐ hùxiāng bāngzhù: nǐ yòng Yīngwén gěi wǒ xiěxìn, wǒ yòng Zhōngwén gěi nǐ xiě xìn.

Wǒ yě yào gàosù nǐ yī gè hǎo xiāoxī: wǒ yǒu nǚ péngyou le! Tā shì Zhōngguórén, yě jiào Xiǎofāng! Míng nián chūntiān wǒmen kěnéng yào qù Zhōngguó. Dào shíhòu, wǒ yīdìng hé Xiǎofāng yīqǐ qù nǐmen jiā wánr.

Wǒ yě hěn xiǎng nǐmen quán jiā. Qǐng dài wǒ xiàng dàjiā wèn hǎo.

Zhù hǎo!

Dàwèi
2005, 8, 10

Exercise 5

a with iv,   b with iii,   c with i,   d with ii

Exercise 6

a 件 jiàn,   b 顿 dùn,   c 辆 liàng,   d 家 jiā,
e 条 tiáo,   f 部 bù,   g 份 fèn

Exercise 7

a 新闻 xīnwén,   b 消息 xiāoxi

Exercise 8

a 我激动得什么话都说不出来。

Wǒ jīdòng de shénme huà dōu shuō bù chūlái.

b 要是他能来和我们一起过春节就好了！

Yàoshì tā néng lái hé wǒmen yīqǐ guò chūnjié jiù hǎo le!

c 虽然他的四声有问题，他总是和当地人说中文。

Suīrán tāde sìshēng yǒu wèntí, tā zǒngshì hé dāngdìrén shuō Zhōngwén.

d 如果你不来参加聚会，小林会很失望的。

Rúguǒ nǐ bù lái cānjiā jùhuì, Xiǎo Lín huì hěn shīwàng de.

e 说真的，我做梦也没想到我们村会有自己的小学。

Shuōzhēnde, wǒ zuòmèng yě méi xiǎngdào wǒmen cūn huì yǒu zìjǐ de xiǎoxué.

Listening comprehension questions

1 a   2 c   3 c   4 c   5 b

Appendix A: Texts, dialogues, reading comprehension texts and listening comprehension scripts in complex characters

Unit 1　中文以及中國

Dialogue 1　學中文

LILI　你會說中文嗎？

TOM　會，不過說得不好。

LILI　你的口音很不錯。

TOM　過獎，過獎。我的四聲總是有問題。

LILI　你太謙虛了。學了幾年中文了？

TOM　整整三年了。

LILI　認識多少個漢字？

TOM　差不多一千個，可是只會寫五百個左右。

LILI　那也很不簡單。我連一句外語也不會說。

Dialogue 2　我對中國的印象

ZHANG XIN　你不是去中國了嗎？什麼時候回來的?

JANE　是啊！去了整整一個月。昨天回來的。

ZHANG XIN　你對中國的印象怎麼樣? 有空聊聊嗎?

JANE　當然有空。總的來說，印象很好。

ZHANG XIN　你能不能具體點?

JANE　北京、上海這些大城市比我想像的現代化得多。給我印象最深的是那些名勝古蹟，比如北京的故宮、西安的碑林等。再就是中國飯菜 – 品種多樣、味道鮮美！

ZHANG XIN　你還去了其他什麼地方?

JANE	差不多七、八個城市。比如青島、成都等。我還游了三峽。真是美極了！
ZHANG XIN	你說的都是好的方面，有什麼是你不喜歡的?
JANE	交通太擁擠，特別是北京；還有就是噪音，到處都吵吵鬧鬧。
ZHANG XIN	我完全同意。

Listening comprehension script

LINFANG	小燕，聽說你的男朋友開始學中文了。是真的嗎？
XIAOYAN	是啊！已經快三個月了。
LINFANG	怎麼樣？他覺得難不難？
XIAOYAN	總的來說，他覺得很難，不過他很喜歡。
LINFANG	你們認識了這麼久，他為什麼現在才學中文？
XIAOYAN	因為我們今年夏天要去北京見我的父母！
LINFANG	難怪！他想給你父母一個好印象。
XIAOYAN	這只是原因之一。他真的想同中國人交流。

Unit 2　在中國旅行

Dialogue 1　準備旅行

MARY	你什麼時候有空？我想請你幫我出出主意。
LI LIANG	什麼方面的主意？
MARY	在中國旅游方面的。聽說你玩了不少地方。
LI LIANG	沒問題。現在就可以。咱們找個地方坐下來慢慢說。
MARY	太好了！剛好快到吃中飯的時間了。我請你吃中飯，咱們一邊吃一邊聊。
LI LIANG	你的這個建議棒極了。走吧！

(After they have sat down with their lunch . . .)

LI LIANG	你先說說，你想去哪幾個城市？准備去多久？
MARY	我有兩個星期的時間，想去西安，三峽，廣州等。
LI LIANG	我覺得，你最好去完三峽後去雲南，不去廣州。
MARY	為什麼？

LI LIANG　　一是因為雲南有許多自然風景，二是因為三峽和雲南都在中國的西南部。廣州你可以下次去桂林的時候再去。

MARY　　　有道理。去雲南坐火車好還是飛機好？

LI LIANG　　坐火車好，因為這樣你可以看到沿途美麗的景色。

......

Dialogue 2　上城牆

MARK　　　　對不起，我想參觀城牆。你知道從哪兒上去嗎？

WANG MENG　真不好意思，我也不太清楚。我也是外地人，剛好也想到城牆上走走。這樣吧，我去打聽一下，然後咱們可以一起去。

MARK　　　　太好了，多謝。

(a few minutes later . . .)

WANG MENG　打聽清楚了，離這兒不遠的南門有個入口處。我們順著這條街一直走到底，就可以看見大門了。

MARK　　　　要走多久？

WANG MENG　大約十分鐘。

(after having visited the Wall . . .)

MARK　　　　多虧了你，我今天玩得高興極了。

WANG MENG　我也是。你的漢語這麼好，而且對中國的文化也有很深的瞭解，真讓我佩服。

MARK　　　　多謝誇獎。我明天准備去兵馬俑。你去過兵馬俑嗎？

WANG MENG　還沒去過呢。

MARK　　　　咱們一起去，好嗎？

WANG MENG　那太棒了！

Reading comprehension　一篇日記

　　我現在正在西安火車站等車去重慶，抽空寫篇日記。我這幾天在西安玩得很開心。這是一個古老的城市，原名叫長安，十多個朝代曾在這兒建都，所以西安的名勝古蹟很多。今天上午我去了著名的兵馬俑，規模那麼大，真讓人不敢相信。展出的兵和馬有上

千個，可每個士兵的面部表情都不一樣。這個城市看上去整整
齊齊，一是因為全城的中心是鐘樓，四面有東、南、西、北四條
大街，二是因為主要街道都很直。西安還保留了古城牆，城牆有
四個入口處，分別為：東門、南門、西門和北門。游人可以到城
牆上參觀，還可以在上面騎自行車呢！

Unit 3　健康

Dialogue 1　看醫生

DOCTOR	你好！請坐。
JANE	你好！大夫。
DOCTOR	你哪兒不舒服？
JANE	我頭疼，嗓子也疼。反正全身沒勁。
DOCTOR	什麼時候開始的？
JANE	兩天前。
DOCTOR	發燒嗎？
JANE	好像有點兒。
DOCTOR	給你量一下體溫。

(having checked the thermometer)

DOCTOR	你發燒了。三十八度五。
JANE	我得了什麼病？
DOCTOR	重感冒。不要緊。我給你開一些退燒藥。再吃幾副中藥。
JANE	熬中藥太麻煩。您給我開一些中成藥吧。
DOCTOR	沒問題。你一定要按時吃藥。多喝水，多休息。過兩天就會好的。
JANE	大夫，您能給我開一張病假條嗎？
DOCTOR	當然可以。我給你開三天。
JANE	謝謝，大夫。

Dialogue 2　談論身體

XIAO LI	老王，您最近氣色不錯。有什麼秘方？
LAO WANG	什麼秘方都沒有，小李。就是生活很有規律。比如早睡早起。而且每天慢跑半個小時。

Xiao Li	我應該向您學習。我最近總是頭暈，睡覺不好。
Lao Wang	看醫生了嗎?
Xiao Li	看了，可是沒查出什麼問題。
Lao Wang	你每天幾點睡覺?
Xiao Li	大概十二點左右。
Lao Wang	鍛煉身體嗎?
Xiao Li	不鍛煉。
Lao Wang	我覺得你應該改變你的生活習慣。晚上早些睡覺，並且做些運動。
Xiao Li	您說的對。我從明天就開始。

Listening comprehension script

在中國，你應該早上去公園看看，那兒特別熱鬧。有打太極拳的，有做健美操的，也有在音樂的伴奏下跳舞的。你如果有興趣的話，也可以跟著一起學。大多數在公園運動的人是退休的老人。就拿我來說吧，今年已經六十八歲了，可我很少感冒生病。你看我的氣色不錯吧。那是因為我每天早上都去公園鍛煉身體。有時候我打太極拳，有時候我跳健美操。如果我孫子和我一起去公園，我們還打打羽毛球。另外，每天吃完晚飯後，我和老伴常常一起出去散步。

Unit 4　聚會和飲食

Dialogue 1　聚會

Jane	麗麗，這個週日，我要請幾個朋友來吃飯。你能來嗎?
Lili	吃午飯還是晚飯?
Jane	晚飯，七點左右。
Lili	那，我能來。
Jane	太好了。這樣，我們可以包餃子吃。
Lili	包餃子很費時間。你最好叫幾個朋友早些到，幫我們一起包。我五點左右可以到你那兒。
Jane	我需要買些什麼?
Lili	買幾斤豬肉末，一顆大白菜，幾根蔥，還有麵粉。
Jane	需要什麼調料?

Lili	醬油，鹽，香油，五香粉和雞蛋。
Jane	這些我都有。
Lili	你會調餡嗎？
Jane	不會，你告訴我怎麼調。
Lili	比較複雜，說不清。還是等我到了你家後，咱們再調餡、和麵。
Jane	好吧。周日五點見。
Lili	需要我帶一些什麼去？
Jane	什麼都不要帶。你幫我包餃子就是最好的禮物。

Dialogue 2   中餐和西餐

Teacher	你喜歡吃中餐還是西餐？
John	'中餐' 是什麼意思？
Teacher	就是 '中國飯'。
John	我十分喜歡中餐。不過早飯，我喜歡吃西式的。
Teacher	你能不能告訴大家 '中餐' 和 '西餐' 有什麼不同的地方？
John	我試試。中餐的主食主要是米飯和麵條，而西餐以土豆和麵包為主。
Teacher	很好，其他同學有什麼需要補充嗎？
Anne	我有。中國飯每頓飯有好幾個菜，西餐一般只有一個菜。
James	我想補充一點。做中國菜準備的時間比較長，比如，要把肉和菜先切成小塊，然後再做。
Teacher	誰能說說中國菜的做法和西餐有什麼不同？
John	中國菜主要是炒，蒸，燉；而西餐主要是用烤箱烤或者煮。
Teacher	大家都說得很好。最後，在吃的方法上，中西餐有什麼不同？
James	老師，這個問題太簡單了。中國人吃飯用筷子，而西方人用刀叉。

Listening comprehension script

Wang Li	麗萍，我特別喜歡吃蛋炒飯。你會做嗎？
Liping	會，非常簡單。
Wang Li	需要什麼作料？
Liping	剩米飯，雞蛋和蔥。
Wang Li	調料呢？

LIPING	菜油，鹽和五香粉。
WANG LI	這些我都有。
LIPING	太好了。準備工作只需要做兩件事，第一：把雞蛋打碎，加點兒鹽一起打。第二：把蔥切碎。
WANG LI	我記住了。然後呢？
LIPING	倒一些菜油在炒鍋裡，等油熱了後，先把蔥倒進去炒幾下，再把打碎的雞蛋倒進去，炒一分鐘左右，最後把剩飯倒進去，炒兩三分鐘後，加一點兒鹽和五香粉，稍微再炒幾下，就可以吃了。
WANG LI	聽上去很容易。今天晚上我就試試。

Unit 5　過年

Text 1　怎麼過年

在中國的傳統節日裡，最重要的就是春節。春節是農曆的新年。很多中國人把它叫'過年'，而西方人把它稱為'中國新年'。春節通常是在一月底或者二月初。中國人是怎麼過年的呢？和西方人過聖誕節差不多，這是一個全家團聚的節日。除夕晚上全家人要吃團圓飯，北方人的飯桌上一定有餃子，南方人一定有春卷。全家人一邊吃一邊看電視，一直看到午夜，然後放鞭砲，歡迎新的一年的到來。有些人家按照老習慣'守夜'，整晚上不睡覺。第二天一大早，也就是大年初一，鄰居朋友和親戚到各家去拜年，互相祝賀新年。從初二開始走親戚，也就是去親戚家拜年，吃飯。比如，去看奶奶，爺爺。也可以跟朋友，同學，同事聚會。在農村，正月十五的元宵節後，春節才算過完。

Dialogue 1　過年好

LAO LI	老王，過年好！
LAO WANG	老李，過年好！這麼早就來拜年了。你的孩子們都回來了嗎？
LAO LI	今年我們家可熱鬧了，兩個兒子和他們的媳婦，還有孫女都回來了。你家呢？
LAO WANG	我家老大今年沒回來，輪到他值班，兩個女兒回來了。
LAO LI	初三你們有空嗎？到我家去吃餃子吧。
LAO WANG	有空。我正要請你們全家過來呢！我們也帶幾個菜去。

LAO LI	那太好了！你夫人的菜是出了名的好吃。
LAO WANG	幾點？
LAO LI	六點怎麼樣？
LAO WANG	行。

Dialogue 2　看朋友

LIPING	你怎麼才來？我還以為你不來了。
MEILI	真對不起。這幾天我都忙暈了。
LIPING	為什麼？你們家有媽媽做飯，又不用你忙。
MEILI	嗨，別提了。我姐姐把他們三歲的女孩帶來了。這兩天，她和我姐夫出去看朋友，我留在家看外甥女。累死我了！
LIPING	今天你可以休息休息。你不用做飯，也不用看孩子！
MEILI	今天吃什麼好吃的？
LIPING	春卷，還有別的菜。馬上就可以吃飯。
MEILI	這麼快就做好了。你太偉大了！

Reading comprehension

老王的大兒子王強是天津一家醫院的醫生。今年輪到他大年初一值班，所以他不能回北京的父母家。初一早上，他打電話給父母拜了年，然後就去了醫院。一直到晚上七點王強才回家。回家後，他五歲的女兒說：'爸爸，我想去看奶奶，爺爺，給他們拜年。' 王強和妻子商量了一下，決定初三去北京住幾天。女兒聽說後，高興極了！

初三他們三個人坐火車到了北京。王強的父母看到大兒子，大兒媳，還有孫女都來了，高興地說 '我們還以為今年春節見不到你們了' 王強的兩個妹妹也激動地說：'這下，我們家也熱鬧了'！

Unit 6　興趣和愛好

Text 1　中國文學

在我們家，我父母喜歡音樂，我哥哥愛好足球，我奶奶特別喜歡養花，我爺爺是個電影迷。至於我呢，我也喜歡電影，但我更喜歡文學。自從學中文以來，我對中國文學越來越感興趣。我已經讀過了一些中國文學作品的英文翻譯，比如《紅樓夢》和《家》。《紅樓夢》是一部古典長篇小說，裡面的人物特別多。剛開始讀的時候，總是記不住有些人的名字。《家》是一部現代小說，裡面的人物不多，比較容易讀。這兩部作品都很有意思。最近，我正在讀老舍的名著《駱駝祥子》。 這一次，我讀的是中文的原著！這是我第一次讀原著，困難可真不小。我不得不一邊查字典，一邊看。有時候，一句話要看好幾遍。但是，看懂了後心裡特別高興。

Dialogue 1 看比賽

DAMING 約翰，你有什麼愛好？
JOHN 體育，特別喜歡球類運動。
DAMING 真的？我也喜歡球類運動，最喜歡足球。
JOHN 我也是！我上小學的時候是校隊的。你呢？
DAMING 我踢得不好，但非常喜歡看比賽。說到比賽，我有兩張明天足球賽的票。你想去看嗎？
JOHN 誰跟誰踢？
DAMING 北京隊跟廣州隊。
JOHN 太好了！這兩個隊都很強。我當然要去看了。比賽幾點開始，在什麼地方？
DAMING 明天早上十一點，在北京首都體育館。
JOHN 什麼？在北京！我還以為在天津呢！
DAMING 那有什麼。坐火車一個小時就到北京了。
JOHN 倒也是。好吧，我明天早點兒起床。八點半去找你，行嗎？
DAMING 行。你起得來嗎？用不用我八點給你打個電話？
JOHN 不用！只要是看球賽，六點起床也可以！

Listening comprehension script

HUAYING 約翰，你看過《駱駝祥子》的電影嗎？
JOHN 沒有。但是我看過這本書的英文翻譯。非常喜歡。
HUAYING 你想看這部電影嗎？
JOHN 有沒有英文字幕？
HUAYING 可惜沒有。

JOHN	那，我看得懂嗎？
HUAYING	你的中文這麼好，一定看得懂。
JOHN:	謝謝你的誇獎。
HUAYING	你同意去看了？
JOHN	同意了。不過，我看不懂的地方，你一定要向我解釋。
HUAYING	那當然了。我現在就去買票。你想看今天晚上的還是明天晚上的？
JOHN	今天晚上的。
HUAYING	沒問題。一會兒我給你打電話。

Unit 7　教育

Text 1　一封信

燕春：

你好！謝謝你的來信。

新的學期剛剛開始，事情特別多。加上我剛來這裡，對一切都不熟悉。好在同事們和家長們都很熱心，給了我很多的幫助。校長讓我當一年級一個班的班主任，並且讓我教一年級所有班的算術課。一年級一共有三個班，每個班有大約四十個學生。

和城裡的孩子一樣，這兒的孩子也是六歲上學。不過，和城裡的學校比起來，這兒的條件差多了。讓我高興的是，這兒的學生十分用功，專一。農村沒有什麼讓他們分心的事，所以他們可以集中注意力。

一會兒我要帶全班去參觀圖書館，不能多寫了。等我有空時再給你寫封長信。

祝好！

陳青

Dialogue 1　中英大學生活

LI LAN	張偉，你在英國學習了三年。能不能給我講講中英大學生活有什麼不同？

ZHANG WEI	中國大學本科一般是四年，而英國大部份學科只需要三年。英國的碩士課程一般只用一年，而中國卻要學三年。
LI LAN	這麼說，和英國的學生比起來，我們在學校花的時間長得多。
ZHANG WEI	沒錯。另外，中國的大學每年有兩個學期，而英國有三個學期，所以有三次假期。放假的時候，許多學生都打工，賺些錢後，出去旅游。
LI LAN	現在，中國的不少大學生假期也出去打工了。英國學生業餘時間常常做什麼？
ZHANG WEI	參加各種俱樂部，比如：辯論俱樂部，戲劇俱樂部等。週末，學生們常去酒吧聚會。他們喝起酒來，比中國學生厲害得多！
LI LAN	大學裡可以談戀愛嗎？
ZHANG WEI	當然可以了。這些事情校方從來不管。再說，英國學生都是一个人一間臥室，談戀愛也比較方便！

Reading comprehension script　在中國教英文

李老師：

您好！

上次給您寫信時，我還在北京學中文。今年九月，一個中國朋友介紹我來太原的一所小學教英文。我已經在這兒工作了三個月了。和北京比起來，太原的生活條件差得多，冬天也冷得多。不過，這兒的孩子特別用功。每天早上八點上課，下午五點才下課。大部份學生回家吃中午飯。孩子們把我叫'老師'，我不太習慣。我讓他們叫我名字，可是他們說不行。學生的家長們也非常熱心，週末常常請我去他們家吃飯。我真的很喜歡我的工作。

我們一月中旬放寒假，到時候我準備去西安旅游，再去北京和我從前學中文時認識的朋友們一起過年。

聖誕節快到了，祝您和全家聖誕快樂！

蘇珊

Unit 8　工作

Text 1　找工作

直到八十年代底，中國的大學生不用自己找工作。即便你想自己
找工作，也不可能。每個畢業生的工作都是由學校分配的。當
然，學校的領導也徵求個人的意見，但是最後的決定是別人為你
做的。所以，那個時候根本沒有選擇的自由，也沒有什麼招聘廣
告，工作面試。現在情況不一樣了。大學畢業後要自己找工作。
這樣一來便出現了招聘廣告，就業網站，人才市場等等。同時也
出現了選擇帶來的煩惱。

Dialogue 1　申請工作

ZHANG LAN　珍妮，今天我在《北京晚報》上看到一份工作，我想
申請。

JANE　是什麼工作？

ZHANG LAN　一家駐京的美國辦事處需要一名經理助理兼翻譯。所有的
申請材料必須用英文。你能幫助我修改一下我的簡歷和
申請信嗎？

JANE　當然可以。如果你帶來了的話，我現在就可以給你看看。

ZHANG LAN　來太棒了。材料都在我的包裡。給你。

(*a few minutes later . . .*)

JANE　簡歷沒有問題。可以加上你的興趣愛好，比如會彈鋼琴
什麼的。申請信裡應該說明你為什麼認為自己能做好這份
工作。

ZHANG LAN　那，他們會不會覺得我不謙虛，在吹牛？

JANE　要是老闆是美國人，你太謙虛的話，他會認為你沒有
自信心。

ZHANG LAN　你的建議太寶貴了。如果我拿到面試，還要再麻煩你幫助
準備。

JANE　沒問題。祝你好運！

Listening comprehension script　換工作

JAMES	你開出租車開了多久了？
DRIVER	只有兩年多。
JAMES	從前你是做什麼工作的？
DRIVER	如果告訴你，你可能不相信。我從前在教育部為領導開車。
JAMES	真的？ 那，為什麼換了這個工作？
DRIVER	原因很多，不過主要是太不自由。我在報紙上看到這個出租車公司在招聘司機，工作時間靈活，而且工資比我從前的高。我便申請了。
JAMES	現在的工作和從前的比，是不是忙一些？
DRIVER	是的，不過，我可以自己決定一天工作多少個小時，比較自由。
JAMES	你一般每天工作多少個小時？
DRIVER	差不多十個小時。
JAMES	這家公司有多少個僱員？
DRIVER	我也不太清楚。大概六十多個司機。
JAMES	是嗎？ 是個不小的公司。

Unit 9　交通與環境

Text 1　自行車與汽車

上個世紀六十年代，七十年代，中國被稱為'自行車王國'。那個時候幾乎沒有私家車，自行車是大多數人的主要交通工具，自行車比汽車多得多。上班的人要騎車，許多上學的學生也得騎車。有些人家每人都有一輛自行車。現在情況不同了，私家車和出租車越來越多，路面上的汽車也就越來越多。汽車數量增加帶來的兩大後果是：交通堵塞和空氣污染。這是中國城市目前急需解決的兩個嚴重問題，特別是在北京和其他一些大城市。

Dialogue 1　騎自行車的好處

LIN MEI	麥克，你為什麼不開車上班？
MIKE	原因很多。主要原因是，我住得離咱們辦公室不遠，騎車只需十五分鐘，可開車的話，這條路常常堵塞。有一次我開車來上班，結果叫車給堵了一個多小時。

LIN MEI	這倒也是。不過,下雨時騎車不太方便。
MIKE	好在北京氣候比較干燥,不常常下雨。從環境保護的角度來說,自行車不消耗能源,不污染環境。
LIN MEI	我完全同意。我認為政府應該限制私家車,提倡騎自行車,並且給騎車人提供安全措施。
MIKE	太對了。比如,騎車人的專用車道。我騎車的另一個原因是為了鍛煉身體。否則,工作那麼忙,沒有時間鍛煉身體。
LIN MEI	有道理,我也應該考慮騎自行車上班。最近,我的體重增加了不少。

Reading comprehension

尊敬的編輯:

　　我的老家在浙江的一個農村。村子邊上有一條小河,我記得河水清清的。小時候,夏天的時候,我和朋友們常在這條小河裡游泳。後來我上大學,離開了家鄉。上個月我回老家看奶奶,高興地看到家鄉的許多變化。但是其中有一個變化真讓我難過: 這條河被污染了! 河水比從前髒得多,而且也臭。我問奶奶這是什麼。她告訴我: 村裡建起了幾個小化工廠,這些工廠把廢水往河裡倒。村裡的人們都提意見,要求這些工廠清理這條河,否則就關門。這幾個廠的廠長們都同意了。我希望這些廠長們說到做到。

王紅

Unit 10　電腦和互聯網

Text 1　信息革命

　　二十年前,大部分中國老百姓家庭連電話都沒有,更別說電腦了。那時候,人們根本沒想到二十年後的今天,在城裡幾乎每家都有電話,手機也十分普及。很多人家不但有電腦,而且還安裝了寬帶。人們不僅可以隨時上網查詢需要的信息,發電子郵件,還可以在網上用信用卡購物,甚至在網上同國外的親戚朋友免費聊天。即便家裡不能上網,去網吧也很方便。這真是一場名副其實的信息革命。

Dialogue 1 去網吧

YUSUKI 嗨,珍妮! 去哪兒?

JANE 別提了。不知是我的電腦出毛病了,還是今天學院的互聯網有問題。反正我怎麼也上不了網。我去校外的網吧試試。

YUSUKI 別急! 你的電腦沒問題,是學院的服務器今天在維修。不瞞你說,我的電腦也上不了網。我也剛從網吧回來。

JANE 這下我放心了。校外的哪個網吧網速快?

YUSUKI 都差不多,不過,咱們學院大門對面的那家叫 '籃天' 的環境比較好。

JANE 謝謝! 我這就去。

Dialogue 2 電子郵件

HUANG WEI 聽說你買了個筆記本電腦,好用嗎?

REN YUAN 挺好用的。我正在學怎麼用。昨天剛學會了怎麼發電子郵件。

HUANG WEI 我早就聽說過電子郵件,可就是不知道是什麼。大姐,你真不簡單。怎麼發電子郵件?

REN YUAN 一時半會兒說不清。下次你到我家來,我給你演示一下。可神啦! 昨晚,我收到了我兒子從法國發回來的郵件,激動得半天睡不著覺。

HUANG WEI 好,我過幾天去你家見識見識。

Listening comprehension script 查電子郵件

MINGFU 約翰,我的電腦壞了。你能不能幫我修一修?

JOHN 我試試吧。我剛好現在有空。

MINGFU 太謝謝你了!

JOHN 明富,我看你的電腦沒有什麼問題。為什麼你說壞了?

MINGFU 因為剛才我想上網,可是上不了。

JOHN 別急! 那是因為學校的服務器今天在維修。

MINGFU 原來如此! 那我就放心了。可是我今天必須查我的電子郵件,那天給我工作面試的公司說今天通知我們。

JOHN 你可以去校外的網吧查。

MINGFU 　　我從來沒有去過。哪家好？
JOHN 　　　都差不多，價錢也差不多。
MINGFU 　　好吧，我這就去。
JOHN 　　　希望你收到好消息！
MINGFU 　　謝謝！

Authentic text

上網聊天是壞事嗎？

　　上網聊天是不是件很壞的事？我這人自製力差，一上網就想聊天，你能幫助我嗎？

心煩女孩

心煩女孩：
　　你好！上網聊天是網絡時代的一種人際溝通和交往的方式，就像打電話一樣，本身沒好壞之分。但是，如果你上網聊天沒有節制，以至於影響了學習，甚至影響身體健康或像報紙上報道的一樣上了壞人的當，那上聊天對你來說就是有害的事情了。我想，你寫這封信就說明上網聊天已經給你的生活帶來了麻煩，你希望能對此有一定的控制，這要求你對上網聊天給自己帶來的害處有深深的反省和認識，並下定決心改變現狀。你的決心越大，見效越快。
　　戒除或者控制上網聊天有兩類辦法：漸進法和厭惡法。如果實行漸進法，你應該逐步減少每天的上網聊天時間。例如，如果你現在每天都要花1小時聊天，那你可以規定下周每天聊天時間不能超過50分鐘，下下周每天聊天不能超過40分鐘等等。逐步減少聊天時間，達到你認為合適的量。. . .

選自《中國青年》2002/3, 64頁

Unit 11 婚姻與子女

Text 1 昨天和今天的婚姻

中國曾是世界上離婚率最低的國家之一。這也許和傳統的婚姻觀念有關係。從前,很多的婚姻是包辦婚姻,也就是說:父母決定你和誰結婚。不管你愛不愛對方,一旦結了婚,就必須白頭到老。許多夫婦說他們是先結婚再戀愛。還有許多夫婦在沒有愛的婚姻中生活了一輩子。如今,年青人重視愛情,追求幸福,比他們的長輩浪漫得多。他們不願意別人給自己介紹對象,因為那樣太不浪漫。他們寧願不結婚,也不願和自己不愛的人結婚。即使結了婚,如果愛情消逝,他們也不願意湊合著過。所以,離婚率開始逐漸上昇。

Text 2 關於子女

傳統的觀念是:多子多福,意思是:孩子越多,福氣越多。生孩子首先是為了傳宗接代,所以就出現了重男輕女的現象;其次是為了老年時有人照顧自己,所以老人總是同子女住在一起。現在的觀念變了:由於獨生子女政策,許多家庭只有一個孩子,所以無論男孩還是女孩,他們都是父母的寶貝。再說,現在的生活條件好了,老人不像從前那麼依靠子女,所以越來越多的老人願意獨立生活。

Dialogue 1 婚禮

LAO LIU 你們什麼時候給寶貝女兒辦喜事?

LAO WANG 本來準備大年初一辦的,可不巧她從初一到初三在醫院值班。只好把婚禮推遲到十五。

LAO LIU 這樣也好,先過年再辦喜事。

LAO WANG 到時候你們兩口子一定要來喝喜酒。

LAO LIU 謝謝,一定來。如果需要我們幫忙,儘管說。

LAO WANG 好的。

Dialogue 2 佈置新房

YING　　　老頭子，昨天我讓你買一束玫瑰花，你買了嗎?
LAO WANG　糟糕! 我把這件事忘了! 我現在馬上去買。
YING　　　快去快回。

(*a little later . . .*)

LAO WANG　花來了! 放在哪兒?
YING　　　你順手把那個水晶花瓶給我拿過來，我來放。
LAO WANG　行。對了，你妹妹送來的那個雙喜剪紙大字到哪兒去了?
YING　　　你轉過身往上看。
LAO WANG　嘿，真棒! 這個新房讓你這麼一佈置，更漂亮了!
YING　　　還是我的老頭子會說話!

Reading comprehension script 我父母的婚姻

我的爺爺奶奶被大家認為是村裡最開明的人，可是，他們就是不同意父親自己找的對象，一定要讓他娶我的母親。父親和母親結婚前只見過一面，根本不瞭解對方，更別說愛情了。父親說，結婚的那天，他很難過，因為他不能和他愛的姑娘結婚。而母親呢，她的心裡也很緊張，因為她不知道父親會不會喜歡她。幸運的是，他們結婚後相處得很好，慢慢地有了感情。而有很多和我父母情況一樣的人結婚後卻相處得不好，在沒有愛的婚姻中湊合了一輩子，一輩子不幸福。

Authentic text

日子 '各過各'

　　傳統觀念認為，老人應該與兒女晚輩生活在一起，共享天倫之樂。然而，如今的老人則不然，他們一個個要與兒女分開過，想享享晚年清閒。'寧願出錢不願心煩' 已經在一些老年人中形成共識。據近期對一些大、中城市的調查結果表明，有70%以上的老人與兒女 '各過各'。

　　現今城市的老人們，經濟上大都獨立支撐，也有自己安身的住房。退休後，他們要參加各種社會活動，有的還根據自己的特長，受聘於各企業、社團去發揮余熱。如果他們與晚輩住在一起，勢必要受一輩子買菜、煮飯、帶孩子等家務雜活的牽累。

一位與兒子分開過的老人直率地說，'我們老了，應把保健身體放在第一位。如果與兒孫住在一起，表面上看熱鬧得很，其實這對我們和兒孫都不利。我們奮鬥大半輩子了，為子女付出了很多，該休息休息了。同時，我們與年輕人在思想認識、生活習慣等諸多方面都存有分歧，如果長期生活在一起，容易產生矛盾。因此，還是分開過好。'

選自《青年一代》, 2004/7, 4

Unit 12　改革和變化

Text 1　成功的鄉鎮企業

中國的經濟改革帶來的成果之一是鄉鎮企業。昨天，我參觀了一家鄉鎮企業，給我留下了很深的印象。這是一家生產皮鞋的廠家。十年前才成立，當時只有十個人，現在已經有兩百個僱員了。他們生產的鞋子款式新穎，質量好，很受消費者的歡迎。百分之五十的產品出口到世界各地。這個廠成功的經驗是：保證質量，注重款式，重視消費者提的意見，並且定期做市場調研。他們成功的另一條經驗是：無論是經理還是普通工人，大家平等相待，互相尊重。

Text 2　一封來自中國農村的信

大衛：

你好！近來學習忙嗎？

好久沒有聯繫。我們家里變化很大，我們村的變化更大。先說說我們家，我上個月結了婚，丈夫在一家鄉鎮企業當會計。我從農業銀行貸款辦了個流動圖書館，每天在附近幾個村來回跑，很受大家的歡迎。在你的影響下，我開始學習英文了！下次，我會用英文給你寫信的。我哥哥和我爸媽還是忙著種菜，今年又增加了兩個新品種 – 西藍花和櫻桃西紅柿。村子里好多人家都蓋起了二層小樓房，裝上了電話，還有幾家買了電腦呢！

你最近有什麼新聞？有空請來信。大家都很想你。

祝好！

小芳

Dialogue 1　小鎮的變化

ZHIYUAN　媽媽，咱們鎮的變化太大了。我都認不出來了。

MAMA　別說你認不出來，就連你哥哥上次回家還差點兒迷了路。你快三年沒回來了吧？

ZHIYUAN　是啊！哥哥多久回來一次？

MAMA　他幾乎每半年回來一次。

ZHIYUAN　我做夢也沒想到人們的生活水平提高得這麼快。

MAMA　誰能想到！要是你父親還活着該多好！

ZHIYUAN　是啊！不過，他會為我們高興的。對了，我和父親最喜歡的那條小河還在嗎？

MAMA　在，前幾年河水被污染了，最近才清理幹淨。

ZHIYUAN　太好了！明天我就去游個泳。

MAMA　雖然清理乾淨了，但是河水不像從前那麼清了。你自己去看看吧。

Dialogue 2　合資企業

WU YU　爸爸，告訴你一個好消息！遠森藥品有限公司給了我一份工作。

FATHER　是嗎？這是一家什麼樣的企業？

WU YU　是中美合資企業。

FATHER　真的！那，你具體做什麼工作？

WU YU　銷售部經理。

FATHER　赫！一個很重要的職務。我的女兒真不簡單！

WU YU　別誇我了。說真的，我昨晚高興得一晚上睡不着覺。

FATHER　那，你今天在家好好休息休息。

Listening comprehension script　開網吧

DAPING　聽說你上個月下崗了？

HUIFENG　是的，不過也許不是一件壞事。我想開一個網吧。

DAPING　你做市場調研了嗎？

HUIFENG　做了，咱們這個區一個網吧都沒有。想上網的人不少，可自己家有寬帶的人很少。

DAPING　聽上去是一個能賺錢的生意。你有足夠的資金嗎？

HUIFENG	我自己有一些存款，還可以從銀行貸一些款。
DAPING	你真不簡單!
HUIFENG	我還沒開始呢，你就誇我了。說真的，我想請你幫個忙。
DAPING	儘管說。
HUIFENG	我對電腦不太熟悉。你能不能抽空給我介紹一些常用的軟件?
DAPING	當然可以。
HUIFENG	你哪天有空?
DAPING	下周三吧。哎呀，不行。下週三我去上海出差。下週末吧。
HUIFENG	可以，過幾天我給你打電話約具體的時間。

Authentic text

江西实现全省村村通电话

江西省宜黃縣仙坪村村民管常福給在廣東南海打工的愛人撥通了電話：'喂！家里裝電話了，以後有事記得就打這個電話。'隨著仙坪村通上電話，江西省17955個行政村實現了村村通電話，成為我國中西部地區第一個實現村村通電話的省份。

到去年底，江西省還有933個行政村未通電話。這些村多半屬於'老、山、邊、窮'地區，自然、交通狀況差，施工難度也大。為幫助電信企業克服資金困難，確保工程按時完成，江西省政府出臺了一系列優惠獎勵措施，....對村村通電話工程大開綠燈。

村村通電話工程不僅給農民生活帶來便利，也為農民創造了實實在在的經濟財富。... 村民胡典發激動地说：'以前，我們都是挑著茶油走20公里的小路到山外去賣，因為沒有事先聯繫好，老賣不出去，還白跑冤枉路。現在有了電話，我們就可以隨時和外面聯繫，做買賣方便多了！'

選自《人民日報》2005年9月25日頭版

Appendix B: English translation of the authentic texts in Units 10, 11 and 12

Unit 10

Is it a bad thing to chat online?

Is it a really bad thing to chat online? I am the kind of person who lacks self-discipline. Whenever I go online, I want to chat. Will you help me please?

A troubled girl

Dear troubled girl:

How do you do!

Online chatting is a type of human communication and interacting in the internet age. It is like making telephone calls, which in itself is neither good nor bad. However, if you exercise no limit over the online chatting (time) to the extent of affecting your school work (or your study), or even affecting your health, or falling prey to bad people as reported in the newspapers, then chatting online would be a harmful thing for you. In my view, the fact that you wrote me this letter itself has indicated that online chatting has already brought trouble to your life, and that you hope to have certain control over the situation. This requires your deep reflection and realisation about the harmfulness brought to yourself, and the determination to change the current situation. The firmer your determination, the sooner it will take effect.

There are two approaches to giving up or controlling online chatting: the gradual approach and the aversion approach. If you carry out the gradual approach, you should progressively reduce the time spent each day online chatting. For example, if at the moment you spend one hour each day on chatting, then you can set the rule that next week the daily chatting time must not exceed 50 minutes, and the week after 40 minutes, etc., etc. The chatting time is gradually reduced until it is down to the duration that you think is right.

Unit 11

Leading one's own life

Traditional views hold that elderly people should live together with their children, enjoying the pleasures of family life. However, elderly people nowadays think differently. Many of them want to live separately from their children as they want to enjoy the happiness of a leisurely and relaxed life-style. The saying that 'We would rather contribute financially than be troubled with work' (i.e. to give children money rather than living together and helping them out with the housework) has become common amongst some elderly people. According to the results of recent surveys on large and middle-sized cities, 70 per cent of elderly people live apart from their children.

These days, the majority of elderly people in cities are financially independent, and they also have their own houses for comfortable shelter. After retirement, they want to take part in various social activities. Some, depending on their strengths, are even employed in various companies and communities. If they live with their children, they are bound to be tied down with household chores such as shopping for food, cooking and looking after grandchildren for the rest of their lives.

One elderly person who lives apart from his son's family said frankly: 'We are getting old, and we should give priority to looking after our own health. If we live with our children and grandchildren, it appears exciting on the surface, but in fact it is harmful to both ourselves and our children and grandchildren. We have worked hard for over half of our life and have done a lot for our children. It is time for us to have a rest. At the same time, there are differences between us and the younger generation in terms of ways of thinking, living habits, and many other aspects. If we live together long-term, conflicts are likely to occur. Therefore, it is better to live apart.'

Unit 12

All the villages in Jiangxi province have had a telephone connection

Guan Changfu, resident of Xianping village of Yihuang county of Jiangxi province, has made a phone call to his wife who is working in Nanhai in Guangdong province: 'Hello, we've installed a telephone in the house now. Please remember to call us in future if there are things to sort out.' Every one of 17,955 villages in Jiangxi province is connected by telephone. It has become the first province in west central China to realise the possibility of having telephones installed in every village.

By the end of last year, there were still 933 administrative villages that had not been connected by telephone. The majority of these villages belong to 'old, mountainous, remote and poor' areas whose natural and transport conditions were poor. Therefore, the level of difficulty in installation was high. In order to help telecommunication companies overcome financial difficulties and guarantee the completion of the project on time, the provincial government came up with a series of measures for preferential treatment and reward, . . . providing help for the telephone installation project in every village.

The telephone being installed in every village has brought convenience to the peasants and also it has created real economic wealth for them. Villager Hu Dianfa said excitedly: 'Before, we all had to walk 20 kilometres on small paths carrying the tea tree oil on a pole, in order to sell it outside the mountain area. Because things were not arranged beforehand, we often couldn't sell it and so made fruitless trips. Now we've got the telephone we can get in touch with people outside the mountain area at any time. Doing business is a lot easier now!'

Chinese–English glossary

The following entries include words under the following headings: Vocabulary, Additional useful words, Useful words for exercises (and some words used in exercises after Unit 8) and Key words for Reading comprehension and Listening comprehension. The numbers indicate the units in which they appear. The * means that the word listed occurred in the Authentic text of the numbered unit.

ài	爱	to love	11
àihào	爱好	to like something as a hobby; hobby	6
àiqíng	爱情	love (noun)	11
āi'yā	哎呀	ah; my God	12
àn zhào	按照	according to	5
ānquán	安全	safety; safe	9
ānshēn	安身	sheltering; take shelter	11*
ànshí	按时	on time; at prescribed intervals; according to time	2, 3
ānzhuāng	安装	to install; to connect	10
áo	熬	to simmer	3
bǎ . . . qiēchéng	把 . . . 切成	to cut . . . into	4
bǎi	百	hundred	1
bài nián	拜年	to exchange New Year's greetings; to wish somebody Happy New Year	5
bái pǎo yuānwang lù	白跑冤枉路	to make a fruitless trip	12*
báicài	白菜	Chinese leaves	4
bǎifēnzhī	百分之	per cent	12
bái-tóu-dào-lǎo	白头到老	grow old together (*lit.* white hair till old)	11
bàn	办	to run; to manage	12
bān	班	class (as a group)	7
bàn tiān	半天	for a long time (*lit.* half a day)	10

bàn xǐ shì	办喜事	to get married (*lit.* sort out a happy event)	11
bān zhǔrèn	班主任	class teacher	7
bāng	帮	to help	2
bàngjíle	棒极了	super	2
bāngzhù	帮助	help	2
bànshì chǔ	办事处	office; agency	8
bāo	包	bag	8
bǎo jiàn	保健	to protect and care for one's health	11*
bāo jiǎozi	包饺子	to make dumplings	4
bāobàn hūnyīn	包办婚姻	arranged marriage	11
bǎobèi	宝贝	treasure; sweetheart	11
bàodào	报道	to report	10*
bǎoguì	宝贵	precious	8
bǎohù	保护	protection; preservation	9
bǎoliú	保留	to preserve	2
bāowéi	包围	to besiege	9
bǎozhèng	保证	to guarantee	12
bàozhǐ	报纸	newspaper	8
bèi	被	(passive marker)	9
Bēi Lín	碑林	Forest of Tablets	1
běifāngde	北方的	northern	1
bèiténg	背疼	backache	3
běnkē	本科	first degree; BA	7
běnkē shēng	本科生	undergraduate student	7
běnlái	本来	originally	11
běnshēn	本身	itself	10*
biàn	变	to change	11
biàn	便	then, therefore	8
biànhuà	变化	change	9
biānjí	编辑	editor	9
biànlì	便利	convenience	12*
biànlùn	辩论	debate; debating	7
biǎo míng	表明	to show; to demonstrate	11*
biǎomiàn shàng	表面上	on surface	11*
bié jí	别急	don't worry	10
bié tí le	别提了	don't mention it!; You can well imagine	5
biérén	别人	others	8
bǐjiào	比较	rather	4
bǐjìběn	笔记本	notebook; laptop	10

bìngjià tiáo	病假条	sick note	3
Bīngmǎyǒng	兵马俑	Terracotta warriors and horses	2
bìngqiě	并且	and	3
bǐ rú	比如	for example	3
bǐsài	比赛	match (as in sports)	6
bìxū	必须	must	3
bìyè	毕业	to graduate	1
bìyè shēng	毕业生	graduate students	8
bízi bùtōng	鼻子不通	blocked nose	3
bō tōng	拨通	to have connected (the call)	12*
bóshì	博士	doctoral; PhD; Dr	7
bóshì shēng	博士生	PhD student	7
bù	部	(measure word for a literary work or film)	6
bù hǎo yìsi	不好意思	I am sorry; I'm a bit embarrassed	2
bù jiǎndān	不简单	extraordinary (lit. very not simple)	1
bù shūfu	不舒服	unwell; not comfortable	3
bú xiàng	不像	be not like	11
bú yàojǐn	不要紧	not serious	3
bú yuàn	不愿	not willing to	11*
bù zhī	不知	do not know; not be sure	10
bǔchōng	补充	to add	4
búcuò	不错	quite good	1
bùgǎn xiāngxìn	不敢相信	unbelievable	2
bùguǎn	不管	regardless; regardless of	3, 11
búguò	不过	however	1
búlì	不利	harmful; detrimental	11*
bùqiǎo	不巧	unfortunately	11
bùrán	不然	be not so; be not like this	11*
bùtóng	不同	difference; different	4
bùzhì	布置	to decorate	11
cái	才	only just	1
cài	菜	vegetables	4
cáifù	财富	wealth	12*
cáiliào	材料	materials	8
cài yóu	菜油	cooking oil	4
cānguān	参观	to visit	2
cānjiā	参加	to take part in	11*

cǎo dì	草地	grass field	1
céng	曾	once; at one time	2
chà	差	not good	10*
chà duō le	差多了	far worse	7
chá yóu	茶油	tea tree oil	12*
chá zìdiǎn	查字典	to look it up in the dictionary	6
chàbuduō	差不多	nearly; more or less the same	1, 10
cháchū	查出	to have found out	3
chàdiǎnr	差点儿	nearly	12
chǎng	场	(measure word for campaigns, matches, etc.)	10
cháng jià	长假	long holiday	7
cháng piān	长篇	long; major (e.g. a major work of fiction)	6
cháng qī	长期	long term	11*
cháng yòng	常用	in everyday use	12
Chángān	长安	(place name) (lit. forever peace)	2
chǎngjiā	厂家	factory; firm	12
chángpǎo	长跑	go jogging; long-distance run	3
chángtúchē	长途车	coach (lit. long-distance bus)	2
chǎngzhǎng	厂长	factory manager	8
chǎnpǐn	产品	product	12
chǎnshēng	产生	to produce; to emerge	11*
chǎo	炒	to stir-fry	4
chǎo-chǎo-nào-nào	吵吵闹闹	noisy; be noisy	1
cháodài	朝代	dynasty	2
chǎoguō	炒锅	wok	4
chāoguò	超过	exceed	10*
cháxún	查询	to check	10
chē	车	car	2
chéng lǐ	城里	in the city	7
chēng wéi	称为	to call something as	5
Chéngdū	成都	(city name)	1
chénggōng	成功	successful; success	12
chéngguǒ	成果	achievement	12
chénglì	成立	to set up; to establish	12

chéng qiáng	城墙	city wall	2
chéngshì	城市	city	9
chéngwéi	成为	to become; turn into	12*
chí	持	to hold; to have	8
Chóngqìng	重庆	(a city in China)	2
chòu	臭	smelly	9
chū	初	the beginning (of a month, year)	5
chū máobìng	出毛病	to break down	10
chū qián	出钱	to contribute financially	11*
chū sān	初三	the third day of the first month	5
chú xī	除夕	Chinese New Year's Eve (*lit.* to get rid of the past)	5
chuàngzào	创造	to create	12*
chuántǒng	传统	tradition; traditional	5
chuán-zōng-jiē-dài	传宗接代	to continue the family line	11
chūchu	出出	to give advice; to come up with . . .	2
chuīniú	吹牛	to boast; be boastful	8
chūkǒu	出口	to export; export	12
chūlemíng	出了名	famously	5
Chūn Jié	春节	Spring Festival	5
chūn juǎn	春卷	spring roll	5
chūtái	出台	to announce (e.g. policy, measures)	12*
chūxiàn	出现	to appear; to occur	8
chūzū qìchē	出租汽车	taxi	2
cǐ	此	this (formal)	10*
cǐ rén	此人	this person	8
cōng	葱	spring onion	4
cóng . . . jiǎodù láishuō	从 . . . 角度来说	looking from the angle of . . . ; in terms of . . .	9
cóng . . . kāishǐ	从 . . . 开始	to start from	3
cóngqián	从前	before; a while back	7
còuhe	凑合	to make do	11
cūn cūn	村村	every village	12*
cúnchē chù	存车处	bike park	9
cúnkuǎn	存款	savings; deposit	12
cūnmín	村民	villager	12*
cúnyǒu	存有	to have; to exist	11*
cūnzi	村子	village	9

cuòshī	措施	measures	9
dǎ gōng	打工	to do part-time work	7
dǎ zhēn	打针	to have an injection	3
dàbùfèn	大部分	majority	7
dádào	达到	to reach	10*
dàdōu	大都	majority	11*
dàduōshù	大多数	majority	9
dàgài	大概	approximately	3
dài háizi	带孩子	to look after children	11*
dài kuǎn	贷款	to get a loan	12
dàifu	大夫	doctor (informal)	3
dàilái	带来	to bring about	8
dàjiā	大家	everybody	12
dàmén	大门	entrance	10
dàn chǎo fàn	蛋炒饭	egg-fried rice	4
dāng	当	to act as; become; be	7
dāngrán	当然	of course	3
dànián chū yī	大年初一	Chinese New Year's Day (*lit.* first day of the new year)	5
dào	倒	to pour	4
dào nǎr qù le	到哪儿去了	where has it gone to	11
dào qù nián dǐ	到去年底	up till the end of last year	12*
dào shíhòu	到时候	when the time comes	11
dāochā	刀叉	knife and fork	4
dàochù	到处	everywhere	1
dàolù	道路	road	7
dàoyěshì	倒也是	you are right; you've got a point	6
dǎsuì	打碎	to beat it up	4
dǎtīng yīxià	打听一下	to find out	2
Dàwèi	大卫	David	12
dàxué	大学	university	7
dé . . . bìng	得 . . . 病	to get/contract (illness)	3
děng	等	etc.	2
děngděng	等等	etc.	10*
dǐ	底	the end (of a month, year)	5
dī	低	low	11
diànnǎo	电脑	computer	10
diànxìn	电信	telecommunications	12*
diànyǐng	电影	film, picture	1

diànyǐng mí	电影迷	film fan	6
diànzǐ yóujiàn	电子邮件	email	10
diàochá	调查	investigation; to investigate	11*
dìngqī	定期	regularly	12
dìqū	地区	area	12*
dú	读	to read	6
dù	度	degree	3
duǎn	短	short	2
duǎn jià	短假	short holiday	7
duànliàn	锻炼	to exercise (body)	3
duì fāng	对方	the other person	11
duì . . . dà kāi lǜdēng	对 . . . 大开绿灯	to provide help to . . . (*lit.* to switch on the green light to . . .)	12*
duì . . . gǎn xìngqu	对 . . . 感兴趣	be interested in . . .	6
duìmiàn	对面	opposite	10
duìxiàng	对象	boyfriend or girlfriend	11
dúlì	独立	independently; independent	11
dùn	顿	(measure word for a meal)	4
dùn	炖	to stew	4
duō	多	more	3
duō bàn	多半	majority	12*
duō yàng	多样	various kinds	1
duōkuīle	多亏了	thanks to . . . , because of . . .	2
duō-zǐ-duō-fú	多子多福	the more children, the more blessing	11
dúshēng zǐnǚ	独生子女	only child	11
dùziténg	肚子疼	stomach ache	3
ér	而	whereas; but	7
èr céng	二层	two-storey	12
ér xífù	儿媳妇	daughter-in-law	11
ěrduǒténg	耳朵疼	earache	3
érnǚ	儿女	children (*lit.* son daughter)	11*
érqiě	而且	furthermore	2
fā	发	to send	10
Fǎguó	法国	France	10
fàn zhuō	饭桌	dining table	5

fàng	放	to put	11
fàng biānpào	放鞭炮	to set off the fireworks	5
fàng jià	放假	to have a holiday; to be on holiday	7
fāng shì	方式	way; method	10*
fàng xīn	放心	to feel at ease; to have no worries	10
fāngbiàn	方便	convenient	7
fāngfǎ	方法	method	4
fāngmiàn	方面	aspect	1
fànguǎn	饭馆	restaurant	1
fánnǎo	烦恼	hassle; worries	8
fǎnxǐng	反省	to reflect	10*
fānyì	翻译	translation; translator; interpreter	6, 8
fǎnzhèng	反正	anyway; in a word	3
fāshāo	发烧	to have a temperature	3
fèi shuǐ	废水	waste water	9
fēijī	飞机	aeroplane	2
fèishíjiān	费时间	time-consuming	4
fèn	份	(measure word for a copy of newspaper)	8
fèn dòu	奋斗	to work hard	11*
fēn kāi guò	分开过	to lead separate lives	11*
fēn xīn	分心	with divided attention	7
fēnbié	分别	respectively	2
fēnpèi	分配	to assign	8
fēnqí	分歧	difference	11*
fǒuzé	否则	otherwise	9
fù	副	(measure word)	3
fùchū	付出	to put in a lot of hard work; to pay	11*
fūfù	夫妇	married couple	11
fùjìn	附近	nearby	12
fùmǔ	父母	parents	1
fúqì	福气	blessing	11
fūrén	夫人	wife	5
fúwùqì	服务器	server	10
fùzá	复杂	complicated; complex	4
fùzé	负责	be in charge of	8
gāi duō hǎo	该多好	would be nice	12
gǎibiàn	改变	to change	3

gàiqǐ	盖起	to build; to erect	12
gānjìng	干净	clean	12
gǎnqíng	感情	affection; emotion; feeling	11
gānzào	干燥	dry	9
gāo xué yā	高血压	high blood pressure	3
gè dì	各地	various places	12
gè guò gè	各过各	to live separately	11*
gémìng	革命	revolution	10
gēn	根	(measure word for slim and long things)	4
gēn	跟	with; against	6
gēnběn	根本	absolutely	8
gèng	更	even more	6
gèng bié shuō	更别说	let alone; not to mention	10
gēnjù	根据	according to	11*
gèrén	个人	individual	8
gòng xiǎng	共享	to enjoy . . . together	11*
gōngchéng	工程	project	12*
gōngchéngshī	工程师	engineer	8
gōnggong	公公	father-in-law (husband's father)	11
gōnggòng qìchē	公共汽车	bus (*lit.* public bus)	2
gōnglǐ	公里	kilometre	12*
gōngrén	工人	worker	8
gòngshí	共识	common belief; common understanding	11*
gōngzī	工资	salary	8
gòu wù	购物	to purchase goods; to make purchase	10
gōutōng	沟通	to communicate	10*
Gù Gōng	故宫	Forbidden City (Palace Museum)	1
guǎn	管	to be in charge; to interfere	7
Guǎn Chángfú	管常福	(personal name)	12*
Guǎngdōng	广东	(a province in southeast China)	12*
guǎnggào	广告	advertisement	8
guǎnggào shèjìshī	广告设计师	copywriter (in advertising)	8
guānniàn	观念	view; concept	11
guānyú	关于	about; on	11
gǔdiǎn	古典	classical	6

guīdìng	规定	to set; to formulate	10*
guīlǜ	规律	routine	3
guīmó	规模	scale	2
gǔlǎode	古老的	ancient	2
gūniang	姑娘	girl	11
guò jǐ tiān	过几天	in a couple of days	10
guò jiǎng	过奖	I am flattered	1
guò nián	过年	to celebrate the New Year; to spend the New Year	5
guò nián hǎo	过年好	Happy New Year	5
guó yǒu qǐyè	国有企业	state-owned enterprise	12
guójì biāozhǔn	国际标准	international standard	7
guójiā	国家	country	11
guówài	国外	abroad	10
gùyuán	雇员	employee	8
gùzhǔ	雇主	employer	8
hāi	嗨	(exclamation word); hey	5, 10
hái yǒu jiù shì	还有就是	another thing is . . .	1
hán jià	寒假	winter vacation (only used for school/university holidays)	7
hǎo jǐ biàn	好几遍	several times	6
hǎo jǐ ge cài	好几个菜	quite a few dishes	4
hǎo yòng	好用	easy to use	10
hǎoxiàng	好像	to seem; to appear; it seems	3
hǎozài	好在	just as well; it is a good job . . .	7
hè	赫	hey	12
hē qǐ jiǔ lái	喝起酒来	when it comes to drinking	7
hē xǐ jiǔ	喝喜酒	to attend the wedding banquet (lit. drink happy wine)	11
hé . . . yǒu guānxì	和 . . . 有关系	to have something to do with; to be related to	11
hé . . . bǐ qǐlái	和 . . . 比起来	compared with . . . ; in comparison with . . .	7
hēi	嘿	gosh!	11
hēiyún	黑云	black cloud	3
hémiàn	和面	to make the dough	4
héshì	合适	appropriate	10*

Hóng Lóu Mèng	红楼梦	*A Dream of Red Mansions* (novel)	6
hòuguǒ	后果	consequence	9
hòulái	后来	later	9
Hú Diǎnfā	胡典发	(personal name)	12*
huā	花	to spend	7
huàféi chǎng	化肥厂	chemical fertiliser factory	9
huài rén	坏人	bad people	10*
huài shì	坏事	a bad thing	10*
huánjìng	环境	environment; environmental	9
huāpíng	花瓶	vase	11
huàzhǎn	画展	art exhibition	2
huì shuōhuà	会说话	to know how to 'sweet talk' people	11
huìhuà	绘画	painting	2
hùliánwǎng	互联网	internet	10
hūnlǐ	婚礼	wedding	3
hūnyīn	婚姻	marriage	11
huǒchē	火车	train	2
huózhe	活着	be alive	12
huòzhě	或者	or	4
hùxiāng	互相	each other	5
jì bu zhù	记不住	cannot remember	6
jí xū	急需	urgently need	9
jià	嫁	to marry (a man)	11
jiā	家	(measure word for an organisation)	5
jiā lǐ	家里	in the family; at home	12
jiā xiāng	家乡	home town	9
jiādiǎnr	加点儿	to add a little	4
jiān	兼	simultaneously (hold two or more jobs at the same time)	8
jiàn xiào	见效	to take effect; be effective	10*
jiǎndān	简单	simple	4
jiǎngshī	讲师	lecturer	7
Jiāngxī	江西	(a province in southwest China)	12*
jiǎngxuéjīn	奖学金	scholarship	12
jiàngyóu	酱油	soya sauce	4
jiànjìn fǎ	渐进法	the gradual approach	10*

jiǎnlì	简历	curriculum vitae	8
jiànměi cāo	健美操	keep-fit exercises (*lit.* healthy beauty exercise)	3
jiànqǐ	建起	to build	9
jiǎnshǎo	减少	to reduce	10*
jiànshi	见识	to widen one's knowledge; to broaden one's experience	10
jiànyì	建议	suggestion	2
jiǎnzhǐ	剪纸	paper-cut	11
jiāo	教	to teach	7
jiāo	交	to hand in	2
jiāoliú	交流	to communicate	1
jiàoshì	教室	classroom	7
jiàoshī	教师	teacher	7
jiàoshòu	教授	professor	7
jiāotōng	交通	traffic	1
jiāotōng dǔsè	交通堵塞	traffic jam	9
jiāotōng gōngjù	交通工具	means of transport	9
jiāotōng jǐng	交通警	traffic police	9
jiāowǎng	交往	to interact	10*
jiàoyù	教育	education	7
jiàoyù bù	教育部	Ministry of Education	8
jiàqī	假期	vacation; holiday	7
jiàqián	价钱	price	10
jiārén	家人	family members; family	6
jiāshàng	加上	besides; on top of this; to add	7, 8
jiātíng	家庭	family	10
jiāwù záhuó	家务杂活	household chore	11*
jiāzhǎng	家长	parents	7
jíbiàn	即便	even if	8
jìde	记得	(still) remember	9
jīdòng	激动	excited; excitedly	5
jiē	街	avenue	2
jiè chú	戒除	to give up	10*
jiēdào	街道	street	2
jiěgù	解雇	to fire; dismiss	9
jiéguǒ	结果	result	11*
jiějué	解决	to resolve	9
jiérì	节日	festival	5

jiěshì	解释	explanation; to explain	6
jiézhì	节制	control; be moderate in	10*
jīhū	几乎	nearly	9
jǐngchá	警察	police; policeman	9
jīngjì gǎigé	经济改革	economic reform	12
jīngjì shàng	经济上	financially	11*
jīnglǐ zhùlǐ	经理助理	assistant manager	8
jǐngsè	景色	scenery	2
jīngtōng	精通	be good at; be an expert on	8
jǐnguǎn shuō	尽管说	to feel free to let us know/speak out	11
jīngyàn	经验	experience; good practice; tip	12
jìnqī	近期	recently	11*
jǐnzhāng	紧张	tense	11
jiǔbā	酒吧	bar	2
jiùyè	就业	employment	8
jíxìng	急性	acute	3
jízhōng	集中	to focus	7
jìzhù	记住	to remember	4
jù	句	sentence	1
jù	据	according to	11*
juéde	觉得	to feel, to think of	1
juédìng	决定	decision	8
jùhuì	聚会	to get together; get-together; party	4
jūlèbù	俱乐部	club	7
jùtǐ	具体	exactly; in detail	12
jùtǐdiǎn(r)	具体点	a bit detailed	1
jùyǒu	具有	to have	7
kāi wǎng	开往	to head for	7
kāi xué	开学	to start the term	7
kāichē	开车	to drive	8
kāimíng	开明	open; liberal	11
kāishǐ	开始	to start	1
kǎlā ōukēi	卡拉OK	karaoke	7
kān	看	to look after	5
kǎolǜ	考虑	to consider	9
kǎoshì	考试	examination	7
kǎoxiāng	烤箱	oven	4
kě	可	very; really	5

kē	颗	(measure word for plants and vegetables)	4
kě shén la	可神啦！	it's amazing	10
kèchéng	课程	course; programme	7
kèfú	克服	to overcome	12*
kěshì	可是	but	1
késòu	咳嗽	to cough	3
kètīng	客厅	sitting room	7
kěxī	可惜	shame; pity	6
kōngqì wūrǎn	空气污染	air pollution	9
kòngzhì	控制	to control	10*
kǒuyīn	口音	accent	1
kuàijì	会计	accountant	12
kuàizi	筷子	chopsticks	4
kuājiǎng	夸奖	praise, compliment	2
kuān	宽	wide	2
kuāndài	宽带	broadband	10
kuǎnshì xīnyǐng	款式新颖	original in style	12
kùnnán	困难	difficulty	6
lādùzi	拉肚子	diarrhoea	3
láihuí pǎo	来回跑	to go around	12
Lán Tiān	蓝天	Blue Sky	10
làngmàn	浪漫	romantic	11
lánqiú	篮球	basketball	3
lánwěiyán	阑尾炎	appendicitis	3
lǎo	老	always	12*
lǎo bǎixìng	老百姓	ordinary people (*lit.* old hundred surnames)	10
Lǎo Shě	老舍	(name of a famous author)	6
lǎo tóuzi	老头子	old man (affectionate term used by one's wife)	11
shān、biān、qióng	山、边、穷	mountainous, remote, poor	12*
lǎobàn	老伴	spouse (used among elderly people)	3
lǎobǎn	老板	boss	8
lǎo dà	老大	the eldest child	5
lǎo jiā	老家	home town	9
lǎonián shí	老年时	in one's old age; when getting old	11
lǎoshī	老师	teacher	7
lì rú	例如	for example	10*

lí . . . bùyuǎn	离 . . . 不远	to be not far from . . .	2
lián . . . yě . . .	连 . . . 也 . . .	even	1
liàn'ài	恋爱	to fall in love; courtship	11
liàng	量	amount; quantity	10*
liǎng kǒuzi	两口子	married couple	11
liáng . . . tǐwēn	量体温	to take the temperature	3
liánxì	联系	be in touch; to contact	12
liánxì hǎo	联系好	to get things arranged	12*
liǎojiě	了解	understanding; to understand	2
liáoliao	聊聊	to chat	1
liáotiān	聊天	to chat	2
lièchēyuán	列车员	assistant on a train	8
lìhai	厉害	serious; aggressive; fierce; impressive	3, 7
líhūn lǜ	离婚率	divorce rate	11
líkāi	离开	to leave	9
lǐngdǎo	领导	leader; management	8
línghuó	灵活	flexible	8
lìngwài	另外	besides	2
línjū	邻居	neighbour	5
liú	留	to be left behind	5
liúdòng	流动	mobile	12
liùshí niándài	六十年代	60s (as in 1960s)	9
liúxià	留下	to leave (behind)	12
liúxué shēng	留学生	overseas student	7
lóufáng	楼房	building	12
lǜlǜde	绿绿的	green	1
lùmiàn shàng	路面上	on the road	9
Luòtuó Xiángzi	骆驼祥子	*Camel Xiangzi* (a famous novel)	6
lǚyóu	旅游	to travel	7
máfán	麻烦	trouble; troublesome; to trouble	3, 8
Màikè	麦克	Mike	9
máodùn	矛盾	conflict	11*
mǎshàng	马上	immediately	5
méicuò	没错	correct; right	7
měifàshī	美发师	hairdresser	8
méiguīhuā	玫瑰花	rose	11
méijìn	没劲	no energy	3
měilì	美丽	beautiful	2

mí le lù	迷了路	got lost	12
miànbāo	面包	bread	4
miànbù biǎoqíng	面部表情	facial expression	2
miǎnfèi	免费	free of charge	10
miànfěn	面粉	flour	4
miànshì	面试	interview	8
mǐfàn	米饭	(cooked) rice	4
mì fāng	秘方	secret recipe	3
míng zhù	名著	famous work	6
míng-fù-qí-shí	名副其实	the name matches the reality; worthy of the name	10
míng-shèng-gǔ-jī	名胜古迹	places of historical interest	1
mótuōchē	摩托车	motorbike	9
mùlù	目录	catalogue	8
mùqián	目前	at the moment; currently	9
nà ge shíhòu	那个时候	at that time	9
ná guòlái	拿过来	to bring over	11
nà yǒu shénme	那有什么	that's not a problem; that is no big deal; so what?	6
ná . . . láishuō	拿 . . . 来说	to take . . . as example	3
nádào	拿到	to have got	8
nánguài	难怪	no wonder	1
nánguò	难过	sad	11
Nánhǎi	南海	(a city in Guangdong province)	12*
néngyuán	能源	energy	9
nǐ nàr	你那儿	your place	4
nián xīn	年薪	annual salary	8
nián yè fàn	年夜饭	Chinese New Year's Eve meal	5
niánlíng	年龄	age	10
niánqīng rén	年青人	young people	11
níngyuàn	宁愿	would rather	11*
níngyuàn . . . yě	宁愿 . . . 也	would rather . . . than	11
nòng huài	弄坏	to break; to damage	9
nóng lì	农历	lunar calendar	5
nóngcūn	农村	countryside	1
nóngyè	农业	agriculture	12
nǚ xù	女婿	son-in-law	11

pèifu	佩服	to admire, admiration	2
pí xié	皮鞋	leather shoes	12
piān	篇	(measure word)	2
píngděng xiāngdài	平等相待	to treat everyone equally	12
pīngpāngqiú	乒乓球	table-tennis	3
pǐnzhǒng	品种	goods; variety	1
pópo	婆婆	mother-in-law (husband's mother)	11
pǔjí	普及	popular	10
pǔtōng	普通	ordinary	12
qǐ de lái	起得来	to be able to get up	6
qǐ yè	企业	enterprise; firm; company	12
qiánbāo	钱包	wallet; purse	9
qiáng	强	strong; capable	6
qiānxū	谦虚	be modest	1
qiàqià xiāngfǎn	恰恰相反	be just the opposite	2
qìchē	汽车	vehicle; car	9
qíchērén	骑车人	cyclist	9
qícì	其次	secondly	11
qìgōng	气功	Chi Kung	3
qìhòu	气候	climate	9
qīng	清	clear	12
Qīngdǎo	青岛	(city name)	1
qīnglǐ	清理	to clear up	9
qǐng-wù-xī-yān	请勿吸烟	No smoking	9
qīnqi	亲戚	relative	5
qìsè	气色	complexion, colour	3
qíshí	其实	in fact	11*
qiú lèi	球类	ball related	6
qiú sài	球赛	(foot)ball match	6
qiúzhí xìn	求职信	job-seeking letter	8
qǐyèjiā	企业家	entrepreneur	12
qīzi	妻子	wife	5
qǔ	娶	to marry (a women)	11
qū	区	district	12
quán jiā	全家	whole family	5
quán shěng	全省	entire province	12*
quánshēn	全身	the whole body	3
què	却	surprisingly, but	7
quèbǎo	确保	to guarantee	12*
rán'ér	然而	however	11*

ránhòu	然后	then	2
rèn bu chūlái	认不出来	cannot recognise	12
rènao	热闹	lively; bustling with noise and excitement	3
réncái shìcháng	人才市场	job market (*lit.* talents market)	8
rénjì	人际	human	10*
rénkǒu	人口	population	11
rénmen	人们	people	10
rènshi	认识	to recognise; to come to understand	1, 10*
rènwéi	认为	to think; to consider	8
rénwù	人物	character	6
rénxíng héngdào	人行横道	pedestrian crossing	9
rèxīn	热心	warm; friendly	7
rìjì	日记	diary	2
rìzi	日子	life	11*
róngyì	容易	easy	4
ròu	肉	meat	4
ruǎnjiàn	软件	software	10
rúguǒ . . . dehuà	如果 . . . 的话	if	8
rújīn	如今	nowadays	11
rùkǒuchù	入口处	entrance	2
Sān Xiá	三峡	The Three Gorges	1
sànbù	散步	to stroll	3
sǎngzi	嗓子	throat	3
shàng kè	上课	to go to class	7
shàng qiāngè	上千个	over a thousand	2
shàng wǎng	上网	to go on the net; to connect to the net	10
shàng xué	上学	to go to school; to start schooling	7
shàng . . . dàng	上 . . . 当	to be tricked by . . .	10*
shàngqu	上去	to go up	2
shàngshēng	上升	to go up; to increase	11
shāowéi	稍微	a little	4
shèhuì huódòng	社会活动	social activity	11*
shéi néng xiǎngdào	谁能想到	who would have thought	12
shēn	深	deep	12
shēng	生	to give birth to	11
shěng fèn	省份	province	12*
shèng mǐfàn	剩米饭	left-over rice	4

shēngchǎn	生产	to produce; production	12
Shèngdànjié	圣诞节	Christmas	5
shēnghuó	生活	life; living; to live	7
shēnghuó tiáojiàn	生活条件	living condition	11
shēnghuó xíguàn	生活习惯	daily routine (lit. living habit)	3
shēngyì	生意	business	12
shēnqǐng	申请	to apply for; application	8
shēnqǐng rén	申请人	applicant	8
shēnshēn de	深深的	deep; in depth	10*
shēntǐ	身体	body	3
shènzhì	甚至	even	10
shètuán	社团	community	11*
shì . . . háishì	是 . . . 还是	is it . . . or . . . ?; whether . . . or . . .	10
shìbì	势必	must; be bound to	11*
shìcháng jīngjì	市场经济	market economy	12
shīgōng	施工	construction	12*
shìjì	世纪	century	9
shìjiè	世界	world	11
shìqing	事情	thing; matter	7
shí-shí-zài-zài	实实在在	concrete; real	12*
shìshi	试试	to give it a try	4
shíxiàn	实现	to realise	12*
shìxiān	事先	in advance	12*
shíxíng	实行	to carry out	10*
shīyè	失业	unemployment; be unemployed	8
shòu guò jiàoyù de rén	受过教育的人	educated person/people	7
shòu huānyíng	受欢迎	be popular (lit. receive welcome)	12
shǒu jī	手机	mobile phone	10
shòu pìn yǔ	受聘与	to be employed with	11*
shǒu yè	守夜	to stay awake for the whole night	5
shòu . . . qiānlèi	受 . . . 牵累	be tied down with . . .	11*
shōudào	收到	to receive; to get; to have received	10
shǒudū	首都	capital	6
shóuxi; shúxí	熟悉	be familiar with	7
shǒuxiān	首先	firstly; first of all	11
shù	束	bunch	11

shǔ jià	暑假	summer vacation (only used for school/university holidays)	2, 7
shuāng xǐ	双喜	double happiness	11
shuì bù zháo jiào	睡不着觉	cannot go to sleep	10
shuǐjīng	水晶	crystal	11
shuìlǎnjiào	睡懒觉	to lie in	7
shūjí	书籍	books	8
shùliàng	数量	amount; quantity	9
shùnshǒu	顺手	on passing	11
shùnzhe	顺着	along	2
shuō bu qīng	说不清	cannot be explained easily	4
shuō dào	说到	talking about	6
shuō zhēn de	说真的	to be honest; honestly	12
shuō-dào-zuò-dào	说到做到	to do as promised	9
shuōhuàrén	说话人	the speaker	3
shuōmíng	说明	to explain; to demonstrate	8, 10*
shuòshì	硕士	master's; MA	7
shǔyú	属于	to belong to	12*
sījī	司机	driver	8
sījiā chē	私家车	private cars	9
sì shēng	四声	four tones	1
sīxiǎng rènshí	思想认识	thinking and understanding	11*
sīyǒu qǐyè	私有企业	private enterprise	12
sòng	送	to give something as present	11
suàn	算	to count as	5
suànshù	算术	arithmetic	7
suí shí	随时	at any time	10
suí zháo	随着	as . . .	12*
suīrán . . . dànshì	虽然 . . . 但是	although . . . but	12
sūnnǚ	孙女	grand-daughter	5
sūnzi	孙子	grandson	3
suǒyǐ	所以	therefore; so	11
tàijíquán	太极拳	Tai-chi	3
Tàiyuán	太原	(city name)	7
tán gāngqín	弹钢琴	to play the piano	8
tán liàn'ài	谈恋爱	to court (lit. to talk about love)	7
tèbié	特别	especially, extremely	1

tècháng	特长	strength; strong point	11*
tī	踢	to kick	6
tí gòng	提供	to provide	9
tí yìjiàn	提意见	to voice one's view (always negative)	9
Tiānjīn	天津	(a city near Beijing)	5
tiānlún zhī lè	天伦之乐	the pleasure of family life	11*
tiáo	条	(measure word for winding and slender objects such as street, river)	2
tiāo	挑	to carry with a pole	12*
tiáojiàn	条件	condition	7
tiáoliào	调料	seasoning; condiment	4
tiàowǔ	跳舞	to dance	3
tiàoxiàn	调馅	to make the filling	4
tíchāng	提倡	to promote; to advocate	9
tígāo	提高	to raise	12
tíngchē chǎng	停车场	car park	9
tīnglì	听力	listening ability	1
tīngshàngqu	听上去	it sounds . . .	12
tǐyù	体育	sport	6
tǐyù guǎn	体育馆	stadium	6
tǐzhòng	体重	weight	9
tōng diànhuà	通电话	to have a telephone installed	12*
tōngcháng	通常	usually	5
tóng shí	同时	at the same time; besides	11*
tóngshì	同事	colleague	5
tóngxué	同学	student (when a teacher addresses a class and means 'any one of you')	4
tōngxùn dìzhǐ	通讯地址	postal address	8
tóngyì	同意	to agree; to approve	1
tōngzhī	通知	to notify	10
tóuténg	头疼	headache	3
tóuyūn	头晕	to feel dizzy (lit. head dizzy)	3
tuánjù	团聚	to get together	5
tuányuán fàn	团圆饭	family reunion meal	5
tǔdòu	土豆	potato	4
tuīchí dào	推迟到	to postpone to	11

tuījiàn xìn	推荐信	letter of reference	8
tuìshāo yào	退烧药	temperature relief medicine	3
tuīxiāoyuán	推销员	sales-person	8
tuìxiū	退休	retired	3
túshū guǎnlǐyuán	图书管理员	librarian	8
túshūguǎn	图书馆	library	7
wàidìrén	外地人	stranger, outsider	2
wàishēngnǚ	外甥女	niece	5
wài yǔ	外语	foreign language	1
wán	玩	to tour	2
wǎn bào	晚报	evening news	8
wǎn bèi	晚辈	a generation below (i.e. children)	11*
wǎn nián	晚年	old age	11*
wánchéng	完成	to complete	12*
wǎng bā	网吧	internet bar	7
wǎng shàng	网上	on the net	10
wǎng shàng kàn	往上看	to look upward	11
wǎng sù	网速	internet speed	10
wǎng . . . dào	往 . . . 倒	to pour into	9
wángguó	王国	kingdom	9
wǎngluò shídài	网络时代	internet era	10*
wǎngqiú	网球	tennis	3
wǎngzhàn	网站	internet site	8
wánquán	完全	completely	1
wèi	未	have not yet	12*
wěidà	伟大	great	5
wèidào	味道	flavour	1
wèikǒu bù hǎo	胃口不好	no appetite	3
wéile	为了	for; in order to	9
wéixiū	维修	to be serviced; to service	10
wénhuà chéngdù	文化程度	level of education; educational qualification	7
wénpíng	文凭	qualification; certificate	8
wénxué	文学	literature	6
wòshì	卧室	bedroom	7
wúlùn . . . háishì	无论 . . . 还是	regardless whether . . . or . . .	11
wǔ xiāng fěn	五香粉	five Chinese spices	4
wǔyè	午夜	midnight	5
xī cān	西餐	Western cuisine; Western food	4

xī shì	西式	Western style	4
xià kè	下课	to finish class	7
xiàdìng juéxīn	下定决心	to have firm determination	10*
xiàgǎng	下岗	be laid off	8
xiān píng cūn	仙坪村	Xianping village	12*
xiàndàihuà	现代化	modernised	1
xiǎnde	显得	to appear	7
xiāng chǔ	相处	to get along; to get on	11
xiǎng dào	想到	to think of; think about	10
xiāng zhèn	乡镇	village and town	12
xiàng . . . xuéxí	向 . . . 学习	to learn from	3
xiāngcūn	乡村	countryside	2
xiǎngxiàng	想像	to imagine	1
xiǎngxiǎng qīngxián	享享清闲	to enjoy the happiness of leisurely and relaxed life	11*
xiāngyóu	香油	sesame oil	4
xiānměi	鲜美	tasty, delicious	1
xián-rén-miǎn-jìn	闲人免进	No entry	9
xiànxiàng	现象	phenomenon	11
xiànzhì	限制	to restrict	9
xiànzhuàng	现状	current situation	10*
xiào duì	校队	school/college team	6
xiào fāng	校方	school authority	7
xiǎo hé	小河	small river	9
xiǎo shíhòu	小时候	when I was small	9
xiào wài	校外	outside the college	10
xiǎo xué	小学	primary school	7
xiāofèizhě	消费者	consumer	12
xiāohào	消耗	to consume, to use up	9
xiǎo kuài	小块	small pieces	4
xiāoshì	消逝	to disappear; to disintegrate	11
xiāoshòu bù	销售部	sales department	12
xiǎoshuō	小说	novel	6
xiāoxi	消息	news (as in 'good news')	10
xiàozhǎng	校长	headmaster	7
xiàtiān	夏天	summer	1
xiàzǎi	下载	to download	10
xiě	写	to write	1
xīfāngrén	西方人	Westerner	5
xífù	媳妇	wife	5
xíguàn	习惯	habit	7

xīhóngshì	西红柿	tomato	12
xìjù	戏剧	drama	7
xīlánhuā	西蓝花	broccoli	12
xīn fán	心烦	troubled	10*
xīn fáng	新房	bridal chamber (*lit.* new room)	11
xīn nián	新年	New Year	5
xīn pǐnzhǒng	新品种	new produce	12
xīnán bù	西南部	southwest part	2
xíngzhèng cūn	行政村	administrative village	12*
xíngchéng	形成	to form; to take shape	11*
xìngfú	幸福	happiness	11
xìngyùn de shì	幸运的是	fortunately	11
xīnláng	新郎	bridegroom (*lit.* new man)	11
xīnniáng	新娘	bride (*lit.* new woman)	11
xīnwén	新闻	news	12
xìnxī	信息	information	10
xìnyòng kǎ	信用卡	credit card	10
xiūgǎi	修改	to polish; to amend	8
xiūxi	休息	to rest	3
xiūyixiū	修一修	to fix it	10
xīwàng	希望	to hope; to wish	9
xuǎnzé	选择	choice	8
xué huì	学会	have learnt to	10
xuékē	学科	subject; major	7
xuéqī	学期	term	7
xuéwèi	学位	degree	7
xuéyuàn	学院	college	10
xùn	训	to tell off	9
yán	盐	salt	4
yǎng huā	养花	to grow flowers	6
yánjiù shēng	研究生	postgraduate student	7
yǎnshì	演示	to demonstrate	10
yántú	沿途	on its way; throughout the journey	2
yànwù fǎ	厌恶法	aversion approach	10*
yánzhòng	严重	serious	9
yàopǐn	药品	medicine; pharmaceutical	12
yāoqiú	要求	to demand; to require	9, 10*
yàoshì	要是	if	8
yáténg	牙疼	toothache	3
yějiù	也就	therefore	9

yèyú	业余	spare (time)	7
yī bèizi	一辈子	the whole life	11
yī niánjí	一年级	year one	7
yī xìliè	一系列	a series	12*
yī . . . jiù . . .	一 . . . 就 . . .	as soon as . . . then	10*
yǐ . . . wéizhǔ	以 . . . 为主	be mainly; to mainly consist of	4
yìbān	一般	normally	4
yìbiān . . . yìbiān . . .	一边 . . . 一边 . . .	(to be doing something) while (doing something else)	2
yídàn . . . jiù . . .	一旦 . . . 就 . . .	once . . . then . . .	11
yídìng	一定	definitely	10*
Yíhuáng Xiàn	宜黄县	Yihuang county	12*
yìjiàn	意见	view; opinion	8
yīkào	依靠	to rely on	11
yīncǐ	因此	therefore	11*
yìng pìn	应聘	to apply for a vacancy	8
yìnggāi	应该	should	3
yìngjiàn	硬件	hardware	10
yīngtáo	樱桃	cherry	12
yǐngxiǎng	影响	influence	12
yǐnshí	饮食	food; cuisine	4
yīnwéi	因为	because	1
yìnxiàng	印象	impression	1
yīnyuè	音乐	music	6
yīshēng	医生	doctor	5
yī-shí-bàn-huìr	一时半会儿	within a short time; a little while	10
yìsi	意思	meaning	4
yǐwéi	以为	thought	5
yīwùsuǒ	医务所	clinic; health centre	3
yīyuàn	医院	hospital	5
yǐzhìyú	以至于	even; go as far as	10*
yòng bú yòng	用不用 . . . ?	Is it necessary . . . ?	6
yònggōng	用功	hardworking	3
yōngjǐ	拥挤	crowded, be crowded	1
yóu	游	to travel	1
yóu	由	by	8
yǒu shíhou	有时候	sometimes	6
yǒu wénhuà de rén	有文化的人	educated person/people	7
yǒu dàolǐ	有道理	you have a point there; it makes sense	2

yòu'ér jiàoshī	幼儿教师	nursery teacher	8
yǒuhài	有害	harmful; detrimental	10*
yōuhuì jiǎnglì	优惠奖励	preferential and with rewards	12*
yóurén	游人	tourist	2
yǒu wèntí	有问题	to have problems	1
yǒuxiàn gōngsī	有限公司	limited company	12
yǒuxiē	有些	some	6
yóuyǒng	游泳	swim; swimming	3
yóuyú	由于	due to; because of	11
Yuǎn Sēn	远森	Far Forest (proper name)	12
yuán zhù	原著	original work	6
yuán-lái-rú-cǐ	原来如此	So that's how it is!	10
yuánmíng	原名	original name	2
yuánxiāo jié	元宵节	Lantern Festival	5
yuànyì	愿意	to be willing	11
yuányīn	原因	reason	1
yùbào	预报	forecast	12
yuē	约	to arrange	12
yuè lái yuè	越来越	more and more	6
Yuēhàn	约翰	John	6
yǔmáoqiú	羽毛球	badminton (*lit.* feather ball)	3
yūn	晕	dizzy	5
yùndòng	运动	exercise; sport	3
Yúnnán	云南	(a province in China)	2
zài . . . shàng	在 . . . 上	in terms of . . . ; regarding	4
zài . . . xià	在 . . . 下	under . . .	12
zài . . . de bànzòu xià	在 . . . 的伴奏下	to be accompanied by (musical instrument)	3
zàijiùshì	再就是	another thing is	1
zàishuō	再说	besides	7
zāng	脏	dirty	9
zǎo diǎnr	早点儿	a bit earlier	6
zǎo jiù	早就	for a long time	10
zàoyīn	噪音	noise, undesired sound	1
zé	则	on the other hand	11*
zēngjiā	增加	increase; to increase	9
zěnme yě	怎么也	no matter how	10
zhàn	站	stop	2
zhǎnchū	展出	to be on display	2
zhǎng bèi	长辈	older generations	11

zhàng rén	丈人	father-in-law (wife's father)	11
zhàngmǔ niáng	丈母娘	mother-in-law (wife's mother)	11
zhǎo	找	to collect; to get (a person)	6
zhǎo gōngzuò	找工作	to look for jobs	8
zhàogù	照顾	to look after	11
zhāopìn	招聘	to invite applications for a job	8
zhè jiù	这就	this minute	10
zhè yàng ba	这样吧	I'll tell you what; let's do it this way	2, 5
zhè yàng yī lái	这样一来	this way; by doing so	8
Zhèjiāng	浙江	(a province in China)	9
zhèn	镇	small town	12
zhēn bàng	真棒	wonderful	11
zhēng	蒸	to steam	4
zhèng yuè	正月	first month of lunar calendar	5
zhěngbiān	整编	sorting-out; cataloguing	8
zhèngcè	政策	policy	11
zhèngfǔ	政府	government	9
zhēngqiú	征求	to ask for; to consult	8
zhèngyào	正要	just about to; just going to	5
zhèngzài	正在	(continuous indicator)	6
zhěngzhěng	整整	exactly	1
zhěng-zhěng-qí-qí	整整齐齐	orderly	2
Zhēnní	珍妮	Jane	8
zhèxià	这下	this way; now	5
zhí	直	straight	2
zhǐ	只	only	1
zhí bān	值班	be on duty	5
zhī fēn	之分	difference	10*
zhǐ hǎo	只好	to have to	11
zhǐ yào	只要	as long as	6
zhī yī	之一	one of	1
zhì yú	至于	as for	6
zhīchēng	支撑	to support	11*
zhídào	直到	until	8
zhìliàng	质量	quality	1

zhíshuài	直率	frankly; directly	11*
zhíwù	职务	position	12
zhǒng	种	kind	1
zhòng cài	种菜	to grow vegetables	12
zhōng cān	中餐	Chinese cuisine; Chinese food	4
zhōng chéngyào	中成药	ready-made traditional Chinese medicine	3
zhòng gǎnmào	重感冒	bad cold	3
Zhōng Lóu	钟楼	bell tower	2
Zhōng Měi hé zī	中美合资	Sino-American joint venture	12
zhòng-nán-qīn-nǚ	重男轻女	favour the boy and discriminate against the girl; regard men as superior to women	11
zhòngshì	重视	to pay attention to; to attach importance to	11
zhōngxīn	中心	centre	2
zhōng xué	中学	secondary school	7
zhōngxún	中旬	mid- (for month)	7
zhòngyào	重要	important	5
zhōngyào	中药	traditional Chinese medicine	3
zhōumò	周末	weekend	7
zhōurì	周日	Sunday	4
zhǔ	煮	to boil	4
zhū	诸	various; all	11*
zhù Jīng	驻京	to be stationed in Beijing	8
zhù nǐ hǎo yùn	祝你好运	to wish you good luck	8
zhǔ yè	主页	home page	10
zhuǎn guò shēn	转过身	to turn (the body) over	11
zhuàn xiē qián	赚些钱	to earn some money	7
zhuān yòng chēdào	专用车道	special designated/ reserved lane	9
zhuàngdǎo	撞倒	to knock down	9
zhuàngkuàng	状况	condition	12*
zhuànqián	赚钱	profitable (*lit.* earn money)	12
zhuānyī	专一	single-minded; concentrating	7
zhúbù	逐步	gradual	10*

zhǔfàn	煮饭	cooking	11*
zhùfáng	住房	house; accommodation	11*
zhùhè	祝贺	to congratulate	5
zhuīqiú	追求	to seek after	11
zhújiàn	逐渐	gradually	11
zhùmíng	著名	well known; famous	2
zhǔnbèi	准备	to be planning	2
zhūròu mò	猪肉末	pork mince	4
zhǔshí	主食	staple food	4
zhǔyào	主要	mainly; main; major	4, 9
zhǔyi	主意	advice; idea	2
zhùyìlì	注意力	attention	7
zhùzhòng	注重	to pay attention to	12
zìcóng . . . yǐlái	自从 . . . 以来	since	6
zījīn	资金	capital; money	12
zìmù	字幕	subtitle	6
zǐnǚ	子女	children (*lit.* son daughter)	11
zìrán	自然	natural	2
zìxìnxīn	自信心	confidence	8
zìyóu	自由	freedom	8
zìzhì lì	自制力	power of self-discipline	10*
zǒngde láishuō	总的来说	generally speaking	1
zǒngshì	总是	always	1
zǒu dào dǐ	走到底	to walk to the very end	2
zǒu qīnqi	走亲戚	to visit family and relatives	5
zūnjìng	尊敬	respected; respectful	9
zūnzhòng	尊重	to respect	12
zuò mǎimài	做买卖	to do business	12*
zuòfǎ	做法	method of cooking	4
zuòliào	作料	ingredient	4
zuòmèng	做梦	to dream	12
zuòpǐn	作品	a work (as in literature or art)	6
zuòyè	作业	homework, assignment	2
zuòzhě	作者	author; writer	6
zúqiú	足球	football	3

Index to language points

The numbers on the right refer to the unit in which each language point appears.

Index to culture notes

The numbers on the right refer to the unit in which each culture note appears.

Related titles from Routledge

Chinese:
A Comprehensive Grammar

Yip Po-Ching and Don Rimmington

Chinese: A Comprehensive Grammar is a complete reference guide
to Chinese grammar.

It presents a fresh and accessible description of the language,
concentrating on the real patterns of use in modern Chinese.
The *Grammar* is an essential reference source for the learner and
user of Chinese, irrespective of level. It is ideal for use in schools,
colleges, universities and adult classes of all types, and will remain
the standard reference work for years to come.

This volume is organized to promote a thorough understanding of
Chinese grammar. It offers a stimulating analysis of the complexities
of the language, and provides full and clear explanations. Throughout,
the emphasis is on Chinese as used by present-day native speakers.

An extensive index and numbered paragraphs provide readers with
easy access to the information they require.

Features include:

▶ Thorough and comprehensive coverage of the modern language
▶ Use of script and romanization throughout
▶ Detailed treatment of common grammatical structures and parts
  of speech
▶ Extensive and wide-ranging use of examples
▶ Particular attention to areas of confusion and difficulty

Yip Po-Ching was Lecturer in Chinese at Leeds University and
Don Rimmington is Emeritus Professor of Chinese, formerly at
Leeds University.

ISBN10: 0-415-15031-0 (hbk)
ISBN10: 0-415–15032-9 (pbk)
ISBN13: 978-0415-15031-6 (hbk)
ISBN13: 978-0-415-15032-3 (pbk)

Available at all good bookshops
For ordering and further information please visit:
www.routledge.com

Related titles from Routledge

Developing Writing Skills in Chinese
Boping Yuan and Kan Qian

Developing Writing Skills in Chinese has been devised for post-intermediate students of Chinese who need to write Chinese in the course of their life, work or study.

Each unit contains a selection of model texts, each followed by clear notes in English on the format, style, grammar or language demonstrated in the text. A variety of exercises allows the student to practise these writing techniques themselves.

Developing Writing Skills in Chinese is suitable for use as a classroom text, or as a self-study resource. The course is functionally based, with each unit focused on a particular form of writing, from New Year cards to business correspondence. Units need not be studied in sequence, so students are free to focus on their particular needs.

Features include:

▶ Glossaries for each chapter, giving Chinese characters, pinyin and English translation
▶ Answer key
▶ Flexible structure
▶ Variety of model texts

Written by experienced teachers of Chinese and thoroughly trialled with non-native students of Chinese, *Developing Writing Skills in Chinese* will help students to write coherently, clearly and appropriately in a variety of contexts.

Boping Yuan is Lecturer in Chinese Studies and **Kan Qian** is Senior Language Teaching Officer in Chinese Studies, both at the University of Cambridge.

ISBN10: 0-415-21583-8 (hbk)
ISBN10: 0-415-21584-6 (pbk)
ISBN13: 978-0-415-21583-1 (hbk)
ISBN13: 978-0-415-21584-8 (pbk)

Available at all good bookshops
For ordering and further information please visit:
www.routledge.com

Related titles from Routledge

Intermediate Chinese
Yip Po-Ching and Don Rimmington

Intermediate Chinese is the ideal reference and practice book for students with some knowledge of the language. Each of the 25 units deals with a particular grammatical point and provides associated exercises.

Features include:

▶ Clear, accessible format
▶ Many useful language examples
▶ Jargon-free grammar explanations
▶ Ample drills and exercises
▶ Full key to exercises

All Chinese entries are presented in both pinyin romanisation and Chinese characters, and are accompanied, in most cases, by English translations to facilitate self-tuition in both the written and spoken language.

Yip Po-Ching was Lecturer in Chinese at Leeds University and **Don Rimmington** is Emeritus Professor of Chinese, formerly at Leeds University.

ISBN10: 0-415-16038-3 (hbk)
ISBN10: 0-415-16039-1 (pbk)
ISBN13: 978-0-415-16038-4 (hbk)
ISBN13: 978-0-415-16039-1 (pbk)

Available at all good bookshops
For ordering and further information please visit:
www.routledge.com

Modern Mandarin Chinese Grammar
Modern Mandarin Chinese Grammar Workbook

Claudia Ross and
Jing-heng Sheng Ma

Modern Mandarin Chinese Grammar: A Practical Guide is an innovative reference guide to Mandarin Chinese, combining traditional and function-based grammar in a single volume.

The *Grammar* is divided into two parts. Part A covers traditional grammatical categories such as phrase order, nouns, verbs and specifiers. Part B is carefully organized around language functions and situations such as communication strategies, making comparisons, giving and seeking information and expressing apologies, regrets and sympathies. The two parts of the *Grammar* are closely linked by extensive cross-references, providing a grammatical and functional perspective on many patterns.

Main features of the *Grammar* include:

▶ Examples given in simplified characters, traditional characters, and romanization (pinyin)
▶ Clear explanations and accessible descriptions
▶ Emphasis on areas of particular difficulty for learners of Mandarin Chinese

This is the ideal reference grammar for learners of Mandarin Chinese at all levels, from elementary to advanced. No prior knowledge of grammatical terminology is assumed and a glossary of grammatical terms is provided.

This Grammar is complemented by the *Modern Mandarin Chinese Grammar Workbook* (ISBN 0-415-70011-6), which features related exercises and activities.

Claudia Ross is Professor of Chinese Language and Linguistics in the Department of Modern Languages at the College of the Holy Cross in Worcester, Massachusetts. **Jing-heng Sheng Ma** is Mayling Soong Professor of Chinese Studies at Wellesley College, Massachusetts.

Grammar ISBN: Pb: 978-0-415-70010-8
Workbook ISBN: Pb: 978-0-415-70011-5

Basic Chinese:
A Grammar and Workbook

Yip Po-Ching and Don Rimmington

Basic Chinese introduces the essentials of Chinese syntax. Each of the twenty-five units deals with a particular grammatical point and provides associated exercises.

Features include:

- clear, accessible format
- many useful language examples
- jargon-free explanations of grammar
- ample drills and exercises
- full key to exercises

All Chinese entries are presented in both *pinyin* romanisation and Chinese characters, and are accompanied, in most cases, by English translations to facilitate self-tuition in both spoken and written Chinese.

Basic Chinese is designed for complete beginners. Together with its sister volume, *Intermediate Chinese*, it forms a compendium of the essentials of Chinese syntax.

Yip Po-Ching is Lecturer in Chinese Studies and **Don Rimmington** is Professor of East Asian Studies and Head of Department, both at the University of Leeds. They are the authors of *Chinese: An Essential Grammar (1996)*.

ISBN: Hb: 978-0-415-16036-0
ISBN: Pb: 978-0-415-16037-7

Available at all good bookshops
For ordering and further information please visit:
www.routledge.com